S. T COLERIDGE

BIOGRAPHIA LITERARIA

S.T Coleridge

BIOGRAPHIA LITERARIA

[Edited with Selected Chapters from the Text, Study Questions and Criticism]

Aditya Nandwani
B.A. English (Hons) , Delhi University;
M.A. (English), IGNOU; Print Journalism (English) YMCA

ANMOL PUBLICATIONS PVT. LTD.
NEW DELHI - 110 002 (INDIA)

ANMOL PUBLICATIONS PVT. LTD.
H.O.: 4374/4B, Ansari Road, Darya Ganj,
New Delhi-110 002 (India)
Ph.: 23278000, 23261597
B.O.: No. 1015, Ist Main Road, BSK IIIrd Stage
IIIrd Phase, IIIrd Block
Bangalore - 560 085 (India)
Visit us at: www.anmolpublications.com

Biographia Literaria

First Published, 2009

PRINTED IN INDIA

Printed at Mehra Offset Press, Delhi.

Contents

Preface

Arthur Symons said it best: *Biographia Literaria* is the greatest book of criticism in English, and one of the most annoying in any language. Many have agreed that Coleridge's brilliance comes shrouded in an obscure, infuriating intricacy. In order to analyze that intricacy, and yet not to write a book as labyrinthine as the *Biographia* itself, it has been all times endeavoured to look steadily at the subject. Wordsworth appears in *Biographia Literaria* partly as an individual, but more centrally as the ideal philosophic poet—and in all instances as Coleridge's idea of him. I step outside that conception only when recourse to Wordsworth's criticism proves requisite to the full understanding of how Coleridge designs his counter-argument.

The data for this work has been gathered with painstaking exactness and it is hoped that its accuracy is commensurate with the efforts that have been put forth to make it so, and that it may be a valuable work of reference for both students' and teachers of literature.

Author

Chapter 1

Introduction

To comprehend Coleridge's work in any one field, one must also understand his work in the others. This is no small task: Coleridge was enormously learned; his writing seldom accommodates to lesser learning and lesser energies than his own. Furthermore, controversy both obscures and complicates anyone's approach.

Another central controversy that concerns Coleridge is plagiarism. This issue is intimately linked to whether one takes seriously Coleridge's Christianity, and, if so, how one understands his faith. Coleridge believed that God sustains the coherent & reliable relations among consciousness, language, and a genuine, knowable, external reality. This was a mature philosophic conviction, not a conventional piety. His Theo centric context often modifies the definitions and philosophic constructions that he incorporates from Immanuel Kant (1724-1804), Friedrich von Schelling (1775-1854) and others. As a result, Coleridge's most severe critics accuse him of misunderstanding what he takes or "distorting" it with religious ideas. His apologists, on the other hand, defend the value of his arguments despite this distressingly "mosaic" verbal surface.

Coleridge's work is also controversial because he took important stands on the major western questions concerning language and the possibility of knowledge. According to Coleridge, the accuracy of a statement—the test of its truth, philosophically—depends upon its precise and vivid use of words. His unfinished "Logosophia" was to demonstrate the basis of this extraordinary claim. But the "Logosophia" was to be an imaginative symbolic encounter, not a formal, closed, logical demonstration. Coleridge fully understood that no closed logical system can adequately reflect the character of reality. Because of this insight, Coleridge is sometimes appropriated by post-structuralists whose basic philosophic positions are inimical to his own. In the same way, the "New Criticism" once appropriated Coleridge, despite its antipathy to Coleridge's vision of the moral value of literature.

Coleridge is most famous for his poetry and his literary criticism. Biographia Literaria is a centrally-important inquiry into the nature of literary imagination. Its discussion of William Wordsworth (1770-1850) remains a classic, as do his 1811 lectures on William Shakespeare (1564-1616). His poetic reputation arises primarily from two groups of poems. Pre-eminent are the visionary poems: "The Rime of the Ancient Mariner," "Kubla Khan" and "Christabel". Second are the "conversation" poems: "The Eolian Harp," "This Lime-Tree Bower My Prison," "Frost at Midnight," "The Nightingale" and "Dejection: An Ode". Beneath the psychological power and musicality of his best lines, the careful reader will recognize Coleridge's considerable technical prowess as a poet. Consider, for instance, the spondaic substitutions in the following lines, from "The Eolian Harp":

> O! the one Life within us and abroad,
> Which meets all motion and becomes its soul,
> A light in sound, a sound-like power in light,
> Rhythm in all thought, and joyance everywhere—
> Methinks, it should have been impossible
> Not to love all things in a world so fill'd;
> Where the breeze warbles, and the mute still air
> Is Music slumbering on her instrument.

In deeply various ways, all Coleridge's work is a celebratory encounter with this "one Life."

Coleridge readily admitted that he demands very much of his readers. Once he called himself a "chamois hunter," who expects that those whom he guides will "cling to the rocks, by the blood of [their] own feet." Any experienced Coleridgean knows just how that feels—and why the journey proves, at last, worth the effort.

"The influence of Coleridge, like that of Bentham, extends far beyond those who share in the peculiarities of his religious or philosophical creed. He has been the great awakener in this country of the spirit of philosophy, within the bounds of traditional opinions. He has been, almost as truly as Bentham, 'the great questioner of things established'; for a questioner needs nor necessarily be an enemy."

Samuel Taylor Coleridge was born in Ottery St. Mary, Devonshire, as the youngest son of the vicar of Ottery St Mary. He was the youngest of ten children, adored by his parents. His father, the Reverend John Coleridge, was already fifty-three years old. Ann Bowdon, the daughter of a farmer, his second wife, was forty-five at that time. Later Coleridge described his childhood as full fantasy: "At six years old I remember to have read Belisarius, Robinson Crusoe, and Philip Quarll - and then I found the Arabian Nights' entertainments - one tale of which (the tale of a man who was compelled to seek for a pure virgin) made so deep an impression on me (I had read it in the evening while my mother was mending stockings) that I was haunted by specters whenever I was in the dark - and I distinctly remember the anxious and fearful eagerness with which I used to watch the window in which the books lay - and whenever the sun lay upon them, I would seize it, carry it by the wall, and bask, and read."

After his father's death, Coleridge was sent away to Christ's Hospital School in London. Coleridge studied at Jesus College. He joined in the reformist movement stimulated by the French Revolution, and abandoned his studies in 1793. In desperation, after an unhappy love-affair and pressed by debt, he enlisted in the 15th Light Dragoons under the name of Silas Tomkin Comberbache. Soon he realised that he was unfit for an army career and he was brought out under 'insanity' clause by his brother, Captain James Coleridge. In Cambridge

Coleridge met the radical, future poet laureate Robert Southey (1774-1843) in 1794. Coleridge moved with him to Bristol to establish a community, but the plan failed. In 1795 he married the sister of Southey's fiancée Sara Fricker, whom he did not really love.

Coleridge's collection POEMS ON VARIOUS SUBJECTS was published in 1796, and in 1797 appeared POEMS. In the same year he began the publication of a short-lived liberal political periodical The Watchman. He started a close friendship with Dorothy and William Wordsworth, one of the most fruitful creative relationships in English literature. From it resulted Lyrical Ballads, which opened with Coleridge's 'Rime of the Ancient Mariner' and ended with Wordsworth's 'Tintern Abbey'.

These poems set a new style by using everyday language and fresh ways of looking at nature. 'The Rime of the Ancient Mariner', a 625-line ballad, is among his essential works. It tells of a sailor who kills an albatross and for that crime against nature endures terrible punishments. The ship upon which the Mariner serves is trapped in a frozen sea. An albatross comes to the aid of the ship; it saves everyone, and stays with the ship until the Mariner shoots it with his crossbow. The motiveless malignity leads to punishment: "And now there came both mist and show, / and it grew wondrous cold; / and ice, mast high, came floating by, / as green as emerald." After a ghost ship passes the crew begins to die but the mariner is eventually rescued. He knows his penance will continue and he is only a machine for dictating always the one story. When Mrs. Barbauld objected to Coleridge that the poem lacked a moral, the poet told her that "in my own judgment the poem had too much; and that the only or chief fault, if I might say so, was the obtrusion of the moral sentiment so openly on the reader as a principle or cause of action in a work of pure imagination."

The brothers Josiah and Thomas Wedge wood granted Coleridge an annuity of 150 pounds, thus enabling him to pursue his literary career. Disenchanted with political developments in France, Coleridge visited Germany in 1798-99 with Dorothy and William Wordsworth, and became interested in the works of Immanuel Kant. He studied philosophy at Göttingen University and mastered the German language. However, he considered his translations of Friedrich von Schiller's plays from the trilogy Wallenstein distasteful. At the end of 1799 Coleridge fell in love with Sara Hutchinson, the sister of Wordsworth's future wife, to whom he devoted his work DEJECTION: AN ODE (1802). During these years Coleridge also began to compile his NOTEBOOKS, daily meditations of his life.

Suffering from neuralgic and rheumatic pains, Coleridge had become addicted to opium, freely prescribed by physicians. In 1804 he sailed to Malta in search of better health. Supplied with an ounce of opium and nine ounces of laudanum, he wrote in his journal: "O dear God! Give me strength of soul to make one thorough Trial - If I land at Malta / spite of all horrors to go through one month of unstipulated nature..." He worked two years as secretary to the governor of Malta, and later traveled through Sicily and Italy, returning then to England. In 1809-10 he wrote and edited with Sara Hutchinson the literary and political magazine The Friend. From 1808 to 1818 he gave several lectures, chiefly in London, and was considered the greatest of Shakespearean critics.

According to the poet, he heard the words to his famous 'Kubla Khan' in a dream. "In Xanadu did Kubla Khan / A stately pleasure dome decree: / Where Alph, the sacred river, ran / through caverns measureless to man / Down to a sunless sea. / so twice five miles of fertile ground / with walls and towers were girdled round: / and there were gardens bright with sinuous rills, / Where blossomed many an incense-bearing tree; / and here were forests ancient as the hills / Enfolding sunny spots of greenery." (From Kubla Khan, 1798) 'Christabel' and 'Kubla Khan' circulated many years in oral form before publication, and especially 'Christabel' influenced later the works of Sir Walter Scott and Lord Byron. In the summer of 1797 the author had retired to a lonely farm-house between Porlock and Linton. He had taken anodyne and after three hours sleep he woke up with a clear image of the poem. Disturbed by a visitor, he lost the vision, with the exception of some eight or ten scattered lines and images. Modern scholarship is skeptical of this story, but it reveals Coleridge's interest in the workings of the subconscious.

In 1810 Coleridge's friendship with Wordsworth came to crisis, and the two poets never fully returned to the relationship they had earlier. During the following years, Coleridge lived in London, on the verge of suicide. REMORSE, a play which he had written many years earlier, was successfully produced at the Drury Lane theatre in 1813. He received £400, which he spent in a few months. After a physical and spiritual crisis at Greyhound Inn, Bath, he submitted himself to a series of medical régimes to free himself from opium. He found a permanent harbor in High gate in the household of Dr. James Gillman, and enjoyed almost legendary reputation among the younger Romantics. During this time he rarely left the house.

In 1816 the unfinished poems 'Christabel' and 'Kubla Khan' were published, and next year appeared SIBYLLINE LEAVES. After 1817 Coleridge devoted himself to theological and politico-sociological works - his final position was that of a Romantic conservative and Christian radical. "Every reform, however necessary, will by weak minds be carried to an excess, that itself will need reforming," he wrote in BIOGRAPHIA LITERARIA (1817). Coleridge contributed to several magazines, among them Blackwood's Edinburgh Magazine. In 1824 Coleridge was elected a fellow of the Royal Society of Literature. He died in High gate, near London on July 25, 1834. Coleridge's daughter Sara (1802-1852) was also a writer and translator. She published children's verse, PRETTY LESSONS IN VERSE FOR GOOD CHILDREN (1834) and PHANTASMION (1837). When her husband died she took up the task of editing her father's works.

Chapter 2

A Note on Coleridge's Life

EARLY LIFE AND EDUCATION

Samuel Taylor Coleridge was born on October 21, 1772 in the rural town of Ottery St Mary, Devonshire. He was the youngest of ten children, and his father, the Reverend John Coleridge, was a well respected vicar. Coleridge suffered from constant ridicule by his older brother Frank, partially due to jealousy, as Samuel was often praised and favoured by his parents. To escape this abuse, he frequently sought refuge at a local library, which led him to discover his passion for poetry.

After the death of his father in 1781, contrary to his desires, he was sent to Christ's Hospital. The school was originally founded in the 16th century in Greyfriars, London and Hertford. [Now a boarding school in West Sussex]. The school was notorious for its unwelcoming atmosphere and strict regimen under The Rev. James Bowyer, many years Head Master of the grammar school, which fostered thoughts of guilt and depression in young Samuel's maturing mind. However, Coleridge seems to have appreciated his teacher, as he wrote in detailed recollections of his schooldays in Biographia Literaria:

I enjoyed the inestimable advantage of a very sensible, though at the same time, a very severe master...At the same time that we were studying the Greek Tragic Poets, he made us read Shakespeare and Milton as lessons: and they were the lessons too, which required most time and trouble to bring up, so as to escape his censure. I learnt from him, that Poetry, even that of the loftiest, and, seemingly, that of the wildest odes, had a logic of its own, as severe as that of science; and more difficult, because more subtle, more complex, and dependent on more, and more fugitive causes....

In our own English compositions (at least for the last three years of our school education) he showed no mercy to phrase, metaphor, or image, unsupported by a sound sense, or where the same sense might have been conveyed with equal force and dignity in plainer words... In fancy I can almost hear him now, exclaiming Harp? Harp? Lyre? Pen and ink, boy, you mean! Muse, boy, Muse? Your Nurse's daughter, you mean! Pierian Spring? Oh aye! The cloister-pump, I suppose!... Be this as it may, there was one custom of our master's, which I cannot pass over in silence, because I think it... worthy of imitation. He would often permit our theme exercises, to accumulate, till each lad had four or five to be looked over. Then placing the whole number abreast on his desk, he would ask the writer, why this or that sentence might not have found as appropriate a place under this or that other thesis: and if no satisfying answer could be returned, and two faults of the same kind were found in one exercise, the irrevocable verdict followed, the exercise was torn up, and another on the same subject to be produced, in addition to the tasks of the day.

Throughout life, Coleridge idealized his father as pious and innocent, but his relationship with his mother was more problematic. His childhood was characterized by attention-seeking, which has been linked to his dependent personality as an adult. He was rarely allowed to return home during the school term, and this distance from his family at such a turbulent time proved emotionally damaging. He later wrote of his loneliness at school in the poem Frost at Midnight: "With unclosed lids, already had I dreamt/of my sweet birthplace"

From 1791 until 1794 Coleridge attended Jesus College, Cambridge. In 1792 he won the Browne Gold Medal for an Ode that he wrote on the slave trade. In November, 1793, he left the college and enlisted in the Royal Dragoons, perhaps because of debt or because the girl that he loved, Mary Evans, had rejected him. His brothers arranged for his discharge a few months later (ironically because of supposed insanity) and he was readmitted to Jesus College, though he would never receive a degree from Cambridge.

PANTISOCRACY AND MARRIAGE

At the university he was introduced to political and theological ideas then considered radical, including those of the poet Robert Southey. Coleridge joined Southey in a plan, soon abandoned, to found a utopian commune-like society, called Pantisocracy, in the wilderness of Pennsylvania. In 1795 the two friends married sisters Sarah and Edith Fricker, but Coleridge's marriage proved unhappy. He grew to detest his wife, whom he only married because of social constraints, and eventually divorced her. During and after his failed marriage, he came to love a woman named Sara Hutchinson, who did not share this passion and consequentially caused him much distress. Sara departed for Portugal, but Coleridge remained in Britain. In 1796 he published Poems on Various Subjects.

In 1795 Coleridge met poet William Wordsworth and his sister Dorothy. They became immediate friends.

Around 1796, Coleridge started taking opium as a pain-reliever. His suffering, caused by many ailments, including toothache and facial neuralgia, is mentioned in his own notebook as well as that of Dorothy Wordsworth. There was no stigma associated with taking opium at the time, but also little understanding of the dangers of addiction.

The years 1797 and 1798, during which he lived in Nether Stowey, Somerset, and Wordsworth, having visited him and being enchanted by the surroundings, rented Alfoxton Park, a little over three miles (5 km) away, were among the most fruitful of Coleridge's life. Besides the Rime of The Ancient Mariner, he composed the symbolic poem Kubla Khan, written—Coleridge himself claimed—as a result of an opium dream, in "a kind of a reverie"; and the first part of the narrative poem Christabel. During this period he also produced his much-praised "conversation" poems This Lime-Tree Bower My Prison, Frost at Midnight, and The Nightingale.

In 1798 Coleridge and Wordsworth published a joint volume of poetry, Lyrical Ballads, which proved to be the starting point for the English Romantic Movement. Though the productive Wordsworth contributed more poems to the volume, Coleridge's first version of The Rime of the Ancient Mariner was the longest poem and drew more immediate attention than anything else. In the spring of 1798, Coleridge temporarily took over for Rev. Joshua Toulmin at Taunton's Mary Street Unitarian Chapel while Rev. Toulmin grieved over the drowning death of his daughter Jane. Poetically commenting on the strength of Rev. Toulmin, Coleridge wrote in a 1798 letter to John Prior Estlin.

In the autumn of 1798, Coleridge and Wordsworth left for a stay in Germany; Coleridge soon went his own way and spent much of his time in university towns. During this period he became interested in German philosophy, especially the transcendental idealism of Immanuel Kant, and in the literary criticism of the 18th century dramatist Gotthold Lessing. Coleridge studied German and, after his return to England, translated the dramatic trilogy Wallenstein by the German Classical poet Friedrich Schiller into English.

Coleridge's greatest intellectual debts were first to William Godwin's Political Justice, especially during his Pantisocratic period, and to David Hartley's Observations on Man, which is the source of the psychology which we find in "Frost at Midnight." Hartley argued that we become aware of sensory events as impressions, and that "ideas" are derived by noticing similarities and differences between impressions and then by naming them. Connections resulting from the coincidence of impressions create linkages, so that the occurrence of one impression triggers those links and calls up the memory of those ideas with which it is associated.Coleridge was critical of the literary taste of his contemporaries, and a literary conservative insofar as he was afraid that the lack of taste in the ever growing masses of literate people would mean a continued desecration of literature itself.

In 1800 he returned to England and shortly thereafter settled with his family and friends at Keswick in the Lake District of Cumberland to be near Grasmere, where Wordsworth had moved. Soon, however, he was beset by marital problems, illnesses, increased opium dependency, tensions with Wordsworth, and a lack of confidence in his poetic powers, all of which fueled the composition of Dejection: An Ode and an intensification of his philosophical studies.

In 1804 he traveled to Sicily and Malta, working for a time as Acting Public Secretary of Malta under the Commissioner, Alexander Ball. He gave this up and returned to England in 1806. Dorothy Wordsworth was shocked at his condition upon his return. From 1807 to 1808, Coleridge returned to Malta and then traveled in Sicily and Italy, in the hope that leaving Britain's damp climate would improve his health and thus enable him to reduce his consumption of opium. Thomas de Quincy alleges in his Recollections of the Lakes and the Lake Poets that it was during this period that Coleridge became a full-blown opium addict, using the drug as a substitute for the lost vigor and creativity of his youth. It has been suggested, however, that this reflects de Quincy's own experiences more than Coleridge's. His opium addiction (he was using as much as two quarts of laudanum a week) now began to take over his life: he separated from his wife in 1808, quarreled with Wordsworth in 1810, lost part of his annuity in 1811, put himself under the care of Dr. Daniel in 1814.Between 1810 and 1820 this "giant among dwarfs", as he was often considered by his contemporaries, gave a series of lectures in London and Bristol – those on Shakespeare renewed interest in the playwright as a model for contemporary writers.

In 1817 Coleridge, with his addiction worsening, his spirits depressed, and his family alienated, took residence in the home of the physician James Gillman, at 3 The Grove, High gate,

London, England. In Gillman's home he finished his major prose work, the Biographia Literaria (1815), a volume composed of 23 chapters of autobiographical notes and dissertations on various subjects, including some incisive literary theory and criticism. He composed much poetry here and had many inspirations – a few of them from opium overdose. Perhaps because he conceived such grand projects, he had difficulty carrying them through to completion, and he berated himself for his "indolence." It is unclear whether his growing use of opium was a symptom or a cause of his growing depression. He published other writings while he was living at the Gillman home, notably Sibylline Leaves (1820), Aids to Reflection (1823), and Church and State (1826). He died of a lung disorder including some heart failure from the opium that he was taking in High gate on July 25, 1834.

POETRY

Coleridge is probably best known for his long poems, The Rime of the Ancient Mariner and Christabel. Even those who have never read the Rime have come under its influence: its words have given the English language the metaphor of an albatross around one's neck, the quotation of "water, water everywhere, nor any drop to drink (almost always rendered as "but not a drop to drink")", and the phrase "a sadder and a wiser man (again, usually rendered as "sadder but wiser man")". Christabel is known for its musical rhythm, language, and its Gothic tale.

Kubla Khan, or, A Vision in a Dream, A Fragment, although shorter, is also widely known and loved. It has strange, dreamy imagery and can be read on many levels. Both Kubla Khan and Christabel have an additional "romantic" aura because they were never finished. Stopford Brooke characterized both poems as having no rival due to their "exquisite metrical movement" and "imaginative phrasing." It is one of history's tragedies that Coleridge was interrupted while writing Kubla Khan by a visitor and could not recall any more of the poem afterwards. However, it is now acknowledged that Coleridge had composed previous drafts of Kubla Khan, perhaps a reflection of his desire to flag the 'power' of imagination. Coleridge's shorter, meditative "conversation poems," however, proved to be the most influential of his work. These include both quiet poems like This Lime-Tree Bower My Prison and Frost at Midnight and also strongly emotional poems like Dejection and The Pains of Sleep. Wordsworth immediately adopted the model of these poems, and used it to compose several of his major poems. Via Wordsworth, the conversation poem became a standard vehicle for English poetic expression, and perhaps the most common approach among modern poets. Coleridge's poetry so impressed the parents of British composer Samuel Coleridge-Taylor (1875-1912) that they named him after the poet.

COLERIDGE AND THE INFLUENCE OF THE GOTHIC

Gothic novels like Polidori's The Vampire, Walpole's The Castle of Otranto, Mrs. Radcliff's The Mysteries of Udolpho and The Italian, and Matthew Lewis's The Monk were the best-sellers of the end of the eighteenth century, and thrilled many young women (who were often strictly forbidden to read them). Jane Austen satirized the style mercilessly in Northanger Abbey. Coleridge wrote reviews of Mrs. Radcliff's books and of The Mad Monk among others. He comments in his reviews:

Situations of torment, and images of naked horror, are easily conceived; and a writer in whose works they abound, deserves our gratitude almost equally with him who should drag us by way of sport through a military hospital, or force us to sit at the dissecting-table of a natural philosopher. To trace the nice boundaries, beyond which terror and sympathy are deserted by the pleasurable emotions, - to reach those limits, yet never to pass them, hic labour, hic opus est.

And:

The horrible and the preternatural have usually seized on the popular taste, at the rise and decline of literature. Most powerful stimulants, they can never be required except by the torpor of an unawakened, or the languor of an exhausted, appetite... We trust, however, that satiety will banish what good sense should have prevented; and that, wearied with fiends, incomprehensible characters, with shrieks, murders, and subterraneous dungeons, the public will learn, by the multitude of the manufacturers, with how little expense of thought or imagination this species of composition is manufactured. However, Coleridge used mysterious and demonic elements in poems such as The Rime of the Ancient Mariner (1798), Christabel and Kubla Khan (published 1816 but known in manuscript form before then) and certainly influenced other poets and writers of the time. Poems like these both drew inspiration from and helped to inflame the craze for Gothic romance.

Mary Shelley, who knew Coleridge well, mentions The Rime of the Ancient Mariner twice directly in Frankenstein and some of the descriptions in the novel echo it indirectly. Although William Godwin, her father, disagreed with Coleridge on some important issues, he respected his opinions and Coleridge often visited the Godwins. Mary Shelley later recalled hiding behind the sofa and hearing his voice chanting The Rime of the Ancient Mariner.

COLERIDGE'S FRIENDSHIP WITH WORDSWORTH

It was the genius of Wordsworth—and, with Wordsworth, we must always think of his 'exquisite sister'—that first revealed him to himself. It was in daily intercourse with a stronger spirit than his own—first at Stowey (1797–8), then, more fitfully, in the lake country (1800–3)—that all his enduring poetry was composed. The spell of Wordsworth, however, went far deeper than this. It not only awakened the younger poet to creative energies which had hitherto lain asleep. It was a transforming influence upon his whole cast of thought, upon the whole character of his soul. His whole nature was roused, for the first time, to a full consciousness of its powers; and powers of which he had hitherto given no suspicion were suddenly called to light. A sense of the beauty of outward things, as deep as Wordsworth's, but still more delicate and more subtle; a sense of the boundless mystery of life—the inner yet more than the outer life—and a power of interpreting it in terms of thought: these were the two gifts which came to him with this new birth; and, however idly he may have used them, they remained with him to the end.

Well might he say that "a new earth and a new heaven" were now "given to him in dower?" For he saw the world with a keener and more radiant vision than had ever been granted to him before; and he saw into it more deeply. In the full sense of the terms, he became, for the first time, both philosopher and poet.

That his use of these magic gifts was not what it might have been is too clear. But it is only just to remember that this applies more to his work as philosopher than as poet. Poetry "comes not with observation." And, if that be true, in a measure, of all poetry, of none is it as true as of that to which the peculiar genius of Coleridge was manifestly ordained. Is it reasonable to suppose that any poet could have gone on living for ever in an air so rarefied as that of The Ancient Mariner, or Kubla Khan, or Christabel? Given circumstances as happy as almost to amount to a miracle, perhaps he might. But the miracle did not happen to Coleridge; and, even if his will had been as strong as it was weak, there is no warrant that it would have happened.

To condemn him on this score, however much he himself would have accepted the condemnation, seems, therefore, unwarrantably harsh. But his other gifts lay in a region more under his control. And, had he been a man of ordinary resolution—above all, had he not let himself become the slave of opium—there was nothing to prevent him from accomplishing a giant's work in philosophy and criticism. In criticism and the theory of criticism, he might have done for his own country the double work which was done for Germany by Lessing and Hegel, and something more besides. In philosophy, he might have recast and even extended the massive fabric of Kant. As it is, in neither field has he left more than a heap of disjointed, but imposing, fragments.

THE FRENCH REVOLUTION

Up to this time, there is nothing beyond the doubtful evidence of a school exercise to show that the revolution in France had roused any deep interest, or even attention, in his mind. Now, under the tenser will of Southey, he became a fiery revolutionist, of a brand, however, peculiarly his own. In hatred of Pitt and the war, he was, no doubt, at one with the other Jacobins of the time. But the Pantisocracy, which the two friends beat out between them, ran decisively athwart the main stream of revolutionary aspirations. It was intended only for the select few; it was no part of a general scheme of social reconstruction.

Again, the "Jacobinism" of Coleridge, though not that of Southey, was always strongly charged with a mystical and religious element, which stands in the sharpest contrast with the purely secular, often atheist, temper more common among the reformers of that day. Lastly—and here, once again, he joins hands with Southey—the whole creed and being of the young convert were drowned in a flood of sentiment which woke in him, for the first time in good earnest, the need of poetic utterance, and which at once sets a barrier between him and most of the leading figures among the rebel band: Godwin, for instance, or Holcroft, or even Thelwall.

It was in pleading the cause of Pantisocracy that he first discovered—to himself, perhaps, as well as to others—his amazing powers of eloquence. His letters of that time are full of boyish delight in the discovery: "Up I arose, terrible in reasoning" is a typical sentence. And, so long as he could convince, or even vanquish, his opponents, it is clear that he did not much trouble himself to put his convictions into act. Even his breach with Southey, who soon became lukewarm in the cause, would seem to have partly sprung from an uneasy sense that he, too, had said more than he was willing or able to make good, and from the consequent impulse, very natural though not very just, to prove that some one else was yet more guilty than himself. Still more ominous, even in an age of overwrought sentiment, is the sentimentalism of his letters. "Since I quitted this room," he writes on his return from the fateful visit to Oxford, "what and how important events have been evolved! America! Southey! Miss Fricker! Yes, Southey, you are right.

Even love is the creature of strong motive. I certainly love her." It is small wondered that the love which began as "the creature of strong motive"—that is, Southey's fiat—should have ended disastrously for both. A year later (October, 1795) the marriage duly took place.

The poetry of these years (1794–6) is a mirror of the man: eloquent, loose-girt, and strongly inclined to preach; in all things, the very reverse of the inspired pieces soon to follow. It is, doubtless, the sincere expression of the generous convictions and aspirations which he held in common with others. But it lacks the individuality which is the soul of poetry; and, only in one passage—some three or four lines of The Eolian Harp 2 —does it offer even a faint promise of the works by which he lives. It is a glorified version of sermons such as Hazlitt heard in the enchanted walls of the Shropshire chapel. It has nothing in common with The Ancient Mariner, or Christabel, or even the ode Dejection.

THE OPIUM HABIT

The opium habit, the beginnings of which go back as far as 1797, seems to have grown upon him during his time at Malta (1804–6); and, by the time he returned to England, the bondage must have been confirmed. Again and again, he strove to throw off the yoke; but only to fall back again more helplessly than before. Degraded in his own eyes, he felt life to be a burden almost too heavy to be borne; and the letters which, now and again, were wrung from him by remorse, are, perhaps, among the most terrible ever written.

Two things alone saved him from total shipwreck: the unwearied tenderness of friends, old and new—Poole, Wordsworth, Mrs. Clarkson and the Morgan's; and the innate rectitude, winged by a strong religious impulse, which did not cease to assert itself against reiterated defeat. At length, after ten years of debasement, he nerved himself to seek refuge with James Gillman, a physician of High gate (1816). And, thanks to the devoted friendship and watchfulness of this man and his wife—he remained their "inmate" till his death—he slowly tore himself loose from the bondage in which he had been held. That he never wholly gave up the drug is tolerably clear. But he so far mastered himself as to take it in rarer and smaller doses; and, for practical purposes, the hard-fought victory was won.

Thus, the last eighteen years of his life were years of inward peace and of fruitful service to others. The old weakness, no doubt, still dogged his steps and prevented the fulfillment of the task—a work on Spiritual Philosophy and half a dozen alternative titles—to which he was conscious of being called. But, in familiar talk, in formal lecturing and even in published writings, this was the richest period of his life; and it left a deep mark upon some of the strongest and most eager spirits of the younger generation.

The victory was won. But the long years of apparently hopeless struggle had left scars which nothing could wholly heal. The prime of his life had been largely wasted. And he had strained the patience of some of his best friends. Josiah Wedgwood had withdrawn, perhaps with undue harshness, his half of the pension that he and his brother had granted in days when nothing seemed beyond the reach of the young poet and thinker. Southey, who had gallantly shouldered the charge of the truant's wife and children, was embittered, if not estranged. Even Wordsworth, by an unguarded utterance made with the best intentions, had caused a breach which could never wholly be made up.

This was probably the deepest sorrow of his life; "all else," he says, "is as a flea-bite." His family life, too—though this was from causes which, in the first instance, at any rate, had little to do with opium—had been entirely broken up. And, though a formal separation was avoided, he never lived with his wife after 1810; and had, in fact, seen as little as he could of her since 1804. The real secret of the estrangement was that, by temperament, the two were ill sorted with each other. But it is impossible not to feel the deepest sympathy with a woman who battled bravely with the hardships of her lot; and hard to check the suspicion that, but for opium, the difficulties might have been smoothed over. In any case, the breach was a worse thing for Coleridge than he was ever willing to acknowledge. It robbed him of the steadying influences of home life, to which he was by nature peculiarly open. And it left a sting in his conscience which he may have ignored, but which, just for that reason, was never healed.

Chapter 3

Chronology

A SAMUEL TAYLOR COLERIDGE CHRONOLOGY

- 1772 born (Oct. 21) at Ottery St. Mary's, Devonshire.
- 1781 father dies.
- 1782-91 at Christ's Hospital (school). [See Lamb, "Christ's Hospital Five- and-Thirty years ago."]
- 1789 reads Bowles's Sonnets.
- 1790-91 Brother Luke and Sister Ann die.
- 1791-94 at Cambridge.
- 1793 in love with Mary Evans; enlists in the 15th Dragoons.
- 1794 returns to Cambridge; meets Southey. Engaged to Sara Fricker. Meets Godwin. STC and Southey plan a "Pantisocracy."
- 1795 meets Wordsworth. Marries Sara Fricker.
- 1796 Poems on Various Subjects. Son Hartley born. Coleridge moves to Nether Stowey. First takes opium.
- 1796-97 preaching at various Unitarian chapels.
- 1797 with Wordsworth at Nether Stowey. Begins The Ancient Mariner.
- 1798 Lyrical Ballads, with Wordsworth. Wedgwood's give Coleridge £150 annuity. Visits Germany with Wordsworth. Writes "Kubla Khan."

- 1799 meets Sara Hutchinson. Tours the Lake District.
- 1799-1802 writes political leaders for Morning Post.
- 1801 health breaks down; opium again.
- 1802 "Dejection, an Ode." Daughter Sara born.
- 1803 tours Scotland with W. & Dorothy Wordsworth.
- 1804 in Malta and Sicily. Private Secretary to Alex. Ball, High Commissioner at Malta.
- 1805 appointed Acting Public Secretary in Malta.
- 1806 returns to England; D. Wordsworth "shocked" at his condition.
- 1808 separates from wife.
- 1809-10 the Friend.
- 1810 quarrel with Wordsworth. Heavily addicted to opium.
- 1811 Josiah Wedge wood withdraws half STC's annuity.
- 1811-12 Lectures on Shakespeare.
- 1812 reconciled to Wordsworth.
- 1812-13 lectures on Belles Letters.
- 1814 in the care of Dr. Daniel for opium addiction. Lectures in Bristol. Turns from Unitarianism to Anglicanism.
- 1814-16 financial difficulties.
- 1816 settles at High gate with Dr. James Gilman. Christabel and Kubla Khan.
- 1817 Biographia Literaria and Lay Sermons.
- 1819 more Lectures on Shakespeare.
- 1825 Aids to Reflection. Appointed Associate of the Royal Society of Literature, begins receiving £125 annuity.
- 1826-34 "High gate Thursdays."
- 1828 continental tour with Wordsworth.
- 1830 Constitution of Church and State.
- 1834 dies July 25.

Chapter 4

Introduction to the Times

LITERARY CONTEXT

The Romantic Movement in Britain, Europe, and America provided the broad literary background for the rise of Transcendentalism. Romanticism permeated American literature between 1820 and the end of the Civil War in 1865. It was expressed not only in the writings of the Transcendentalists, but also by their literary contemporaries—James Fenimore Cooper, Edgar Allan Poe, Henry Wadsworth Longfellow, Nathaniel Hawthorne, Herman Melville, and Walt Whitman—who worked in a variety of genres. Romanticism informed the literature of the period and also gave direction to developments in art, architecture, and music. The landscape paintings of the Hudson River School, for example, and of Washington Allston whose work defined art for Margaret Fuller, Elizabeth Peabody, and others among the Transcendentalists—grew out of European Romanticism.

Romanticism (or "Romanticisms," as some literary scholars have preferred to term the multiplicity of expressions of the movement) emerged in England and Germany in the late eighteenth century. Influenced by the intuitive philosophy of Kant, Romantic writers looked at literature as an outpouring of the inner spirit, and saw imagination as the means of summoning this spirit. They reacted against classical formalism and symmetry, against rationalism, and against other restrictions on individual expression and imagination.

Romantic writers celebrated the freedom of the individual, whom they placed at the centre of life and art, and the expression of personal emotion. Perceiving physical objects as representative of spiritual, moral, and intellectual reality, Romantic writers relied heavily on symbolism and allegory. Romantic literature displayed a number of recurrent motifs: the theme of the individual in rebellion; the symbolic interpretation of the historic past; subjects from myth and folklore; the glorification of nature; faraway settings; sentimentalism; the nobility of the uncivilized man; admiration for the simple life; the elevation of the common man; a fascination with Gothic themes, with the supernatural and mysterious, with introspection, melancholy, and horror; and a humanitarian political and social outlook. The American experience provided much raw material suited to Romantic interpretation.

British Romantic authors William Wordsworth, Samuel Taylor Coleridge, and Thomas Carlyle greatly influenced the New England Transcendentalists. Poets Wordsworth (1770–1850) and Coleridge (1772–1834) together wrote Lyrical Ballads, the first edition of which was issued in 1798. In these poems, Wordsworth and Coleridge presented personal feeling, employed language that reflected the spoken rather than the stylized written word, and focused on both the supernatural and ordinary experience. In his Biographia Literaria (1817) and his Aids to Reflection (1825), Coleridge presented the Kantian distinction between knowledge gained through the senses ("Understanding") and that grasped intuitively ("Reason") and discussed German philosophy. Carlyle (1795–1881) impressed the Transcendentalists with his essays on German literature and philosophy, his translations from Goethe, his Sartor Resartus (1836), The French Revolution (1837), and On Heroes and Hero-Worship (1841). Some of the Transcendentalists had the opportunity to meet Wordsworth, Coleridge, and Carlyle. Emerson met all three of them on his first trip abroad (1832–1833). The Transcendentalists also read German and French Romantic authors, among them Goethe, Richter, Schlegel, Cousin, Chateaubriand, and Madame de Stäel.

American Romanticism was powerfully expressed with the anonymous publication of Emerson's Nature in 1836. This manifesto of Transcendentalism, based on earlier journal entries, sermons, and lectures, was soon followed by the important addresses "The American Scholar" (1837) and the "Divinity School Address" (1838). In "The American Scholar," delivered before the Phi Beta Kappa Society at Harvard on August 31, 1837, and published in the same year, Emerson urged self-reliance, self-knowledge, and closeness to nature in the forging of an original American thought and literature. In the "Divinity School Address," delivered at Harvard on July 15, 1838, and first printed in the same year, he exhorted the pursuit of spiritual truth by the individual through intuition rather than through the passive acceptance of traditional religion. The publication of these three "scriptures" of Transcendentalism imparted energy and momentum to the efforts of the movement's proponents. The Transcendental Club was formed in 1836, the year in which Nature was published, providing the opportunity for Emerson, Alcott, Clarke, Parker, Fuller, Ripley, Brownson, Peabody, Thoreau, Very, Crunch, and others to explore their philosophical similarities and differences.

Romanticism in the form of Transcendentalism was communicated foremost through the writings of the faithful. Emerson, Thoreau, Fuller, and others published lengthy works of a range of types on a variety of subjects, each in its own way an expression of Romantic ideals. The Transcendentalists also conveyed their philosophy, concerns, and creativity through shorter pieces printed in the periodical publications that were important to the intellectual life of the mid-nineteenth century. The Western Messenger, published in Cincinnati and Louisville from 1835 to 1841, included pieces on Unitarianism, Transcendentalism, and German and Oriental literature. In 1838, Orestes Brownson began the Boston Quarterly Review. The Dial, the best-known organ of Transcendentalism, edited by Emerson and Margaret Fuller and published for a time by Elizabeth Palmer Peabody, was issued between 1840 and 1844. The Brook Farm publication

The Harbinger commenced in 1845. Theodore Parker founded the Massachusetts Quarterly Review in 1847. The single issue of Elizabeth Peabody's Aesthetic Papers appeared in 1849. The North American Review began publication in 1854, Atlantic Monthly in 1857. Both were later bought by the Boston publishing firm of Ticknor and Fields. Neither publication was strictly a periodical of American Transcendentalism, but both included pieces by Emerson, Thoreau, and others.

The flowering of Transcendentalism was only one American expression of Romanticism—albeit the strongest one—in the period between 1820 and 1865. Moreover, the literary presentation of Romantic themes and ideas was not confined only to New England authors. Novelist James Fenimore Cooper (1789–1851) vividly wrote about the frontier experience, life at sea, America's past, the wilderness, and the individual's relation to society. His Leatherstocking Series was published between 1823 and 1841. A critic of Transcendentalism and an opponent of abolition and reform, Edgar Allan Poe (1809–1849) had nevertheless been influenced by Coleridge in his approach to literary criticism. His poetry conveyed intense emotion; his stories were full of mystery and horror. Popular poet Henry Wadsworth Longfellow (1807–1882) wrote personal sonnets, took history as subject matter (his narrative poem Evangeline was published in 1847), and drew upon Native American legend in his poem The Song of Hiawatha (1855). Although not a Transcendentalist, Nathaniel Hawthorne (1804–1864) spent a substantial portion of his life among Transcendentalists. Married to Sophia Peabody, sister of Elizabeth Palmer Peabody, he lived in Concord from 1842 to 1845, at the height of the transcendental movement, and again later in life. He was also a resident of Brook Farm. His romances and stories, rich with symbolism and allegory, focused on the individual, explored morality, dealt with historical subjects, and examined the effect of the past upon the present. Herman Melville (1819–1891) wrote narratives drawing upon his personal experiences in exotic places and his knowledge of life at sea. His Moby-Dick (1851) was atmospheric, evocative, allegorical, symbolic, an exploration of good and evil—the embodiment of Romantic literature. Poet Walt Whitman (1819–1892) was deeply moved by Emerson's thought and writing. His Leaves of Grass (1855) extolled the individual in the person of the poet himself and celebrated personal expression, freedom, and the intuitive understanding of the world. Whitman went far beyond the transcendental vision in assigning a place of importance to sensuality.

All of these voices of Romanticism, and other writers as well (Washington Irving, William Gilmore Simms, William Cullen Bryant, Nathaniel Parker Willis, and John Greenleaf Whittier among them), contributed to the development of that vigorous national thought and expression that Emerson had envisioned in 1837 in "The American Scholar." The Romantic impulse played a major role in the mid-nineteenth century blossoming of American literature and art that has been called the American Renaissance

Chapter 5

Biographia Literaria: An Introduction

The Biographia Literaria was one of Coleridge's main critical studies. In this work, he discussed the elements of writing and what writing should be to be considered genius. Although the work is not written from Coleridge's poetic mind, it is still written with the qualities and rhythm of the poetic. Not only does he discuss literature itself he discusses the many variables that influence and inspire writers. Through this discussion, he makes many value judgments, leaving his audience with a clear understand of his stance on certain issues. Some of the issues he tackles include politics, religion, social values, and human identity. His treatment of these issues tends to be conservative in its foundation, yet also blatant and original. He does not cater to one certain audience; rather he expresses his own thoughts from a personal viewpoint. Coleridge delivers the Biographia Literaria without a second thought of whether or not there will be any disagreement from his audience.

"Imagination" and "Fancy"

Rejecting the empiricist assumption that the mind was a tabula rasa on which external experiences and sense impressions were imprinted, stored, recalled, and combined through a process of association, Coleridge divided the "mind" into two distinct faculties. He labeled these the "Imagination" and "Fancy."

The Imagomatopm then, I consider either as primary, or secondary. The primary IMAGINATION I hold to be the living Power and prime Agent of all human Perception, and as a repetition in the finite mind of the eternal act of creation in the infinite I AM. The secondary Imagination I consider as an echo of the former, co-existing with the conscious will, yet still as identical with the primary in the kind of its agency, and differing only in degree, and in the mode of operation. It dissolves, diffuses, dissipates, in order to recreate; or where this process is rendered impossible, yet still at all events it struggles to idealize and unify. It is essentially vital, even as all objects (as objects) are essentially fixed and dead.

Fancy, on the contrary, has no other counters to play with, but fixities and definite. The Fancy is indeed no other than a mode of Memory emancipated from the order of time and space; while it is blended with, and modified by that empirical phenomenon of the will, which we express by the word Choice. But equally with the ordinary memory the Fancy must receive all its materials ready made from the law of association.

"Fancy," in Coleridge's eyes was employed for tasks that were "passive" and "mechanical", the accumulation of fact and documentation of what is seen. "Always the ape," Fancy, Coleridge argued, was "too often the adulterator and counterfeiter of memory."59 The Imagination on the other hand was "vital" and transformative, "a repetition in the finite mind of the eternal act of creation." For Coleridge, it was the Imagination that was responsible for acts that were truly creative and inventive and, in turn, that identified true instances of fine or noble art.

The Distinction B/W Fancy and the Imagination

The distinction made by Coleridge between Fancy and the Imagination rested on the fact that Fancy was concerned with the mechanical operations of the mind, those which are responsible for the passive accumulation of data and the storage of such data in the memory. Imagination, on the other hand, described the "mysterious power," which extracted from such data, "hidden ideas and meaning." It also determined "the various operations of constructive and inventive genius."

Engel has demonstrated that Coleridge's division of the imagination into the "primary" and "secondary" draws a distinction between creative acts that are unconscious and those that are intentional and deliberate. "The Primary Imagination" was for Coleridge, the "necessary imagination" as it "automatically balances and fuses the innate capacities and powers of the mind with the external presence of the objective world that the mind receives through the senses." It represents man's ability to learn from nature. The over arching property of the primary imagination was that it was common to all people. The Secondary imagination, on the other hand, represents a superior faculty which could only be associated with artistic genius. It was this aspect of the imagination, one which could break down what was perceived in order to recreate by an autonomous willful act of the mind that has no analog in the natural world—which Coleridge associated with art and poetry. A key and defining attribute of the secondary imagination was a free and deliberate will; "superior voluntary control... co-existing with the conscious will." The secondary imagination, once activated by the will, "dissolves, dissipates in order to recreate." Coleridge, Biographia Literaria.

Significance of the Imagination:

The significance of the Imagination for Coleridge was that it represented the sole faculty within man that was able to achieve the romantic ambition of reuniting the subject and the object; the world of the self and the world of nature. By establishing the creative act as mimicking the "organic principle" or "one"—a divine principle believed to underlie all reality—the romantic theorist sought to establish a harmonious relationship between the ideal world of the subject and the real world of the object. Baker has demonstrated that Coleridge was convinced that the Imagination acted as "a repetition in the finite mind of the eternal act of creation in the infinite I AM," and that it not only reinforced the notion that perception was active and creative, it established the cosmos as an organic entity.

For Coleridge, the most important aspect of the imagination was that it was active to the highest degree. The creative act called the whole soul of man into activity. As Baker has argued: "the creative act, on the contrary, is a godlike-act-of-power and causing-to-be, imagination being the divine potency in man. The creative act by which the poet writes the poem is similar to the creative act by which God ordered the world out of chaos; if the poet's creative act is not a creation xenophile, it is a process of organic becoming through which the materials are transformed into something absolutely new, and also very likely, strange." James Volant Baker, the Sacred River. Coleridge's Theory of the Imagination

"Imagination" as "ESEMPLASTIC,"

Coleridge explained this property of the "Imagination" as "ESEMPLASTIC," to "shape into one" and to "convey a new sense." Coleridge in the tenth chapter of Biographia Literaria described this ability of the imagination as "Esemplastic." Noting that esemplastic was a word he borrowed from the Greek "to shape," Coleridge explained that it referred to the imagination's ability to "shape into one, having to convey a new sense." He felt such a term was necessary as "it would aid the recollection of my meaning and prevent it being confounded with the usual import of the word imagination." Biographia Literaria, vol. 1, p. 86

If you really want to use a pretentious-sounding term, try esemplastic. Derived from Greek words meaning "into" and "one" and "mold," and coined by Coleridge in 1817, the word means "having the function of molding into unity; unifying." The picture derived from the word is of someone, probably a poet, taking images and words and feelings from a number of realms of human endeavor and thought and bringing them all together into a poem s/he writes. This requires a huge effort of the imagination, which we might call the "esemplastic power of the poetic imagination." A decade after its first appearance a writer could remark, "Nor I trust will Coleridge's favourite word esemplastic...ever become current."

Not only did the subject subsume the object it can also be argued that Imagination subsumed the role of Fancy within the creative work. Thus while Coleridge argued that the poet relied on both Fancy and Imagination when inventing a poem, and that the poet should seek a balance of these two faculties, (Coleridge, Biographia Literaria, Volume 1, p. 194) the "active" and "transformative" powers of the Imagination negated the contribution of, and representation of Fancy. In Coleridge's system, the Imagination is ultimately the only faculty which contributed to the creative process.

Chapter 6

Selected Chapters: Biographia Literaria

CHAPTER

- Motives to the present work—Reception of the Author's first publication—Discipline of his taste at school—Effect of contemporary writers on youthful minds—Bowles's Sonnets-Comparison between the poets before and since
- Supposed irritability of genius brought to the test of facts—Causes and occasions of the charge—Its injustice
- The Author's obligations to Critics, and the probable occasion—Principles of modern criticism—Mr. Southey's works and character
- The Lyrical Ballads with the Preface—Mr. Wordsworth's earlier poems—On Fancy and Imagination—The investigation of the distinction important to the Fine Arts
- On the law of Association—Its history traced from Aristotle to Hartley
- That Hartley's system, as far as it differs from that of Aristotle, is neither tenable in theory, nor founded in facts
- Of the necessary consequences of the Hartleian Theory—Of the original mistake or equivocation which procured its admission—Memoriatechnica

- The system of Dualism introduced by Des Cartes—Refined first by Spinoza and afterwards by Leibnitz into the doctrine of Harmonia praestabilita-Hylozoism—Materialism —None of these systems, or any possible theory of Association, supplies or supersedes a theory of Perception, or explains the formation of the Associable
- Is Philosophy possible as a science, and what are its conditions?—Giordano Bruno—Literary Aristocracy, or the existence of a tacit compact among the learned as a privileged order—The Author's obligations to the Mystics- To Immanuel Kant—The difference between the letter and The spirit of Kant's writings, and a vindication of Prudence in the teaching of Philosophy—Fichte's attempt to complete the Critical system-Its partial success and ultimate failure—Obligations to Schelling; and among English writers to Saumarez
- A Chapter of digression and anecdotes, as an interlude preceding that on the nature and genesis of the Imagination or Plastic Power—On Pedantry and pedantic expressions—Advice to young authors respecting publication—Various anecdotes of the Author's literary life, and the progress of his opinions in Religion and Politics
- An affectionate exhortation to those who in early life feel themselves disposed to become authors
- A Chapter of requests and premonitions concerning the perusal or omission of the chapter that follows
- On the Imagination, or Esemplastic power
- Occasion of the Lyrical Ballads, and the objects originally proposed—Preface to the second edition—The ensuing controversy, its causes and acrimony—Philosophic definitions of a Poem and Poetry with scholia
- The specific symptoms of poetic power elucidated in a Critical analysis of Shakespeare's Venus and Adonis, and Rape of Lucrece

- Striking points of difference between the Poets of the present age and those of the fifteenth and sixteenth centuries—Wish expressed for the union of the characteristic merits of both
- Examination of the tenets peculiar to Mr. Wordsworth— Rustic life (above all, low and rustic life) especially unfavourable to the formation of a human diction-The best parts of language the product of philosophers, not of clowns or shepherds—Poetry essentially ideal and generic-The language of Milton as much the language of real life, yea, incomparably more so than that of the cottager
- Language of metrical composition, why and wherein essentially different from that of prose—Origin and elements of metre-Its necessary consequences, and the conditions thereby imposed on the metrical writer in the choice of his diction
- Continuation—Concerning the real object, which, it is probable, Mr. Wordsworth had before him in his critical preface—Elucidation and application of this
- The former subject continued—The neutral style, or that common to Prose and Poetry, exemplified by specimens from Chaucer, Herbert, and others
- Remarks on the present mode of conducting critical journals
- The characteristic defects of Wordsworth's poetry, with the principles from which the judgment, that they are defects, is deduced—Their proportion to the beauties—For the greatest part characteristic of his theory only

SATYRANE'S LETTERS

- Critique on Bertram
- Conclusion

BIOGRAPHIA LITERARIA

CHAPTER I

Motives to the present work—Reception of the Author's first publication—Discipline of his taste at school—Effect of contemporary writers on youthful minds—Bowles's Sonnets—Comparison between the poets before and since Pope.

It has been my lot to have had my name introduced both in conversation, and in print, more frequently than I find it easy to explain, whether I consider the fewness, unimportance, and limited circulation of my writings, or the retirement and distance, in which I have lived, both from the literary and political world. Most often it has been connected with some charge which I could not acknowledge, or some principle which I had never entertained. Nevertheless, had I had no other motive or incitement, the reader would not have been troubled with this exculpation. What my additional purposes were will be seen in the following pages. It will be found, that the least of what I have written concerns myself personally. I have used the narration chiefly for the purpose of giving a continuity to the work, in part for the sake of the miscellaneous reflections suggested to me by particular events, but still more as introductory to a statement of my principles in Politics, Religion, and Philosophy, and an application of the rules, deduced from philosophical principles, to poetry and criticism. But of the objects, which I proposed to myself, it was not the least important to effect, as far as possible, a settlement of the long continued controversy concerning the true nature of poetic diction; and at the same time to define with the utmost impartiality the real poetic character of the poet, by whose writings this controversy was first kindled, and has been since fuelled and fanned.

In the spring of 1796, when I had but little passed the verge of manhood, I published a small volume of juvenile poems. They were received with a degree of favour, which, young as I was, I well know was bestowed on them not so much for any positive merit, as because they were considered buds of hope, and promises of better works to come. The critics of that day, the most flattering, equally with the severest, concurred in objecting to them obscurity, a general turgid ness of diction, and a profusion of new coined double epithets. The first is the fault which a writer is the least able to detect in his own compositions: and my mind was not then sufficiently disciplined to receive the authority of others, as a substitute for my own conviction. Satisfied that the thoughts, such as they were, could not have been expressed otherwise, or at least more perspicuously, I forgot to inquire, whether the thoughts themselves did not demand a degree of attention unsuitable to the nature and objects of poetry.

This remark however applies chiefly, though not exclusively, to the Religious Musings. The remainder of the charge I admitted to its full extent and not without sincere acknowledgments both to my private and public censors for their friendly admonitions. In the after editions, I pruned the double epithets with no sparing hand, and used my best efforts to tame the swell and glitter both of thought and diction; though in truth, these parasite plants of youthful poetry had insinuated themselves into my longer poems with such intricacy of union, that I was often obliged to omit disentangling the weed, from the fear of snapping the flower. From that period to the date of the present work I have published nothing, with my name, which could by any possibility have come before the board of anonymous criticism. Even the three or four poems, printed with the works of a friend, as far as they were censured at all, were charged with the same or similar defects, (though I am persuaded not with equal justice),—with an excess of ornament, in addition to strained and elaborate diction.

I must be permitted to add, that, even at the early period of my juvenile poems, I saw and admitted the superiority of an austere and more natural style, with an insight not less clear, than I at present possess. My judgment was stronger than were my powers of realizing its dictates; and the faults of my language, though indeed partly owing to a wrong choice of subjects, and the desire of giving a poetic colouring to abstract and metaphysical truths, in which a new world then seemed to open upon me, did yet, in part likewise, originate in unfeigned diffidence of my own comparative talent.—During several years of my youth and early manhood, I reverenced those who had re- introduced the manly simplicity of the Greek, and of our own elder poets, with such enthusiasm as made the hope seem presumptuous of writing successfully in the same style. Perhaps a similar process has happened to others; but my earliest poems were marked by an ease and simplicity, which I have studied, perhaps with inferior success, to impress on my later compositions.

At school, (Christ's Hospital,) I enjoyed the inestimable advantage of a very sensible, though at the same time, a very severe master, the Reverend James Bowyer. He early molded my taste to the preference of Demosthenes to Cicero, of Homer and Theocritus to Virgil, and again of Virgil to Ovid. He habituated me to compare Lucretius, (in such extracts as I then read,) Terence, and above all the chaster poems of Catullus, not only with the Roman poets of the, so called, silver and brazen ages; but with even those of the Augustan aera: and on grounds of plain sense and universal logic to see and assert the superiority of the former in the truth and native ness both of their thoughts and diction.

At the same time that we were studying the Greek tragic poets, he made us read Shakespeare and Milton as lessons: and they were the lessons too, which required most time and trouble to bring up, so as to escape his censure. I learned from him, that poetry, even that of the loftiest and, seemingly, that of the wildest odes, had a logic of its own, as severe as that of science; and more difficult, because more subtle, more complex, and dependent on more, and more fugitive causes. In the truly great poets, he would say, there is a reason assignable, not only for every word, but for the position of every word; and I well remember that, availing himself of the synonyms to the Homer of Didymus, he made us attempt to show, with regard to each, why it would not have answered the same purpose; and wherein consisted the peculiar fitness of the word in the original text. In our own English compositions, (at least for the last three years of our school education,) he showed no mercy to phrase, metaphor, or image, unsupported by a sound sense, or where the same sense might have been conveyed with equal force and dignity in plainer words.

Lute, harp, and lyre, Muse, Muses, and inspirations, Pegasus, Parnassus, and Hippocrene were all an abomination to him. In fancy I can almost hear him now, exclaiming "Harp? Harp? Lyre? Pen and ink, boy, you mean! Muse, boy, Muse? Your nurse's daughter, you mean! Pierian Spring? Oh aye! The cloister-pump, I suppose!" Nay certain introductions, similes, and examples, were placed by name on a list of interdiction. Among the similes, there was, I remember, that of the manchineel fruit, as suiting equally well with too many subjects; in which however it yielded the palm at once to the example of Alexander and Clytus, which was equally good and apt, whatever might be the theme. Was it ambition? Alexander and Clytus!-Flattery? Alexander and Clytus!—anger—drunkenness—pride—friendship—ingratitude—late repentance? Still, still Alexander and Clytus! At length, the praises of agriculture having been exemplified in the sagacious observation that, had Alexander been holding the plough, he would not have run his friend Clytus through with a spear, this tried, and serviceable old friend was banished by public edict in saecula saeculorum.

I have sometimes ventured to think, that a list of this kind, or an index expurgatorius of certain well-known and ever-returning phrases, both introductory, and transitional, including a large assortment of modest egoisms, and flattering illeisms, and the like, might be hung up in our Law-courts, and both Houses of Parliament, with great advantage to the public, as an important saving of national time, an incalculable relief to his Majesty's ministers, but above all, as insuring the thanks of country attornies, and their clients, who have private bills to carry through the House.

Be this as it may, there was one custom of our master's, which I cannot pass over in silence, because I think it imitable and worthy of imitation. He would often permit our exercises, under some pretext of want of time, to accumulate, till each lad had four or five to be looked over. Then placing the whole number abreast on his desk, he would ask the writer, why this or that sentence might not have found as appropriate a place under this or that other thesis: and if no satisfying answer could be returned, and two faults of the same kind were found in one exercise, the irrevocable verdict followed, the exercise was torn up, and another on the same subject to be produced, in addition to the tasks of the day. The reader will, I trust, excuse this tribute of recollection to a man, whose severities, even now, not seldom furnish the dreams, by which the blind fancy would fain interpret to the mind the painful sensations of distempered sleep; but neither lessen nor dim the deep sense of my moral and intellectual obligations. He sent us to the University excellent Latin and Greek scholars, and tolerable Hebraists. Yet our classical knowledge was the least of the good gifts, which we derived from his zealous and conscientious tutorage. He is now gone to his final reward, full of years, and full of honours, even of those honours, which were dearest to his heart, as gratefully bestowed by that school, and still binding him to the interests of that school, in which he had been himself educated, and to which during his whole life he was a dedicated thing.

From causes, which this is not the place to investigate, no models of past times, however perfect, can have the same vivid effect on the youthful mind, as the productions of contemporary genius. The discipline, my mind had undergone, Ne falleretur rotundo sono et versuum cursu, cincinnis, et floribus; sed ut inspiceret quidnam subesset, quae, sedes, quod firmamentum, quis fundus verbis; an figures essent mera ornatura et orationis fucus; vel sanguinis emateriae ipsius corde effluentis rubor quidam nativus et incalescentia genuina;—removed all obstacles to the appreciation of excellence in style without diminishing my delight. That I was thus prepared for the perusal of Mr. Bowles's sonnets and earlier poems, at once increased their influence, and my enthusiasm. The great works of past ages seem to a young man things of another race, in respect to which his faculties must remain passive and submiss, even as to the stars and mountains.

But the writings of a contemporary, perhaps not many years older than himself, surrounded by the same circumstances, and disciplined by the same manners, possess a reality for him, and inspire an actual friendship as of a man for a man. His very admiration is the wind which fans and feeds his hope. The poem sthemselves assume the properties of flesh and blood. To recite, to extol, to contend for them is but the payment of a debt due to one, who exists to receive it.

There are indeed modes of teaching which have produced, and are producing, youths of a very different stamp; modes of teaching, in comparison with which we have been called on to despise our great public schools, and universities, in whose halls are hung Armoury of the invincible knights of old—modes, by which children are to be metamorphosed into prodigies. And prodigies with a vengeance have I known thus produced; prodigies of self-conceit, shallowness, arrogance, and infidelity! Instead of storing the memory, during the period when the memory is the predominant faculty, with facts for the after exercise of the judgment; and instead of awakening by the noblest models the fond and unmixed love and admiration, which is the natural and graceful temper of early youth; these nurslings of improved pedagogy are taught to dispute and decide; to suspect all but their own and their lecturer's wisdom; and to hold nothing sacred from their contempt, but their own contemptible arrogance; boy-graduates in all the technicals, and in all the dirty passions and impudence of anonymous criticism. To such dispositions alone can the admonition of Pliny be requisite, Neque enim debet operibus ejus obesse, quod vivit. An si inter eos, quos nunquam vidimus, floruisset, non solum libros ejus, verum etiam imagines conquireremus, ejusdem nunc honor prasentis, et gratia quasi satietate languescet? At hoc pravum, malignumque est, non admirari hominem admiratione dignissimum, quia videre, complecti, nec laudare tantum, verum etiam amare contingit.

I had just entered on my seventeenth year, when the sonnets of Mr. Bowles, twenty in number, and just then published in a quarto pamphlet, were first made known and presented to me, by a schoolfellow who had quitted us for the University, and who, during the whole time that he was in our first form (or in our school language a Grecian,) had been my patron and protector. I refer to Dr. Middleton, the truly learned, and every way excellent Bishop of Calcutta:

qui laudibus amplis
Ingenium celebrare meum, calamumque solebat,
Calcar agens animo validum. Non omnia terra
Obruta; vivit amor, vivit dolor; ora negatur
Dulcia conspicere; at fiere et meminisse relictum est.

It was a double pleasure to me, and still remains a tender recollection, that I should have received from a friend so revered the first knowledge of a poet, by whose works, year after year, I was so enthusiastically delighted and inspired. My earliest acquaintances will not have forgotten the undisciplined eagerness and impetuous zeal, with which I laboured to make proselytes, not only of my companions, but of all with whom I conversed, of whatever rank, and in whatever place. As my school finances did not permit me to purchase copies, I made, within less than a year and a half, more than forty transcriptions, as the best presents I could offer to those, who had in any way won my regard. And with almost equal delight did I receive the three or four following publications of the same author.

Though I have seen and known enough of mankind to be well aware, that I shall perhaps stand alone in my creed, and that it will be well, if I subject myself to no worse charge than that of singularity; I am not therefore deterred from avowing, that I regard, and ever have regarded the obligations of intellect among the most sacred of the claims of gratitude. A valuable thought, or a particular train of thoughts, gives me additional pleasure, when I can safely refer and attribute it to the conversation or correspondence of another. My obligations to Mr. Bowles were indeed important, and for radical good. At a very premature age, even before my fifteenth year, I had bewildered myself in metaphysics, and in theological controversy. Nothing else pleased me. History, and particular facts, lost all interest in my mind.

Poetry—(though for a school-boy of that age, I was above par in English versification, and had already produced two or three compositions which, I may venture to say, without reference to my age, were somewhat above mediocrity, and which had gained me more credit than the sound, good sense of my old master was at all pleased with,) —poetry itself, yea, novels and romances, became insipid to me. In my friendless wanderings on our leave-days, (for I was an orphan, and had scarcely any connections in London,) highly was I delighted, if any passenger, especially if he were dressed in black, would enter into conversation with me. For I soon found the means of directing it to my favourite subjects

Of providence, fore-knowledge, will, and fate,
Fixed fate, free will, fore-knowledge absolute,
And found no end in wandering mazes lost.

This preposterous pursuit was, beyond doubt, injurious both to my natural powers, and to the progress of my education. It would perhaps have been destructive, had it been continued; but from this I was auspiciously withdrawn, partly indeed by an accidental introduction to an amiable family, chiefly however, by the genial influence of a style of poetry, so tender and yet so manly, so natural and real, and yet so dignified and harmonious, as the sonnets and other early poems of Mr. Bowles. Well would it have been for me, perhaps, had I never relapsed into the same mental disease; if I had continued to pluck the flower and reap the harvest from the cultivated surface, instead of delving in the unwholesome quicksilver mines of metaphysic lore. And if in after time I have sought a refuge from bodily pain and mismanaged sensibility in abstruse researches, which exercised the strength and subtilty of the understanding without awakening the feelings of the heart; still there was a long and blessed interval, during which my natural faculties were allowed to expand, and my original tendencies to develop themselves;—my fancy, and the love of nature, and the sense of beauty in forms and sounds.

The second advantage, which I owe to my early perusal, and admiration of these poems, (to which let me add,) though known to me at a somewhat later period, the Lewesdon Hill of Mr. Crowe bears more immediately on my present subject. Among those with whom I conversed, there were, of course, very many who had formed their taste, and their notions of poetry, from the writings of Pope and his followers; or to speak more generally, in that school of French poetry, condensed and invigorated by English understanding, which had predominated from the last century. I was not blind to the merits of this school, yet, as from inexperience of the world, and consequent want of sympathy with the general subjects of these poems, they gave me little pleasure, I doubtless undervalued the kind, and with the presumption of youth withheld from its masters the legitimate name of poets. I saw that the excellence of this kind consisted in just and acute observations on men and manners in an artificial state of society, as its matter and substance; and in the logic of wit, conveyed in smooth and strong epigrammatic couplets, as its form: that even when the subject was addressed to the fancy, or the intellect, as in the Rape of the Lock, or the Essay on Man; nay, when it was a consecutive narration, as in that astonishing product of matchless talent and ingenuity Pope's Translation of the Iliad; still a point was looked for at the end of each second line, and the whole was, as it were, a sorites, or, if I may exchange a logical for a grammatical metaphor, a conjunction disjunctive, of epigrams. Meantime the matter and diction seemed to me characterized not so much by poetic thoughts, as by thoughts translated into the language of poetry. On this last point, I had occasion to render my own thoughts gradually more and more plain to myself, by frequent amicable disputes concerning Darwin's Botanic Garden, which, for some years, was greatly extolled, not only by the reading public in general, but even by those, whose genius and natural robustness of understanding enabled them afterwards to act foremost in dissipating these "painted mists" that occasionally rise from the marshes at the foot of Parnassus. During my first Cambridge vacation, I assisted a friend in a contribution for a literary society in Devonshire: and in this I remember to have compared Darwin's work to the Russian palace of ice, glittering, cold and transitory. In the same essay too, I assigned sundry reasons, chiefly drawn from a comparison of passages in the Latin poets with the original Greek, from which they were borrowed, for the preference of Collins's odes to those of Gray; and of the simile in Shakespeare

> How like a younker or a prodigal
> The scarfed bark puts from her native bay,
> Hugg'd and embraced by the strumpet wind!
> How like the prodigal doth she return,
> With over-weather'd ribs and ragged sails,
> Lean, rent, and beggar'd by the strumpet wind!
>
> *(Merch. of Ven. Act II. sc. 6.)*

to the imitation in the Bard;

> Fair laughs the morn, and soft the zephyr blows
> While proudly riding o'er the azure realm
> In gallant trim the gilded vessel goes,
> Youth at the prow and pleasure at the helm;
> Regardless of the sweeping whirlwind's sway,
> That hush'd in grim repose, expects it's evening prey.

(in which, by the bye, the words "realm" and "sway" are rhymes dearly purchased)—I preferred the original on the ground, that in the imitation it depended wholly on the compositor's putting, or not putting, a small capital, both in this, and in many other passages of the same poet, whether the words should be personifications, or mere abstractions. I mention this, because, in referring various lines in Gray to their original in Shakespeare and Milton, and in the clear perception how completely all the propriety was lost in the transfer, I was, at that early period, led to a conjecture, which, many years afterwards was recalled to me from the same thought having been started in conversation, but far more ably, and developed more fully, by Mr. Wordsworth;—namely, that this style of poetry, which I have characterized above, as translations of prose thoughts into poetic language, had been kept up by, if it did not wholly arise from, the custom of writing Latin verses, and the great importance attached to these exercises, in our public schools.

Whatever might have been the case in the fifteenth century, when the use of the Latin tongue was so general among learned men, that Erasmus is said to have forgotten his native language; yet in the present day it is not to be supposed, that a youth can think in Latin, or that he can have any other reliance on the force or fitness of his phrases, but the authority of the writer from whom he has adopted them. Consequently he must first prepare his thoughts, and then pick out, from Virgil, Horace, Ovid, or perhaps more compendiously from his Gradus, halves and quarters of lines, in which to embody them.

I never object to a certain degree of disputatiousness in a young man from the age of seventeen to that of four or five and twenty, provided I find him always arguing on one side of the question. The controversies, occasioned by my unfeigned zeal for the honour of a favourite contemporary, then known to me only by his works, were of great advantage in the formation and establishment of my taste and critical opinions. In my defence of the lines running into each other, instead of closing at each couplet; and of natural language, neither bookish, nor vulgar, neither redolent of the lamp, nor of the kennel, such as I will remember thee; instead of the same thought tricked up in the rag-fair finery of,

———thy image on her wing
Before my fancy's eye shall memory bring,—

I had continually to adduce the metre and diction of the Greek poets, from Homer to Theocritus inclusively; and still more of our elder English poets, from Chaucer to Milton. Nor was this all. But as it was my constant reply to authorities brought against me from later poets of great name, that no authority could avail in opposition to Truth, Nature, Logic, and the Laws of Universal Grammar; actuated too by my former passion for metaphysical investigations; I laboured at a solid foundation, on which permanently to ground my opinions, in the component faculties of the human mind itself, and their comparative dignity and importance.

According to the faculty or source, from which the pleasure given by any poem or passage was derived, I estimated the merit of such poem or passage. As the result of all my reading and meditation, I abstracted two critical aphorisms, deeming them to comprise the conditions and criteria of poetic style;—first, that not the poem which we have read, but that to which we return, with the greatest pleasure, possesses the genuine power, and claims the name of essential poetry;—secondly, that whatever lines can be translated into other words of the same language, without diminution of their significance, either in sense or association, or in any worthy feeling, are so far vicious in their diction.

Be it however observed, that I excluded from the list of worthy feelings, the pleasure derived from mere novelty in the reader, and the desire of exciting wonderment at his powers in the author. Oftentimes since then, in pursuing French tragedies, I have fancied two marks of admiration at the end of each line, as hieroglyphics of the author's own admiration at his own cleverness.

Our genuine admiration of a great poet is a continuous undercurrent of feeling! it is everywhere present, but seldom anywhere as a separate excitement. I was wont boldly to affirm, that it would be scarcely more difficult to push a stone out from the Pyramids with the bare hand, than to alter a word, or the position of a word, in Milton or Shakespeare, (in their most important works at least,) without making the poet say something else, or something worse, than he does say. One great distinction, I appeared to myself to see plainly between even the characteristic faults of our elder poets, and the false beauty of the moderns. In the former, from Donne to Cowley, we find the most fantastic out-of-the-way thoughts, but in the most pure and genuine mother English, in the latter the most obvious thoughts, in language the most fantastic and arbitrary. Our faulty elder poets sacrificed the passion and passionate flow of poetry to the subtleties of intellect and to the stars of wit; the moderns to the glare and glitter of a perpetual, yet broken and heterogeneous imagery, or rather to an amphibious something, made up, half of image, and half of abstract meaning. The one sacrificed the heart to the head; the other both heart and head to point and drapery.

The reader must make himself acquainted with the general style of composition that was at that time deemed poetry, in order to understand and account for the effect produced on me by the Sonnets, the Monody at Matlock, and the Hope, of Mr. Bowles; for it is peculiar to original genius to become less and less striking, in proportion to its success in improving the taste and judgment of its contemporaries. The poems of West, indeed, had the merit of chaste and manly diction; but they were cold, and, if I may so express it, only dead-coloured; while in the best of Warton's there is a stiffness, which too often gives them the appearance of imitations from the Greek. Whatever relation, therefore, of cause or impulse Percy's collection of Ballads may bear to the most popular poems of the present day; yet in a more sustained and elevated style, of the then living poets, Cowper and Bowles were, to the best of my knowledge, the first who combined natural thoughts with natural diction; the first who reconciled the heart with the head.

It is true, as I have before mentioned, that from diffidence in my own powers, I for a short time adopted a labourious and florid diction, which I myself deemed, if not absolutely vicious, yet of very inferior worth. Gradually, however, my practice conformed to my better judgment; and the compositions of my twenty-fourth and twenty-fifth years—(for example, the shorter blank verse poems, the lines, which now form the middle and conclusion of the poem entitled the

Destiny of Nations, and the tragedy of Remorse)—are not more below my present ideal in respect of the general tissue of the style than those of the latest date.

Their faults were at least a remnant of the former leaven, and among the many who have done me the honour of putting my poems in the same class with those of my betters, the one or two, who have pretended to bring examples of affected simplicity from my volume, have been able to adduce but one instance, and that out of a copy of verses half ludicrous, half splenetic, which I intended, and had myself characterized, as sermoni propiora.

Every reform, however necessary, will by weak minds be carried to an excess, which will itself need reforming. The reader will excuse me for noticing, that I myself was the first to expose risu honesto the three sins of poetry, one or the other of which is the most likely to beset a young writer. So long ago as the publication of the second number of the Monthly Magazine, under the name of Nehemiah Higginbottom, I contributed three sonnets, the first of which had for its object to excite a good-natured laugh at the spirit of doleful egotism, and at the recurrence of favourite phrases, with the double defect of being at once trite and licentious;—the second was on low creeping language and thoughts, under the pretence of simplicity; the third, the phrases of which were borrowed entirely from my own poems, on the indiscriminate use of elaborate and swelling language and imagery.

The reader will find them in the note below, and will I trust regard them as reprinted for biographical purposes alone, and not for their poetic merits. So general at that time, and so decided was the opinion concerning the characteristic vices of my style, that a celebrated physician (now, alas! no more) speaking of me in other respects with his usual kindness, to a gentleman, who was about to meet me at a dinner party, could not however resist giving him a hint not to mention 'The house that Jack built' in my presence, for "that I was as sore as a boil about that sonnet;" he not knowing that I was myself the author of it.

CHAPTER III

The Author's obligations to critics, and the probable occasion.

Principles of modern criticism—Mr. Southey's works and character.

To anonymous critics in reviews, magazines, and news-journals of various name and rank, and to satirists with or without a name in verse or prose, or in verse-text aided by prose-comment, I do seriously believe and profess, that I owe full two-thirds of whatever reputation and publicity I happen to possess.

For when the name of an individual has occurred so frequently, in so many works, for so great a length of time, the readers of these works—(which with a shelf or two of beauties, elegant Extracts and Anas, form nine-tenths of the reading of the reading Public)—cannot but be familiar with the name, without distinctly remembering whether it was introduced for eulogy or for censure. And this becomes the more likely, if (as I believe) the habit of perusing periodical works may be properly added to Averroes' catalogue of Anti-Mnemonics, or weakeners of the memory.

But where this has not been the case, yet the reader will be apt to suspect that there must be something more than usually strong and extensive in a reputation, that could either require or stand so merciless and long-continued a cannonading. Without any feeling of anger therefore—(for which indeed, on my own account, I have no pretext)—I may yet be allowed to express some degree of surprise, that, after having run the critical gauntlet for a certain class of faults which I had, nothing having come before the judgment-seat in the interim, I should, year after year, quarter after quarter, month after month—(not to mention sundry petty periodicals of still quicker revolution, "or weekly or diurnal")—have been, for at least seventeen years consecutively, dragged forth by them into the foremost ranks of the proscribed, and forced to abide the brunt of abuse, for faults directly opposite, and which I certainly had not. How shall I explain this?

Whatever may have been the case with others, I certainly cannot attribute this persecution to personal dislike, or to envy, or to feelings of vindictive animosity. Not to the former, for with the exception of a very few who are my intimate friends, and were so before they were known as authors, I have had little other acquaintance with literary characters, than what may be implied in an accidental introduction, or casual meeting in a mixed company. And as far as words and looks can be trusted, I must believe that, even in these instances, I had excited no unfriendly disposition. Neither by letter, nor in conversation, have I ever had dispute or controversy beyond the common social interchange of opinions. Nay, where I had reason to suppose my convictions fundamentally different, it has been my habit, and I may add, the impulse of my nature, to assign the grounds of my belief, rather than the belief itself; and not to express dissent, till I could establish some points of complete sympathy, some grounds common to both sides, from which to commence its explanation.

Still less can I place these attacks to the charge of envy. The few pages which I have published, are of too distant a date, and the extent of their sale a proof too conclusive against their having been popular at any time, to render probable, I had almost said possible, the excitement of envy on their account; and the man who should envy me on any other, verily he must be envy-mad!

Lastly, with as little semblance of reason, could I suspect any animosity towards me from vindictive feelings as the cause. I have before said, that my acquaintance with literary men has been limited and distant; and that I have had neither dispute nor controversy. From my first entrance into life, I have, with few and short intervals, lived either abroad or in retirement. My different essays on subjects of national interest, published at different times, first in the Morning Post and then in the Courier, with my courses of Lectures on the principles of criticism as applied to Shakespeare and Milton, constitute my whole publicity; the only occasions on which I could offend any member of the republic of letters. With one solitary exception in which my words were first misstated and then wantonly applied to an individual, I could never learn that I had excited the displeasure of any among my literary contemporaries. Having announced my intention to give a course of Lectures on the characteristic merits and defects of English poetry in its different aeras; first, from Chaucer to Milton; second, from Dryden inclusively to Thomson; and third, from Cowper to the present day; I changed my plan, and confined my disquisition to the former two periods, that I might furnish no possible pretext for the unthinking to misconstrue, or the malignant to misapply my words, and having stamped their own meaning on them, to pass them as current coin in the marts of garrulity or detraction.

Praises of the unworthy are felt by ardent minds as robberies of the deserving; and it is too true, and too frequent, that Bacon, Harrington, Machiavel, and Spinoza, are not read, because Hume, Condillac, and Voltaire are. But in promiscuous company no prudent man will oppugn the merits of a contemporary in his own supposed department; contenting himself with praising in his turn those whom he deems excellent. If I should ever deem it my duty at all to oppose the pretensions of individuals, I would oppose them in books which could be weighed and answered, in which I could evolve the whole of my reasons and feelings, with their requisite limits and modifications; not in irrecoverable conversation, where however strong the reasons might be, the feelings that prompted them would assuredly be attributed by some one or other to envy and discontent. Besides I well know, and, I trust, have acted on that knowledge, that it must be the ignorant and injudicious who extol the unworthy; and the eulogies of critics without taste or judgment are the natural reward of authors without feeling or genius. Sint unicuique sua praemia.

How then, dismissing, as I do, these three causes, am I to account for attacks, the long continuance and inveteracy of which it would require all three to explain? The solution seems to be this,—I was in habits of intimacy with Mr. Wordsworth and Mr. Southey! This, however, transfers, rather than removes the difficulty. Be it, that, by an unconscionable extension of the old adage, noscitur a socio, my literary friends are never under the water-fall of criticism, but I must be wet through with the spray; yet how came the torrent to descend upon them?

First then, with regard to Mr. Southey. I well remember the general reception of his earlier publications; namely, the poems published with Mr. Lovell under the names of Moschus and Bion; the two volumes of poems under his own name, and the Joan of Arc. The censures of the critics by profession are extant, and may be easily referred to:— careless lines, inequality in the merit of the different poems, and (in the lighter works) a predilection for the strange and whimsical; in short, such faults as might have been anticipated in a young and rapid writer, were indeed sufficiently enforced.

Nor was there at that time wanting a party spirit to aggravate the defects of a poet, who with all the courage of uncorrupted youth had avowed his zeal for a cause, which he deemed that of liberty, and his abhorrence of oppression by whatever name consecrated. But it was as little objected by others, as dreamed of by the poet himself, that he preferred careless and prosaic lines on rule and of forethought, or indeed that he pretended to any other art or theory of poetic diction, except that which we may all learn from Horace, Quinctilian, the admirable dialogue, De Oratoribus, generally attributed to Tacitus, or Strada's Prolusions; if indeed natural good sense and the early study of the best models in his own language had not infused the same maxims more securely, and, if I may venture the expression, more vitally.

All that could have been fairly deduced was, that in his taste and estimation of writers Mr. Southey agreed far more with Thomas Warton, than with Dr. Johnson. Nor do I mean to deny, that at all times Mr. Southey was of the same mind with Sir Philip Sidney in preferring an excellent ballad in the humblest style of poetry to twenty indifferent poems that strutted in the highest. And by what have his works, published since then, been characterized, each more strikingly than the preceding, but by greater splendour, a deeper pathos, profounder reflections, and a more sustained dignity of language and of metre?

Distant may the period be, but whenever the time shall come, when all his works shall be collected by some editor worthy to be his biographer, I trust that an appendix of excerpta of all the passages, in which his writings, name, and character have been attacked, from the pamphlets and periodical works of the last twenty years, may be an accompaniment. Yet that it would prove medicinal in after times I dare not hope; for as long as there are readers to be delighted with calumny, there will be found reviewers to calumniate.

And such readers will become in all probability more numerous, in proportion as a still greater diffusion of literature shall produce an increase of sciolists, and sciolism bring with it petulance and presumption. In times of old, books were as religious oracles; as literature advanced, they next became venerable preceptors; they then descended to the rank of instructive friends; and, as their numbers increased, they sank still lower to that of entertaining companions; and at present they seem degraded into culprits to hold up their hands at the bar of every self-elected, yet not the less peremptory, judge, who chooses to write from humour or interest, from enmity or arrogance, and to abide the decision "of him that reads in malice, or him that reads after dinner."

The same retrograde movement may be traced, in the relation which the authors themselves have assumed towards their readers. From the lofty address of Bacon: "these are the meditations of Francis of Verulam, which that posterity should be possessed of, he deemed their interest:" or from dedication to Monarch or Pontiff, in which the honour given was asserted in equipoise to the patronage acknowledged: from Pindar's

> ———'ep' alloi-
> -si d'alloi megaloi: to d'eschaton kory-
> phoutai basilensi. Maeketi

paptaine porsion.
Eiae se te touton
upsou chronon patein, eme
te tossade nikaphorois
omilein, prophanton sophian kath' El-
lanas eonta panta.

—*OLYMP. OD. I.*

there was a gradual sinking in the etiquette or allowed style of pretension.

Poets and Philosophers, rendered diffident by their very number, addressed themselves to "learned readers;" then aimed to conciliate the graces of "the candid reader;" till, the critic still rising as the author sank, the amateurs of literature collectively were erected into a municipality of judges, and addressed as the Town! And now, finally, all men being supposed able to read, and all readers able to judge, the multitudinous Public, shaped into personal unity by the magic of abstraction, sits nominal despot on the throne of criticism.

But, alas! as in other despotisms, it but echoes the decisions of its invisible ministers, whose intellectual claims to the guardianship of the Muses seem, for the greater part, analogous to the physical qualifications which adapt their oriental brethren for the superintendence of the Harem. Thus it is said, that St. Nepomuc was installed the guardian of bridges, because he had fallen over one, and sunk out of sight; thus too St. Cecilia is said to have been first propitiated by musicians, because, having failed in her own attempts, she had taken a dislike to the art and all its successful professors.

But I shall probably have occasion hereafter to deliver my convictions more at large concerning this state of things, and its influences on taste, genius and morality.

In the Thalaba, the Madoc, and still more evidently in the unique Cid, in the Kehama, and, as last, so best, the Roderick; Southey has given abundant proof, se cogitare quam sit magnum dare aliquid in manus hominum: nec persuadere sibi posse, non saepe tractandum quod placere et semper et omnibus cupiat. But on the other hand, I conceive, that Mr. Southey was quite unable to comprehend, wherein could consist the crime or mischief of printing half a dozen or more playful poems; or to speak more generally, compositions which would be enjoyed or passed over, according as the taste and humour of the reader might chance to be; provided they contained nothing immoral. In the present age periturae parcere chartae is emphatically an unreasonable demand.

The merest trifle he ever sent abroad had tenfold better claims to its ink and paper than all the silly criticisms on it, which proved no more than that the critic was not one of those, for whom the trifle was written; and than all the grave exhortations to a greater reverence for the public—as if the passive page of a book, by having an epigram or doggerel tale impressed on it, instantly assumed at once loco-motive power and a sort of ubiquity, so as to flutter and buz in the ear of the public to the sore annoyance of the said mysterious personage.

But what gives an additional and more ludicrous absurdity to these lamentations is the curious fact, that if in a volume of poetry the critic should find poem or passage which he deems more especially worthless, he is sure to select and reprint it in the review; by which, on his own grounds, he wastes as much more paper than the author, as the copies of a fashionable review are more numerous than those of the original book; in some, and those the most prominent instances, as ten thousand to five hundred.

I know nothing that surpasses the vileness of deciding on the merits of a poet or painter,—(not by characteristic defects; for where there is genius, these always point to his characteristic beauties; but)—by accidental failures or faulty passages; except the impudence of defending it, as the proper duty, and most instructive part, of criticism. Omit or pass slightly over the expression, grace, and grouping of Rafael's figures; but ridicule in detail the knitting-needles and broom-twigs, that are to represent trees in his back grounds; and never let him hear the last of his galli-pots! Admit that the Allegro and Penseroso of Milton are not without merit; but repay yourself for this concession, by reprinting at length the two poems on the University Carrier! As a fair specimen of his Sonnets, quote

> "A Book was writ of late called Tetrachordon;"
>
> and, as characteristic of his rhythm and metre, cite his literal translation of the first and second Psalm! In order to justify yourself, you need only assert, that had you dwelt chiefly on the beauties and excellencies of the poet, the admiration of these might seduce the attention of future writers from the objects of their love and wonder, to an imitation of the few poems and passages in which the poet was most unlike himself.

But till reviews are conducted on far other principles, and with far other motives; till in the place of arbitrary dictation and petulant sneers, the reviewers support their decisions by reference to fixed canons of criticism, previously established and deduced from the nature of man; reflecting minds will pronounce it arrogance in them thus to announce themselves to men of letters, as the guides of their taste and judgment. To the purchaser and mere reader it is, at all events, an injustice. He who tells me that there are defects in a new work, tells me nothing which I should not have taken for granted without his information. But he, who points out and elucidates the beauties of an original work does indeed give me interesting information, such as experience would not have authorized me in anticipating. And as to compositions which the authors themselves announce with

> Haec ipsi novimus esse nihil,

why should we judge by a different rule two printed works, only because the one author is alive, and the other in his grave? What literary man has not regretted the prudery of Spratt in refusing to let his friend Cowley appear in his slippers and dressing gown? I am not perhaps the only one who has derived an innocent amusement from the riddles, conundrums, tri-syllable lines, and the like, of Swift and his correspondents, in hours of languor, when to have read his more finished works would have been useless to myself, and, in some sort, an act of injustice to the author. But I am at a loss to conceive by what perversity of judgment, these relaxations of his genius could be employed to diminish his fame as the writer of Gulliver, or the Tale of a Tub. Had Mr. Southey written twice as many poems of inferior merit, or partial interest, as have enlivened the journals of the day, they would have added to his honour with good and wise men, not merely or principally as proving the versatility of his talents, but as evidences of the purity of that mind, which even in its levities never dictated a line which it need regret on any moral account.

I have in imagination transferred to the future biographer the duty of contrasting Southey's fixed and well-earned fame, with the abuse and indefatigable hostility of his anonymous critics from his early youth to his ripest manhood. But I cannot think so ill of human nature as not to believe, that these critics have already taken shame to themselves, whether they consider the object of their abuse in his moral or his literary character. For reflect but on the variety and extent of his acquirements! He stands second to no man, either as an historian or as a bibliographer; and when I regard him as a popular essayist,—(for the articles of his compositions in the reviews are, for the greater part, essays on subjects of deep or curious interest rather than criticisms on particular works)—I look in vain for any writer, who has conveyed so much information, from so many and such recondite sources, with so many just and original reflections, in a style so lively and poignant, yet so uniformly classical and perspicuous; no one, in short, who has combined so much wisdom with so much wit; so much truth and knowledge with so much life and fancy. His prose is always intelligible and always entertaining. In poetry he has attempted almost every species of composition known before, and he has added new ones; and if we except the highest lyric,—(in which how few, how very few even of the greatest minds have been fortunate)—he has attempted every species successfully; from the political song of the day, thrown off in the playful overflow of honest joy and patriotic exultation, to the wild ballad; from epistolary ease and graceful narrative, to austere and impetuous moral declamation; from the pastoral charms and wild streaming lights of the Thalaba, in which sentiment and imagery have given permanence even to the excitement of curiosity; and from the full blaze of the Kehama,—(a gallery of finished pictures in one splendid fancy piece, in which, notwithstanding, the moral grandeur rises gradually above the brilliance of the colouring and the boldness and novelty of the machinery)—to the more sober beauties of the Madoc; and lastly, from the Madoc to his Roderick, in which, retaining all his former excellencies of a poet eminently inventive and picturesque, he has surpassed himself in language and metre, in the construction of the whole, and in the splendour of particular passages.

Here then shall I conclude? No! The characters of the deceased, like the encomia on tombstones, as they are described with religious tenderness, so are they read, with allowing sympathy indeed, but yet with rational deduction. There are men, who deserve a higher record; men with whose characters it is the interest of their contemporaries, no less than that of posterity, to be made acquainted; while it is yet possible for impartial censure, and even for quick-sighted envy, to cross-examine the tale without offence to the courtesies of humanity; and while the eulogist, detected in exaggeration or falsehood, must pay the full penalty of his baseness in the contempt which brands the convicted flatterer.

Publicly has Mr. Southey been reviled by men, who, as I would fain hope for the honour of human nature, hurled fire-brands against a figure of their own imagination; publicly have his talents been depreciated, his principles denounced; as publicly do I therefore, who have known him intimately, deem it my duty to leave recorded, that it is Southey's almost unexampled felicity, to possess the best gifts of talent and genius free from all their characteristic defects. To those who remember the state of our public schools and universities some twenty years past, it will appear no ordinary praise in any man to have passed from innocence into virtue, not only free from all vicious habit, but unstained by one act of intemperance, or the degradations akin to intemperance.

That scheme of head, heart, and habitual demeanour, which in his early manhood, and first controversial writings, Milton, claiming the privilege of self- defence, asserts of himself, and challenges his calumniators to disprove; this will his school-mates, his fellow-collegians, and his maturer friends, with a confidence proportioned to the intimacy of their knowledge, bear witness to, as again realised in the life of Robert Southey.

But still more striking to those, who by biography or by their own experience are familiar with the general habits of genius, will appear the poet's matchless industry and perseverance in his pursuits; the worthiness and dignity of those pursuits; his generous submission to tasks of transitory interest, or such as his genius alone could make otherwise; and that having thus more than satisfied the claims of affection or prudence, he should yet have made for himself time and power, to achieve more, and in more various departments, than almost any other writer has done, though employed wholly on subjects of his own choice and ambition. But as Southey possesses, and is not possessed by, his genius, even so is he master even of his virtues.

The regular and methodical tenor of his daily labours, which would be deemed rare in the most mechanical pursuits, and might be envied by the mere man of business, loses all semblance of formality in the dignified simplicity of his manners, in the spring and healthful cheerfulness of his spirits. Always employed, his friends find him always at leisure. No less punctual in trifles, than steadfast in the performance of highest duties, he inflicts none of those small pains and discomforts which irregular men scatter about them, and which in the aggregate so often become formidable obstacles both to happiness and utility; while on the contrary he bestows all the pleasures, and inspires all that ease of mind on those around him or connected with him, which perfect consistency, and (if such a word might be framed) absolute reliability, equally in small as in great concerns, cannot but inspire and bestow; when this too is softened without being weakened by kindness and gentleness. I know few men who so well deserve the character which an antient attributes to Marcus Cato, namely, that he was likest virtue, in as much as he seemed to act aright, not in obedience to any law or outward motive, but by the necessity of a happy nature, which could not act otherwise. As son, brother, husband, father, master, friend, he moves with firm yet light steps, alike unostentatious, and alike exemplary.

As a writer, he has uniformly made his talents subservient to the best interests of humanity, of public virtue, and domestic piety; his cause has ever been the cause of pure religion and of liberty, of national independence and of national illumination. When future critics shall weigh out his guerdon of praise and censure, it will be Southey the poet only, that will supply them with the scanty materials for the latter. They will likewise not fail to record, that as no man was ever a more constant friend, never had poet more friends and honorees among the good of all parties; and that quacks in education, quacks in politics, and quacks in criticism were his only enemies.

CHAPTER IV

The Lyrical Ballads with the Preface—Mr. Wordsworth's earlier poems—On fancy and imagination—The investigation of the distinction important to the Fine Arts.

I have wandered far from the object in view, but as I fancied to myself readers who would respect the feelings that had tempted me from the main road; so I dare calculate on not a few, who will warmly sympathize with them. At present it will be sufficient for my purpose, if I have proved, that Mr. Southey's writings no more than my own furnished the original occasion to this fiction of a new school of poetry, and to the clamours against its supposed founders and proselytes.

As little do I believe that Mr. Wordsworth's Lyrical Ballads were in themselves the cause. I speak exclusively of the two volumes so entitled. A careful and repeated examination of these confirms me in the belief, that the omission of less than a hundred lines would have precluded nine-tenths of the criticism on this work. I hazard this declaration, however, on the supposition, that the reader has taken it up, as he would have done any other collection of poems purporting to derive their subjects or interests from the incidents of domestic or ordinary life, intermingled with higher strains of meditation which the poet utters in his own person and character; with the proviso, that these poems were perused without knowledge of, or reference to, the author's peculiar opinions, and that the reader had not had his attention previously directed to those peculiarities.

In that case, as actually happened with Mr. Southey's earlier works, the lines and passages which might have offended the general taste, would have been considered as mere inequalities, and attributed to inattention, not to perversity of judgment. The men of business who had passed their lives chiefly in cities, and who might therefore be expected to derive the highest pleasure from acute notices of men and manners conveyed in easy, yet correct and pointed language; and all those who, reading but little poetry, are most stimulated with that species of it, which seems most distant from prose, would probably have passed by the volumes altogether.

Others more catholic in their taste, and yet habituated to be most pleased when most excited, would have contented themselves with deciding, that the author had been successful in proportion to the elevation of his style and subject. Not a few, perhaps, might, by their admiration of the Lines written near Tintern Abbey, on revisiting the Wye, those Left upon a Yew Tree Seat, The Old Cumberland Beggar, and Ruth, have been gradually led to peruse with kindred feeling The Brothers, the Hart-leap Well, and whatever other poems in that collection may be described as holding a middle place between those written in the highest and those in the humblest style; as for instance between the Tintern Abbey, and The Thorn, or

Simon Lee. Should their taste submit to no further change, and still remain unreconciled to the colloquial phrases, or the imitations of them, that are, more or less, scattered through the class last mentioned; yet even from the small number of the latter, they would have deemed them but an inconsiderable subtraction from the merit of the whole work; or, what is sometimes not unpleasing in the publication of a new writer, as serving to ascertain the natural tendency, and consequently the proper direction of the author's genius.

In the critical remarks, therefore, prefixed and annexed to the Lyrical Ballads, I believe, we may safely rest, as the true origin of the unexampled opposition which Mr. Wordsworth's writings have been since doomed to encounter. The humbler passages in the poems themselves were dwelt on and cited to justify the rejection of the theory. What in and for themselves would have been either forgotten or forgiven as imperfections, or at least comparative failures, provoked direct hostility when announced as intentional, as the result of choice after full deliberation. Thus the poems, admitted by all as excellent, joined with those which had pleased the far greater number, though they formed two-thirds of the whole work, instead of being deemed (as in all right they should have been, even if we take for granted that the reader judged aright) an atonement for the few exceptions, gave wind and fuel to the animosity against both the poems and the poet. In all perplexity there is a portion of fear, which predisposes the mind to anger. Not able to deny that the author possessed both genius and a powerful intellect, they felt very positive,—but yet were not quite certain that he might not be in the right, and they themselves in the wrong; an unquiet state of mind, which seeks alleviation by quarrelling with the occasion of it, and by wondering at the perverseness of the man, who had written a long and argumentative essay to persuade them, that

Fair is foul, and foul is fair;

in other words, that they had been all their lives admiring without judgment, and were now about to censure without reason.

That this conjecture is not wide from the mark, I am induced to believe from the noticeable fact, which I can state on my own knowledge, that the same general censure has been grounded by almost every different person on some different poem. Among those, whose candour and judgment I estimate highly, I distinctly remember six who expressed their objections to the Lyrical Ballads almost in the same words, and altogether to the same purport, at the same time admitting, that several of the poems had given them great pleasure; and, strange as it might seem, the composition which one cited as execrable, another quoted as his favourite. I am indeed convinced in my own mind, that could the same experiment have been tried with these volumes, as was made in the well known story of the picture, the result would have been the same; the parts which had been covered by black spots on the one day, would be found equally albo lapide notatae on the succeeding.

However this may be, it was assuredly hard and unjust to fix the attention on a few separate and insulated poems with as much aversion, as if they had been so many plague-spots on the whole work, instead of passing them over in silence, as so much blank paper, or leaves of a bookseller's catalogue; especially, as no one pretended to have found in them any immorality or indelicacy; and the poems, therefore, at the worst, could only be regarded as so many light or inferior coins in a rouleau of gold, not as so much alloy in a weight of bullion. A friend whose talents I hold in the highest respect, but whose judgment and strong sound sense I have had almost continued occasion to revere, making the usual complaints to me concerning both the style and subjects of Mr. Wordsworth's minor poems; I admitted that there were some few of the tales and incidents, in which I could not myself find a sufficient cause for their having been recorded in metre. I mentioned Alice Fell as an instance; "Nay," replied my friend with more than usual quickness of manner, "I cannot agree with you there!—that, I own, does seem to me a remarkably pleasing poem." In the Lyrical Ballads, (for my experience does not enable me to extend the remark equally unqualified to the two subsequent volumes,) I have heard at different times, and from different individuals, every single poem extolled and reprobated, with the exception of those of loftier kind, which as was before observed, seem to have won universal praise. This fact of itself would have made me diffident in my censures, had not a still stronger ground been furnished by the strange contrast of the heat and long continuance of the opposition, with the nature of the faults stated as justifying it. The seductive faults, the dulcia vitia of Cowley, Marine, or Darwin might reasonably be thought capable of corrupting the public judgment for half a century, and require a twenty years war, campaign after campaign, in order to dethrone the usurper and re-establish the legitimate taste. But that a downright simpleness, under the affectation of simplicity, prosaic words in feeble metre, silly thoughts in childish phrases, and a preference of mean, degrading, or at best trivial associations and characters, should succeed in forming a school of imitators, a company of almost religious admirers, and this too among young men of ardent minds, liberal education, and not

———with academic laurels unbestowed;

and that this bare and bald counterfeit of poetry, which is characterized as below criticism, should for nearly twenty years have well-nigh engrossed criticism, as the main, if not the only, butt of review, magazine, pamphlet, poem, and paragraph; this is indeed matter of wonder. Of yet greater is it, that the contest should still continue as undecided as that between Bacchus and the frogs in Aristophanes; when the former descended to the realms of the departed to bring back the spirit of old and genuine poesy;—

CH. Brekekekex, koax, koax.
D. All' exoloisth' auto koax.
Ouden gar est' all', hae koax.
Oimozet' ou gar moi melei.
CH. Alla maen kekraxomestha
g', oposon hae pharynx an haemon
chandanae di' haemeras,

brekekekex, koax, koax!
D. Touto gar ou nikaesete.
CH. Oude men haemas su pantos.
D. Oude maen humeis ge dae m'
oudepote. Kekraxomai gar,
kan me deae, di' haemeras,
eos an humon epikrataeso tou koax!
CH. Brekekekex, KO'AX, KOAX!

During the last year of my residence at Cambridge, 1794, I became acquainted with Mr. Wordsworth's first publication entitled Descriptive Sketches; and seldom, if ever, was the emergence of an original poetic genius above the literary horizon more evidently announced. In the form, style, and manner of the whole poem, and in the structure of the particular lines and periods, there is a harshness and acerbity connected and combined with words and images all a-glow, which might recall those products of the vegetable world, where gorgeous blossoms rise out of a hard and thorny rind and shell, within which the rich fruit is elaborating. The language is not only peculiar and strong, but at times knotty and contorted, as by its own impatient strength; while the novelty and struggling crowd of images, acting in conjunction with the difficulties of the style, demands always a greater closeness of attention, than poetry,—at all events, than descriptive poetry—has a right to claim. It not seldom therefore justified the complaint of obscurity. In the following extract I have sometimes fancied, that I saw an emblem of the poem itself, and of the author's genius as it was then displayed.—

'Tis storm; and hid in mist from hour to hour,
All day the floods a deepening murmur pour;
The sky is veiled, and every cheerful sight
Dark is the region as with coming night;
Yet what a sudden burst of overpowering light!
Triumphant on the bosom of the storm,
Glances the fire-clad eagle's wheeling form;
Eastward, in long perspective glittering, shine

The wood-crowned cliffs that o'er the lake recline;
Those Eastern cliffs a hundred streams unfold,
At once to pillars turned that flame with gold;
Behind his sail the peasant strives to shun
The west, that burns like one dilated sun,
Where in a mighty crucible expire
The mountains, glowing hot, like coals of fire.

The poetic Psyche, in its process to full development, undergoes as many changes as its Greek namesake, the butterfly. And it is remarkable how soon genius clears and purifies itself from the faults and errors of its earliest products; faults which, in its earliest compositions, are the more obtrusive and confluent, because as heterogeneous elements, which had only a temporary use, they constitute the very ferment, by which themselves are carried off.

Or we may compare them to some diseases, which must work on the humours, and be thrown out on the surface, in order to secure the patient from their future recurrence. I was in my twenty-fourth year, when I had the happiness of knowing Mr. Wordsworth personally, and while memory lasts, I shall hardly forget the sudden effect produced on my mind, by his recitation of a manuscript poem, which still remains unpublished, but of which the stanza and tone of style were the same as those of the Female Vagrant, as originally printed in the first volume of the Lyrical Ballads.

There was here no mark of strained thought, or forced diction, no crowd or turbulence of imagery; and, as the poet hath himself well described in his Lines on revisiting the Wye, manly reflection and human associations had given both variety, and an additional interest to natural objects, which, in the passion and appetite of the first love, they had seemed to him neither to need nor permit. The occasional obscurities, which had risen from an imperfect control over the resources of his native language, had almost wholly disappeared, together with that worse defect of arbitrary and illogical phrases, at once hackneyed and fantastic, which hold so distinguished a place in the technique of ordinary poetry, and will, more or less, alloy the earlier poems of the truest genius, unless the attention has been specially directed to their worthlessness and incongruity.

I did not perceive anything particular in the mere style of the poem alluded to during its recitation, except indeed such difference as was not separable from the thought and manner; and the Spenserian stanza, which always, more or less, recalls to the reader's mind Spenser's own style, would doubtless have authorized, in my then opinion, a more frequent descent to the phrases of ordinary life, than could without an ill effect have been hazarded in the heroic couplet. It was not however the freedom from false taste, whether as to common defects, or to those more properly his own, which made so unusual an impression on my feelings immediately, and subsequently on my judgment.

It was the union of deep feeling with profound thought; the fine balance of truth in observing, with the imaginative faculty in modifying, the objects observed; and above all the original gift of spreading the tone, the atmosphere, and with it the depth and height of the ideal world around forms, incidents, and situations, of which, for the common view, custom had bedimmed all the lustre, had dried up the sparkle and the dew drops.

This excellence, which in all Mr. Wordsworth's writings is more or less predominant, and which constitutes the character of his mind, I no sooner felt, than I sought to understand. Repeated meditations led me first to suspect,—(and a more intimate analysis of the human faculties, their appropriate marks, functions, and effects matured my conjecture into full conviction,)—that Fancy and Imagination were two distinct and widely different faculties, instead of being, according to the general belief, either two names with one meaning, or, at furthest, the lower and higher degree of one and the same power. It is not, I own, easy to conceive a more apposite translation of the Greek phantasia than the Latin imaginatio; but it is equally true that in all societies there exists an instinct of growth, a certain collective, unconscious good sense working progressively to desynonymize those words originally of the same meaning, which the conflux of dialects supplied to the more homogeneous languages, as the Greek and German: and which the same cause, joined with accidents of translation from original works of different countries, occasion in mixed languages like our own. The first and most important point to be proved is, that two conceptions perfectly distinct are confused under one and the same word, and—this done—to appropriate that word exclusively to the one meaning, and the synonyme, should there be one, to tne other. But if,—(as will be often the case in the arts and sciences,)—no synonyme exists, we must either invent or borrow a word. In the present instance the appropriation has already begun, and been legitimated in the derivative adjective: Milton had a highly imaginative, Cowley a very fanciful mind. If therefore I should succeed in establishing the actual existence of two faculties generally different, the nomenclature would be at once determined. To the faculty by which I had characterized Milton, we should confine the term 'imagination;' while the other would be contra-distinguished as

> 'fancy.' Now were it once fully ascertained, that this division is no less grounded in nature than that of delirium from mania, or Otway's Lutes, laurels, seas of milk, and ships of amber, from Shakespeare's
>
> What! have his daughters brought him to this pass?

or from the preceding apostrophe to the elements; the theory of the fine arts, and of poetry in particular, could not but derive some additional and important light. It would in its immediate effects furnish a torch of guidance to the philosophical critic; and ultimately to the poet himself. In energetic minds, truth soon changes by domestication into power; and from directing in the discrimination and appraisal of the product, becomes influencive in the production. To admire on principle, is the only way to imitate without loss of originality.

It has been already hinted, that metaphysics and psychology have long been my hobby-horse. But to have a hobby-horse, and to be vain of it, are so commonly found together, that they pass almost for the same. I trust therefore, that there will be more good humour than contempt, in the smile with which the reader chastises my self-complacency, if I confess myself uncertain, whether the satisfaction from the perception of a truth new to myself may not have been rendered more poignant by the conceit, that it would be equally so to the public.

There was a time, certainly, in which I took some little credit to myself, in the belief that I had been the first of my countrymen, who had pointed out the diverse meaning of which the two terms were capable, and analysed the faculties to which they should be appropriated. Mr. W. Taylor's recent volume of synonymes I have not yet seen ; but his specification of the terms in question has been clearly shown to be both insufficient and erroneous by Mr. Wordsworth in the Preface added to the late collection of his Poems.

The explanation which Mr. Wordsworth has himself given, will be found to differ from mine, chiefly, perhaps as our objects are different. It could scarcely indeed happen otherwise, from the advantage I have enjoyed of frequent conversation with him on a subject to which a poem of his own first directed my attention, and my conclusions concerning which he had made more lucid to myself by many happy instances drawn from the operation of natural objects on the mind. But it was Mr. Wordsworth's purpose to consider the influences of fancy and imagination as they are manifested in poetry, and from the different effects to conclude their diversity in kind; while it is my object to investigate the seminal principle, and then from the kind to deduce the degree. My friend has drawn a masterly sketch of the branches with their poetic fruitage. I wish to add the trunk, and even the roots as far as they lift themselves above ground, and are visible to the naked eye of our common consciousness.

Yet even in this attempt I am aware that I shall be obliged to draw more largely on the reader's attention, than so immethodical a miscellany as this can authorize; when in such a work (the Ecclesiasical Polity) of such a mind as Hooker's, the judicious author, though no less admirable for the perspicuity than for the port and dignity of his language,—and though he wrote for men of learningin a learned age,—saw nevertheless occasion to anticipate and guardagainst "complaints of obscurity," as often as he was to trace his subject "to the highest well-spring and fountain." Which, (continues he) "because men are not accustomed to, the pains we take are more needful a great deal, than acceptable; and the matters we handle, seem by reason of newness (till the mind grow better acquainted with them) dark and intricate." I would gladly therefore spare both myself and others this labour, if I knew how without it to present an intelligible statement of my poetic creed,—not as my opinions, which weigh for nothing, but as deductions from established premises conveyed in such a form, as is calculated either to effect a fundamental conviction, or to receive a fundamental confutation. If I may dare once more adopt the words of Hooker, "they, unto whom we shall seem tedious, are in no wise injured by us, because it is in their own hands to spare that labour, which they are not willing to endure." Those at least, let me be permitted to add, who have taken so much pains to render me ridiculous for a perversion of taste, and have supported the charge by attributing strange notions to me on no other authority than their own conjectures, owe it to themselves as well as to me not to refuse their attention to my own statement of the theory which I do acknowledge; or shrink from the trouble of examining the grounds on which I rest it, or the arguments which I offer in its justification.

CHAPTER XIII

On the imagination, or esemplastic power

O Adam, One Almighty is, from whom
All things proceed, and up to him return,
If not deprav'd from good, created all
Such to perfection, one first matter all,
Endued with various forms, various degrees
Of substance, and, in things that live, of life;

But more refin'd, more spiritous and pure,
As nearer to him plac'd, or nearer tending,
Each in their several active spheres assigu'd,
Till body up to spirit work, in bounds
Proportion'd to each kind. So from the root
Springs lighter the green stalk, from thence the leaves
More aery: last the bright consummate flower
Spirits odorous breathes: flowers and their fruit,
Man's nourishment, by gradual scale sublim'd,
To vital spirits aspire: to animal:
To intellectual!—give both life and sense,
Fancy and understanding; whence the soul
REASON receives, and reason is her being,
Discursive or intuitive.

"Sane dicerentur si res corporales nil nisi materiale continerent, verissime in fluxu consistere, neque habere substantiale quicquam, quemadmodum et Platonici olim recte agnovere."

"Hinc igitur, praeter pure mathematica et phantasiae subjecta, collegi quaedam metaphysica solaque mente perceptibilia, esse admittenda et massae materiali principium quoddam superius et, ut sic dicam, formale addendum: quandoquidem omnes veritates rerum corporearum ex solis axiomatibus logisticis et geometricis, nempe de magno et parvo, toto et parte, figura et situ, colligi non possint; sed alia de causa et effectu, actioneque et passione, accedere debeant, quibus ordinis rerum rationes salventur. Id principium rerum, an entelecheian an vim appellemus, non refert, modo meminerimus, per solam Virium notionem intelligibiliter explicari."

Sebomai noeron
Kruphian taxin
Chorei TI MESON
Ou katachuthen.

Des Cartes, speaking as a naturalist, and in imitation of Archimedes, said, give me matter and motion and I will construct you the universe. We must of course understand him to have meant; I will render the construction of the universe intelligible. In the same sense the transcendental philosopher says; grant me a nature having two contrary forces, the one of which tends to expand infinitely, while the other strives to apprehend or find itself in this infinity, and I will cause the world of intelllgences with the whole system of their representations to rise up before you. Every other science presupposes intelligence as already existing and complete: the philosopher contemplates it in its growth, and as it were represents its history to the mind from its birth to its maturity.

The venerable sage of Koenigsberg has preceded the march of this master-thought as an effective pioneer in his essay on the introduction of negative quantities into philosophy, published 1763. In this he has shown, that instead of assailing the science of mathematics by metaphysics, as Berkeley did in his ANALYST, or of sophisticating it, as Wolf did, by the vain attempt of deducing the first principles of geometry from supposed deeper grounds of ontology, it behoved the metaphysician rather to examine whether the only province of knowledge, which man has succeeded in erecting into a pure science, might not furnish materials, or at least hints, for establishing and pacifying the unsettled, warring, and embroiled domain of philosophy. An imitation of the mathematical method had indeed been attempted with no better success than attended the essay of David to wear the armour of Saul.

Another use however is possible and of far greater promise, namely, the actual application of the positions which had so wonderfully enlarged the discoveries of geometry, mutatis mutandis, to philosophical subjects. Kant having briefly illustrated the utility of such an attempt in the questions of space, motion, and infinitely small quantities, as employed by the mathematician, proceeds to the idea of negative quantities and the transfer of them to metaphysical investigation. Opposites, he well observes, are of two kinds, either logical, that is, such as are absolutely incompatible; or real, without being contradictory. The former he denominates Nihil negativum irrepraesentabile, the connection of which produces nonsense.

A body in motion is something— Aliquid cogitabile; but a body, at one and the same time in motion and not in motion, is nothing, or, at most, air articulated into nonsense. But a motory force of a body in one direction, and an equal force of the same body in an opposite direction is not incompatible, and the result, namely, rest, is real and representable. For the purposes of mathematical calculus it is indifferent which force we term negative, and which positive, and consequently we appropriate the latter to that, which happens to be the principal object in our thoughts.

Thus if a man's capital be ten and his debts eight, the subtraction will be the same, whether we call the capital negative debt, or the debt negative capital. But in as much as the latter stands practically in reference to the former, we of course represent the sum as 10-8. It is equally clear that two equal forces acting in opposite directions, both being finite and each distinguished from the other by its direction only, must neutralize or reduce each other to inaction.

Now the transcendental philosophy demands; first, that two forces should be conceived which counteract each other by their essential nature; not only not in consequence of the accidental direction of each, but as prior to all direction, nay, as the primary forces from which the conditions of all possible directions are derivative and deducible: secondly, that these forces should be assumed to be both alike infinite, both alike indestructible.

The problem will then be to discover the result or product of two such forces, as distinguished from the result of those forces which are finite, and derive their difference solely from the circumstance of their direction. When we have formed a scheme or outline of these two different kinds of force, and of their different results, by the process of discursive reasoning, it will then remain for us to elevate the thesis from notional to actual, by contemplating intuitively this one power with its two inherent indestructible yet counteracting forces, and the results or generations to which their inter-penetration gives existence, in the living principle and in the process of our own self- consciousness. By what instrument this is possible the solution itself will discover, at the same time that it will reveal to and for whom it is possible. Non omnia possumus omnes. There is a philosophic no less than a poetic genius, which is differenced from the highest perfection of talent, not by degree but by kind.

The counteraction then of the two assumed forces does not depend on their meeting from opposite directions; the power which acts in them is indestructible; it is therefore inexhaustibly re-ebullient; and as something must be the result of these two forces, both alike infinite, and both alike indestructible; and as rest or neutralization cannot be this result; no other conception is possible, but that the product must be a tertium aliquid, or finite generation. Consequently this conception is necessary. Now this tertium aliquid can be no other than an inter-penetration of the counteracting powers, partaking of both.

Thus far had the work been transcribed for the press, when I received the following letter from a friend, whose practical judgment I have had ample reason to estimate and revere, and whose taste and sensibility preclude all the excuses which my self-love might possibly have prompted me to set up in plea against the decision of advisers of equal good sense, but with less tact and feeling.

"Dear C.

"You ask my opinion concerning your Chapter on the Imagination, both as to the impressions it made on myself, and as to those which I think it will make on the Public, i.e. that part of the public, who, from the title of the work and from its forming a sort of introduction to a volume of poems, are likely to constitute the great majority of your readers.

"As to myself, and stating in the first place the effect on my understanding, your opinions and method of argument were not only so new to me, but so directly the reverse of all I had ever been accustomed to consider as truth, that even if I had comprehended your premises sufficiently to have admitted them, and had seen the necessity of your conclusions, I should still have been in that state of mind, which in your note in Chap. IV you have so ingeniously evolved, as the antithesis to that in which a man is, when he makes a bull. In your own words, I should have felt as if I had been standing on my head.

"The effect on my feelings, on the other hand, I cannot better represent, than by supposing myself to have known only our light airy modern chapels of ease, and then for the first time to have been placed, and left alone, in one of our largest Gothic cathedrals in a gusty moonlight night of autumn. 'Now in glimmer, and now in gloom;' often in palpable darkness not without a chilly sensation of terror; then suddenly emerging into broad yet visionary lights with coloured shadows of fantastic shapes, yet all decked with holy insignia and mystic symbols; and ever and anon coming out full upon pictures and stone-work images of great men, with whose names I was familiar, but which looked upon me with countenances and an expression, the most dissimilar to all I had been in the habit of connecting with those names. Those whom I had been taught to venerate as almost super-human in magnitude of intellect, I found perched in little fret-work niches, as grotesque dwarfs; while the grotesques, in my hitherto belief, stood guarding the high altar with all the characters of apotheosis. In short, what I had supposed substances were thinned away into shadows, while everywhere shadows were deepened into substances:

> If substance might be call'd that shadow seem'd,
> For each seem'd either!

"Yet after all, I could not but repeat the lines which you had quoted from a MS. poem of your own in the FRIEND, and applied to a work of Mr. Wordsworth's though with a few of the words altered:

> ———An Orphic tale indeed,
> A tale obscure of high and passionate thoughts
> To a strange music chanted!

"Be assured, however, that I look forward anxiously to your great book on the CONSTRUCTIVE PHILOSOPHY, which you have promised and announced: and that I will do my best to understand it. Only I will not promise to descend into the dark cave of Trophonius with you, there to rub my own eyes, in order to make the sparks and figured flashes, which I am required to see.

"So much for myself. But as for the Public I do not hesitate a moment in advising and urging you to withdraw the Chapter from the present work, and to reserve it for your announced treatises on the Logos or communicative intellect in Man and Deity. First, because imperfectly as I understand the present Chapter, I see clearly that you have done too much, and yet not enough. You have been obliged to omit so many links, from the necessity of compression, that what remains, looks (if I may recur to my former illustration) like the fragments of the winding steps of an old ruined tower. Secondly, a still stronger argument (at least one that I am sure will be more forcible with you) is, that your readers will have both right and reason to complain of you.

This Chapter, which cannot, when it is printed, amount to so little as an hundred pages, will of necessity greatly increase the expense of the work; and every reader who, like myself, is neither prepared nor perhaps calculated for the study of so abstruse a subject so abstrusely treated, will, as I have before hinted, be almost entitled to accuse you of a sort of imposition on him.

For who, he might truly observe, could from your title-page, to wit, "My Literary Life and Opinions," published too as introductory to a volume of miscellaneous poems, have anticipated, or even conjectured, a long treatise on Ideal Realism which holds the same relation in abstruseness to Plotinus, as Plotinus does to Plato. It will be well, if already you have not too much of metaphysical disquisition in your work, though as the larger part of the disquisition is historical, it will doubtless be both interesting and instructive to many to whose unprepared minds your speculations on the esemplastic power would be utterly unintelligible. Be assured, if you do publish this Chapter in the present work, you will be reminded of Bishop Berkeley's Siris, announced as an Essay on Tar-water, which beginning with Tar ends with the Trinity, the omne scibile forming the interspace. I say in the present work. In that greater work to which you have devoted so many years, and study so intense and various, it will be in its proper place. Your prospectus will have described and announced both its contents and their nature; and if any persons purchase it, who feel no interest in the subjects of which it treats, they will have themselves only to blame.

"I could add to these arguments one derived from pecuniary motives, and particularly from the probable effects on the sale of your present publication; but they would weigh little with you compared with the preceding. Besides, I have long observed, that arguments drawn from your own personal interests more often act on you as narcotics than as stimulants, and that in money concerns you have some small portion of pig-nature in your moral idiosyncrasy, and, like these amiable creatures, must occasionally be pulled backward from the boat in order to make you enter it. All success attend you, for if hard thinking and hard reading are merits, you have deserved it. Your affectionate, etc." In consequence of this very judicious letter, which produced complete conviction on my mind, I shall content myself for the present with stating the main result of the chapter, which I have reserved for that future publication, a detailed prospectus of which the reader will find at the close of the second volume.

The Imagination then I consider either as primary, or secondary. The primary Imagination I hold to be the living power and prime agent of all human perception, and as a repetition in the finite mind of the eternal act of creation in the infinite I AM. The secondary Imagination I consider as an echo of the former, co-existing with the conscious will, yet still as identical with the primary in the kind of its agency, and differing only in degree, and in the mode of its operation. It dissolves, diffuses, dissipates, in order to recreate: or where this process is rendered impossible, yet still at all events it struggles to idealize and to unify. It is essentially vital, even as all objects (as objects) are essentially fixed and dead.

FANCY, on the contrary, has no other counters to play with, but fixities and definite. The fancy is indeed no other than a mode of memory emancipated from the order of time and space; while it is blended with, and modified by that empirical phaenomenon of the will, which we express by the word Choice. But equally with the ordinary memory the Fancy must receive all its materials ready made from the law of association.

CHAPTER XVI

Striking points of difference between the Poets of the present age and those of the fifteenth and sixteenth centuries—Wish expressed for the union of the characteristic merits of both.

Christendom, from its first settlement on feudal rights, has been so far one great body, however imperfectly organized, that a similar spirit will be found in each period to have been acting in all its members. The study of Shakespeare's poems—(I do not include his dramatic works, eminently as they too deserve that title)—led me to a more careful examination of the contemporary poets both in England and in other countries. But my attention was especially fixed on those of Italy, from the birth to the death of Shakespeare; that being the country in which the fine arts had been most sedulously, and hitherto most successfully cultivated.

Abstracted from the degrees and peculiarities of individual genius, the properties common to the good writers of each period seem to establish one striking point of difference between the poetry of the fifteenth and sixteenth centuries, and that of the present age. The remark may perhaps be extended to the sister art of painting. At least the latter will serve to illustrate the former. In the present age the poet—(I would wish to be understood as speaking generally, and without allusion to individual names)—seems to propose to himself as his main object, and as that which is the most characteristic of his art, new and striking images; with incidents that interest the affections or excite the curiosity. Both his characters and his descriptions he renders, as much as possible, specific and individual, even to a degree of portraiture. In his diction and metre, on the other hand, he is comparatively careless.

The measure is either constructed on no previous system, and acknowledges no justifying principle but that of the writer's convenience; or else some mechanical movement is adopted, of which one couplet or stanza is so far an adequate specimen, as that the occasional differences appear evidently to arise from accident, or the qualities of the language itself, not from meditation and an intelligent purpose. And the language from Pope's translation of Homer, to Darwin's Temple of Nature, may, notwithstanding some illustrious exceptions, be too faithfully characterized, as claiming to be poetical for no better reason, than that it would be intolerable in conversation or in prose.

Though alas! even our prose writings, nay even the style of our more set discourses, strive to be in the fashion, and trick themselves out in the soiled and over-worn finery of the meretricious muse. It is true that of late a great improvement in this respect is observable in our most popular writers. But it is equally true, that this recurrence to plain sense and genuine mother English is far from being general; and that the composition of our novels, magazines, public harangues, and the like is commonly as trivial in thought, and yet enigmatic in expression, as if Echo and Sphinx had laid their heads together to construct it.

Nay, even of those who have most rescued themselves from this contagion, I should plead inwardly guilty to the charge of duplicity or cowardice, if I withheld my conviction, that few have guarded the purity of their native tongue with that jealous care, which the sublime Dante in his tract De la volgare Eloquenza, declares to be the first duty of a poet. For language is the armoury of the human mind; and at once contains the trophies of its past, and the weapons of its future conquests. Animadverte, says Hobbes, quam sit ab improprietate verborum pronum hominihus prolabi in errores circa ipsas res! Sat [vero], says Sennertus, in hac vitae brevitate et naturae obscuritate, rerum est, quibus cognoscendis tempus impendatur, ut [confusis et multivotis] sermonibus intelligendis illud consumere opus non sit. [Eheu! quantas strages paravere verba nubila, quae tot dicunt ut nihil dicunt;—nubes potius, e quibus et in rebus politicis et in ecclesia turbines et tonitrua erumpunt!] Et proinde recte dictum putamus a Platone in Gorgia: os an ta onomata eidei, eisetai kai ta pragmata: et ab Epicteto, archae paideuseos hae ton onomaton episkepsis: et prudentissime Galenus scribit, hae ton onomaton chraesis tarachtheisa kai taen ton pragmaton epitarattei gnosin.

Egregie vero J. C. Scaliger, in Lib. I. de Plantis: Est primum, inquit, sapientis officium, bene sentire, ut sibi vivat: proximum, bene loqui, ut patriae vivat.

Something analogous to the materials and structure of modern poetry I seem to have noticed—(but here I beg to be understood as speaking with the utmost diffidence)—in our common landscape painters. Their foregrounds and intermediate distances are comparatively unattractive: while the main interest of the landscape is thrown into the background, where mountains and torrents and castles forbid the eye to proceed, and nothing tempts it to trace its way back again.

But in the works of the great Italian and Flemish masters, the front and middle objects of the landscape are the most obvious and determinate, the interest gradually dies away in the background, and the charm and peculiar worth of the picture consists, not so much in the specific objects which it conveys to the understanding in a visual language formed by the substitution of figures for words, as in the beauty and harmony of the colours, lines, and expression, with which the objects are represented. Hence novelty of subject was rather avoided than sought for. Superior excellence in the manner of treating the same subjects was the trial and test of the artist's merit.

Not otherwise is it with the more polished poets of the fifteenth and sixteenth centuries, especially those of Italy. The imagery is almost always general: sun, moon, flowers, breezes, murmuring streams, warbling songsters, delicious shades, lovely damsels cruel as fair, nymphs, naiads, and goddesses, are the materials which are common to all, and which each shaped and arranged according to his judgment or fancy, little solicitous to add or to particularize. If we make an honourable exception in favour of some English poets, the thoughts too are as little novel as the images; and the fable of their narrative poems, for the most part drawn from mythology, or sources of equal notoriety, derive their chief attractions from the manner of treating them; from impassioned flow, or picturesque arrangement. In opposition to the present age, and perhaps in as faulty an extreme, they placed the essence of poetry in the art.

The excellence, at which they aimed, consisted in the exquisite polish of the diction, combined with perfect simplicity. This their prime object they attained by the avoidance of every word, which a gentleman would not use in dignified conversation, and of every word and phrase, which none but a learned man would use; by the studied position of words and phrases, so that not only each part should be melodious in itself, but contribute to the harmony of the whole, each note referring and conducting to the melody of all the foregoing and following words of the same period or stanza; and lastly with equal labour, the greater because unbetrayed, by the variation and various harmonies of their metrical movement.

Their measures, however, were not indebted for their variety to the introduction of new metres, such as have been attempted of late in the Alonzo and Imogen, and others borrowed from the German, having in their very mechanism a specific overpowering tune, to which the generous reader humours his voice and emphasis, with more indulgence to the author than attention to the meaning or quantity of the words; but which, to an ear familiar with the numerous sounds of the

Greek and Roman poets, has an effect not unlike that of galloping over a paved road in a German stage-waggon without springs. On the contrary, the elder bards both of Italy and England produced a far greater as well as more charming variety by countless modifications, and subtle balances of sound in the common metres of their country.

A lasting and enviable reputation awaits that man of genius, who should attempt and realise a union;—who should recall the high finish, the appropriateness, the facility, the delicate proportion, and above all, the perfusive and omnipresent grace, which have preserved, as in a shrine of precious amber, the Sparrow of Catullus, the Swallow, the Grasshopper, and all the other little loves of Anacreon; and which, with bright, though diminished glories, revisited the youth and early manhood of Christian Europe, in the vales of Arno, and the groves of Isis and of Cam; and who with these should combine the keener interest, deeper pathos, manlier reflection, and the fresher and more various imagery, which give a value and a name that will not pass away to the poets who have done honour to our own times, and to those of our immediate predecessors.

CHAPTER XXII

The characteristic defects of Wordsworth's poetry, with the principles from which the judgment, that they are defects, is deduced—Their proportion to the beauties—For the greatest part characteristic of his theory only.

If Mr. Wordsworth have set forth principles of poetry which his arguments are insufficient to support, let him and those who have adopted his sentiments be set right by the confutation of those arguments, and by the substitution of more philosophical principles. And still let the due credit be given to the portion and importance of the truths, which are blended with his theory; truths, the too exclusive attention to which had occasioned its errors, by tempting him to carry those truths beyond their proper limits. If his mistaken theory have at all influenced his poetic compositions, let the effects be pointed out, and the instances given. But let it likewise be shown, how far the influence has acted; whether diffusively, or only by starts; whether the number and importance of the poems and passages thus infected be great or trifling compared with the sound portion; and lastly, whether they are inwoven into the texture of his works, or are loose and separable. The result of such a trial would evince beyond a doubt, what it is high time to announce decisively and aloud, that the supposed characteristics of Mr. Wordsworth's poetry, whether admired or reprobated; whether they are simplicity or simpleness; faithful adherence to essential nature, or wilful selections from human nature of its meanest forms and under the least attractive associations; are as little the real characteristics of his poetry at large, as of his genius and the constitution of his mind.

In a comparatively small number of poems he chose to try an experiment; and this experiment we will suppose to have failed. Yet even in these poems it is impossible not to perceive that the natural tendency of the poet's mind is to great objects and elevated conceptions. The poem entitled FIDELITY is for the greater part written in language, as unraised and naked as any perhaps in the two volumes. Yet take the following stanza and compare it with the preceding stanzas of the same poem.

"There sometimes doth a leaping fish
Send through the tarn a lonely cheer;
The crags repeat the raven's croak,
In symphony austere;
Thither the rainbow comes—the cloud—
And mists that spread the flying shroud;
And sun-beams; and the sounding blast,
That, if it could, would hurry past;
But that enormous barrier holds it fast."

Or compare the four last lines of the concluding stanza with the former half.

"Yes, proof was plain that, since the day
On which the Traveller thus had died,

The Dog had watched about the spot,
Or by his Master's side:
How nourish'd here through such long time
He knows, who gave that love sublime,—
And gave that strength of feeling, great
Above all human estimate!"

Can any candid and intelligent mind hesitate in determining, which of these best represents the tendency and native character of the poet's genius? Will he not decide that the one was written because the poet would so write, and the other because he could not so entirely repress the force and grandeur of his mind, but that he must in some part or other of every composition write otherwise? In short, that his only disease is the being out of his element; like the swan, that, having amused himself, for a while, with crushing the weeds on the river's bank, soon returns to his own majestic movements on its reflecting and sustaining surface. Let it be observed that I am here supposing the imagined judge, to whom I appeal, to have already decided against the poet's theory, as far as it is different from the principles of the art, generally acknowledged.

I cannot here enter into a detailed examination of Mr. Wordsworth's works; but I will attempt to give the main results of my own judgment, after an acquaintance of many years, and repeated perusals. And though, to appreciate the defects of a great mind it is necessary to understand previously its characteristic excellences, yet I have already expressed myself with sufficient fulness, to preclude most of the ill effects that might arise from my pursuing a contrary arrangement. I will therefore commence with what I deem the prominent defects of his poems hitherto published.

The first characteristic, though only occasional defect, which I appear to myself to find in these poems is the inconstancy of the style. Under this name I refer to the sudden and unprepared transitions from lines or sentences of peculiar felicity—(at all events striking and original)—to a style, not only unimpassioned but undistinguished. He sinks too often and too abruptly to that style, which I should place in the second division of language, dividing it into the three species; first, that which is peculiar to poetry; second, that which is only proper in prose; and third, the neutral or common to both. There have been works, such as Cowley's Essay on Cromwell, in which prose and verse are intermixed (not as in the Consolation of Boetius, or the ARGENIS of Barclay, by the insertion of poems supposed to have been spoken or composed on occasions previously related in prose, but) the poet passing from one to the other, as the nature of the thoughts or his own feelings dictated. Yet this mode of composition does not satisfy a cultivated taste.

There is something unpleasant in the being thus obliged to alternate states of feeling so dissimilar, and this too in a species of writing, the pleasure from which is in part derived from the preparation and previous expectation of the reader. A portion of that awkwardness is felt which hangs upon the introduction of songs in our modern comic operas; and to prevent which the judicious Metastasio (as to whose exquisite taste there can be no hesitation, whatever doubts may be entertained as to his poetic genius) uniformly placed the aria at the end of the scene, at the same time that he almost always raises and impassions the style of the recitative immediately preceding.

Even in real life, the difference is great and evident between words used as the arbitrary marks of thought, our smooth market-coin of intercourse, with the image and superscription worn out by currency; and those which convey pictures either borrowed from one outward object to enliven and particularize some other; or used allegorically to body forth the inward state of the person speaking; or such as are at least the exponents of his peculiar turn and unusual extent of faculty.

So much so indeed, that in the social circles of private life we often find a striking use of the latter put a stop to the general flow of conversation, and by the excitement arising from concentred attention produce a sort of damp and interruption for some minutes after. But in the perusal of works of literary art, we prepare ourselves for such language; and the business of the writer, like that of a painter whose subject requires unusual splendour and prominence, is so to raise the lower and neutral tints, that what in a different style would be the commanding colours, are here used as the means of that gentle degradation requisite in order to produce the effect of a whole. Where this is not achieved in a poem, the metre merely reminds the reader of his claims in order to disappoint them; and where this defect occurs frequently, his feelings are alternately startled by anticlimax and hyperclimax.

I refer the reader to the exquisite stanzas cited for another purpose from THE BLIND HIGHLAND BOY; and then annex, as being in my opinion instances of this disharmony in style, the two following:

"And one, the rarest, was a shell,
Which he, poor child, had studied well:
The shell of a green turtle, thin
And hollow;—you might sit therein,
It was so wide, and deep."

"Our Highland Boy oft visited
The house which held this prize; and, led
By choice or chance, did thither come
One day, when no one was at home,
And found the door unbarred."
Or page 172, vol. I.

"'Tis gone forgotten, let me do
My best. There was a smile or two—
I can remember them, I see
The smiles worth all the world to me.
Dear Baby! I must lay thee down:
Thou troublest me with strange alarms;
Smiles hast thou, sweet ones of thine own;
I cannot keep thee in my arms;
For they confound me: as it is,
I have forgot those smiles of his!"
Or page 269, vol. I.

"Thou hast a nest, for thy love and thy rest
And though little troubled with sloth
Drunken lark! thou would'st be loth
To be such a traveller as I.

Happy, happy liver!

_With a soul as strong as a mountain river
Pouring out praise to th' Almighty giver,_
Joy and jollity be with us both!
Hearing thee or else some other,
As merry a brother
I on the earth will go plodding on
By myself cheerfully till the day is done."

The incongruity, which I appear to find in this passage, is that of the two noble lines in italics with the preceding and following. So vol. II. page 30.

"Close by a Pond, upon the further side,
He stood alone; a minute's space I guess,
I watch'd him, he continuing motionless
To the Pool's further margin then I drew;
He being all the while before me full in view."

Compare this with the repetition of the same image, the next stanza but two.

"And, still as I drew near with gentle pace,
Beside the little pond or moorish flood
Motionless as a Cloud the Old Man stood,
That heareth not the loud winds when they call;
And moveth altogether, if it move at all."

Or lastly, the second of the three following stanzas, compared both with the first and the third.

"My former thoughts returned; the fear that kills;
And hope that is unwilling to be fed;
Cold, pain, and labour, and all fleshly ills;
And mighty Poets in their misery dead.

But now, perplex'd by what the Old Man had said,
My question eagerly did I renew,
'How is it that you live, and what is it you do?'

"He with a smile did then his words repeat;
And said, that gathering Leeches far and wide
He travell'd; stirring thus about his feet
The waters of the Ponds where they abide.

'Once I could meet with them on every side;
'But they have dwindled long by slow decay;
'Yet still I persevere, and find them where I may.'

While he was talking thus, the lonely place,
The Old Man's shape, and speech, all troubled me
In my mind's eye I seemed to see him pace
About the weary moors continually,
Wandering about alone and silently."

Indeed this fine poem is especially characteristic of the author. There is scarce a defect or excellence in his writings of which it would not present a specimen. But it would be unjust not to repeat that this defect is only occasional. From a careful reperusal of the two volumes of poems, I doubt whether the objectionable passages would amount in the whole to one hundred lines; not the eighth part of the number of pages. In the excursion the feeling of incongruity is seldom excited by the diction of any passage considered in itself, but by the sudden superiority of some other passage forming the context.

The second defect I can generalize with tolerable accuracy, if the reader will pardon an uncouth and new-coined word. There is, I should say, not seldom a matter-of-factness in certain poems. This may be divided into, first, a labourious minuteness and fidelity in the representation of objects, and their positions, as they appeared to the poet himself; secondly, the insertion of accidental circumstances, in order to the full explanation of his living characters, their dispositions and actions; which circumstances might be necessary to establish the probability of a statement in real life, where nothing is taken for granted by the hearer; but appear superfluous in poetry, where the reader is willing to believe for his own sake. To this actidentality I object, as contravening the essence of poetry, which Aristotle pronounces to be spoudaiotaton kai philosophotaton genos, the most intense, weighty and philosophical product of human art; adding, as the reason, that it is the most catholic and abstract.

The following passage from Davenant's prefatory letter to Hobbes well expresses this truth. "When I considered the actions which I meant to describe; (those inferring the persons), I was again persuaded rather to choose those of a former age, than the present; and in a century so far removed, as might preserve me from their improper examinations, who know not the requisites of a poem, nor how much pleasure they lose, (and even the pleasures of heroic poesy are not unprofitable), who take away the liberty of a poet, and fetter his feet in the shackles of an historian.

For why should a poet doubt in story to mend the intrigues of fortune by more delightful conveyances of probable fictions, because austere historians have entered into bond to truth? An obligation, which were in poets as foolish and unnecessary, as is the bondage of false martyrs, who lie in chains for a mistaken opinion. But by this I would imply, that truth, narrative and past, is the idol of historians, (who worship a dead thing), and truth operative, and by effects continually alive, is the mistress of poets, who hath not her existence in matter, but in reason."

For this minute accuracy in the painting of local imagery, the lines in the excursion, pp. 96, 97, and 98, may be taken, if not as a striking instance, yet as an illustration of my meaning. It must be some strong motive—(as, for instance, that the description was necessary to the intelligibility of the tale)—which could induce me to describe in a number of verses what a draughtsman could present to the eye with incomparably greater satisfaction by half a dozen strokes of his pencil, or the painter with as many touches of his brush. Such descriptions too often occasion in the mind of a reader, who is determined to understand his author, a feeling of labour, not very dissimilar to that, with which he would construct a diagram, line by line, for a long geometrical proposition. It seems to be like taking the pieces of a dissected map out of its box. We first look at one part, and then at another, then join and dove-tail them; and when the successive acts of attention have been completed, there is a retrogressive effort of mind to behold it as a whole. The poet should paint to the imagination, not to the fancy; and I know no happier case to exemplify the distinction between these two faculties. Master-pieces of the former mode of poetic painting abound in the writings of Milton, for example:

"The fig-tree; not that kind for fruit renown'd,
"But such as at this day, to Indians known,
"In Malabar or Decan spreads her arms
"Branching so broad and long, that in the ground
"The bended twigs take root, and daughters grow
"About the mother tree, a pillar'd shade
"High over-arch'd and ECHOING WALKS BETWEEN;
"There oft the Indian herdsman, shunning heat,
"Shelters in cool, and tends his pasturing herds
"At hoop-holes cut through thickest shade."

This is creation rather than painting, or if painting, yet such, and with such co-presence of the whole picture flashed at once upon the eye, as the sun paints in a camera obscura. But the poet must likewise understand and command what Bacon calls the vestigia communia of the senses, the latency of all in each, and more especially as by a magical penny duplex, the excitement of vision by sound and the exponents of sound. Thus, "The echoing walks between," may be almost said to reverse the fable in tradition of the head of Memnon, in the Egyptian statue. Such may be deservedly entitled the creative words in the world of imagination.

The second division respects an apparent minute adherence to matter- of-fact in character and Incidents; a biographical attention to probability, and an anxiety of explanation and retrospect. Under this head I shall deliver, with no feigned diffidence, the results of my best reflection on the great point of controversy between Mr. Wordsworth and his objectors; namely, on the choice of his characters. I have already declared, and, I trust justified, my utter dissent from the mode of argument which his critics have hitherto employed. To their question, "Why did you choose such a character, or a character from such a rank of life?"—the poet might in my opinion fairly retort: why with the conception of my character did you make wilful choice of mean or ludicrous associations not furnished by me, but supplied from your own sickly and fastidious feelings?

How was it, indeed, probable, that such arguments could have any weight with an author, whose plan, whose guiding principle, and main object it was to attack and subdue that state of association, which leads us to place the chief value on those things on which man differs from man, and to forget or disregard the high dignities, which belong to Human Nature, the sense and the feeling, which may be, and ought to be, found in all ranks? The feelings with which, as Christians, we contemplate a mixed congregation rising or kneeling before their common Maker, Mr. Wordsworth would have us entertain at all times, as men, and as readers; and by the excitement of this lofty, yet prideless impartiality in poetry, he might hope to have encouraged its continuance in real life.

The praise of good men be his! In real life, and, I trust, even in my imagination, I honour a virtuous and wise man, without reference to the presence or absence of artificial advantages. Whether in the person of an armed baron, a laurelled bard, or of an old Pedlar, or still older Leech-gatherer, the same qualities of head and heart must claim the same reverence. And even in poetry I am not conscious, that I have ever suffered my feelings to be disturbed or offended by any thoughts or images, which the poet himself has not presented.

But yet I object, nevertheless, and for the following reasons. First, because the object in view, as an immediate object, belongs to the moral philosopher, and would be pursued, not only more appropriately, but in my opinion with far greater probability of success, in sermons or moral essays, than in an elevated poem. It seems, indeed, to destroy the main fundamental distinction, not only between a poem and prose, but even between philosophy and works of fiction, inasmuch as it proposes truth for its immediate object, instead of pleasure. Now till the blessed time shall come, when truth itself shall be pleasure, and both shall be so united, as to be distinguishable in words only, not in feeling, it will remain the poet's office to proceed upon that state of association, which actually exists as general; instead of attempting first to make it what it ought to be, and then to let the pleasure follow. But here is unfortunately a small hysteron-proteron. For the communication of pleasure is the introductory means by which alone the poet must expect to moralize his readers. Secondly: though I were to admit, for a moment, this argument to be groundless: yet how is the moral effect to be produced, by merely attaching the name of some low profession to powers which are least likely, and to qualities which are assuredly not more likely, to be found in it? The Poet, speaking in his own person, may at once delight and improve us by sentiments, which teach us the independence of goodness, of wisdom, and even of genius, on the favours of fortune. And having made a due reverence before the throne of Antonine, he may bow with equal awe before Epictetus among his fellow-slaves

———"and rejoice
In the plain presence of his dignity."

Who is not at once delighted and improved, when the Poet Wordsworth himself exclaims,

"Oh! many are the Poets that are sown
By Nature; men endowed with highest gifts
The vision and the faculty divine,
Yet wanting the accomplishment of verse,
Nor having e'er, as life advanced, been led
By circumstance to take unto the height
The measure of themselves, these favoured Beings,
All but a scattered few, live out their time,
Husbanding that which they possess within,
And go to the grave, unthought of. Strongest minds

Are often those of whom the noisy world
Hears least."

To use a colloquial phrase, such sentiments, in such language, do one's heart good; though I for my part, have not the fullest faith in the truth of the observation. On the contrary I believe the instances to be exceedingly rare; and should feel almost as strong an objection to introduce such a character in a poetic fiction, as a pair of black swans on a lake, in a fancy landscape. When I think how many, and how much better books than Homer, or even than Herodotus, Pindar or Aeschylus, could have read, are in the power of almost every man, in a country where almost every man is instructed to read and write; and how restless, how difficultly hidden, the powers of genius are; and yet find even in situations the most favourable, according to Mr. Wordsworth, for the formation of a pure and poetic language; in situations which ensure familiarity with the grandest objects of the imagination; but one Burns, among the shepherds of Scotland, and not a single poet of humble life among those of English lakes and mountains; I conclude, that Poetic Genius is not only a very delicate but a very rare plant.

But be this as it may, the feelings with which,
"I think of Chatterton, the marvellous Boy,
The sleepless Soul, that perished in his pride;
Of Burns, who walk'd in glory and in joy
Behind his plough, upon the mountain-side"—

are widely different from those with which I should read a poem, where the author, having occasion for the character of a poet and a philosopher in the fable of his narration, had chosen to make him a chimney-sweeper; and then, in order to remove all doubts on the subject, had invented an account of his birth, parentage and education, with all the strange and fortunate accidents which had concurred in making him at once poet, philosopher, and sweep! Nothing, but biography, can justify this. If it be admissible even in a novel, it must be one in the manner of De Foe's, that were meant to pass for histories, not in the manner of Fielding's: In THE LIFE OF

MOLL FLANDERS, Or COLONEL JACK, not in a TOM JONES, or even a JOSEPH ANDREWS. Much less then can it be legitimately introduced in a poem, the characters of which, amid the strongest individualization, must still remain representative.

The precepts of Horace, on this point, are grounded on the nature both of poetry and of the human mind. They are not more peremptory, than wise and prudent. For in the first place a deviation from them perplexes the reader's feelings, and all the circumstances which are feigned in order to make such accidents less improbable, divide and disquiet his faith, rather than aid and support it. Spite of all attempts, the fiction will appear, and unfortunately not as fictitious but as false.

The reader not only knows, that the sentiments and language are the poet's own, and his own too in his artificial character, as poet; but by the fruitless endeavors to make him think the contrary, he is not even suffered to forget it. The effect is similar to that produced by an Epic Poet, when the fable and the characters are derived from Scripture history, as in THE MESSIAH of Klopstock, or in CUMBERLAND'S CALVARY; and not merely suggested by it as in the PARADISE LOST of Milton.

That illusion, contradistinguished from delusion, that negative faith, which simply permits the images presented to work by their own force, without either denial or affirmation of their real existence by the judgment, is rendered impossible by their immediate neighbourhood to words and facts of known and absolute truth. A faith, which transcends even historic belief, must absolutely put out this mere poetic analogon of faith, as the summer sun is said to extinguish our household fires, when it shines full upon them. What would otherwise have been yielded to as pleasing fiction, is repelled as revolting falsehood. The effect produced in this latter case by the solemn belief of the reader, is in a less degree brought about in the instances, to which I have been objecting, by the balked attempts of the author to make him believe.

Add to all the foregoing the seeming uselessness both of the project and of the anecdotes from which it is to derive support. Is there one word, for instance, attributed to the pedlar in THE EXCURSION, characteristic of a Pedlar? One sentiment, that might not more plausibly, even without the aid of any previous explanation, have proceeded from any wise and beneficent old man, of a rank or profession in which the language of learning and refinement are natural and to be expected? Need the rank have been at all particularized, where nothing follows which the knowledge of that rank is to explain or illustrate? When on the contrary this information renders the man's language, feelings, sentiments, and information a riddle, which must itself be solved by episodes of anecdote? Finally when this, and this alone, could have induced a genuine Poet to inweave in a poem of the loftiest style, and on subjects the loftiest and of most universal interest, such minute matters of fact, (not unlike those furnished for the obituary of a magazine by the friends of some obscure "ornament of society lately deceased" in some obscure town,) as

"Among the hills of Athol he was born
There, on a small hereditary Farm,
An unproductive slip of rugged ground,
His Father dwelt; and died in poverty;
While He, whose lowly fortune I retrace,
The youngest of three sons, was yet a babe,
A little One—unconscious of their loss.

But ere he had outgrown his infant days
His widowed Mother, for a second Mate,
Espoused the teacher of the Village School;
Who on her offspring zealously bestowed
Needful instruction."

"From his sixth year, the Boy of whom I speak,
In summer tended cattle on the Hills;
But, through the inclement and the perilous days
Of long-continuing winter, he repaired
To his Step-father's School,"-etc.

For all the admirable passages interposed in this narration, might, with trifling alterations, have been far more appropriately, and with far greater verisimilitude, told of a poet in the character of a poet; and without incurring another defect which I shall now mention, and a sufficient illustration of which will have been here anticipated.

Third; an undue predilection for the dramatic form in certain poems, from which one or other of two evils result. Either the thoughts and diction are different from that of the poet, and then there arises an incongruity of style; or they are the same and indistinguishable, and then it presents a species of ventriloquism, where two are represented as talking, while in truth one man only speaks.

The fourth class of defects is closely connected with the former; but yet are such as arise likewise from an intensity of feeling disproportionate to such knowledge and value of the objects described, as can be fairly anticipated of men in general, even of the most cultivated classes; and with which therefore few only, and those few particularly circumstanced, can be supposed to sympathize: In this class, I comprise occasional prolixity, repetition, and an eddying, instead of progression, of thought. As instances, see pages 27, 28, and 62 of the Poems, vol. I. and the first eighty lines of the VIth Book of THE EXCURSION.

Fifth and last; thoughts and images too great for the subject. This is an approximation to what might be called mental bombast, as distinguished from verbal: for, as in the latter there is a disproportion of the expressions to the thoughts so in this there is a disproportion of thought to the circumstance and occasion. This, by the bye, is a fault of which none but a man of genius is capable. It is the awkwardness and strength of Hercules with the distaff of Omphale.

It is a well-known fact, that bright colours in motion both make and leave the strongest impressions on the eye. Nothing is more likely too, than that a vivid image or visual spectrum, thus originated, may become the link of association in recalling the feelings and images that had accompanied the original impression. But if we describe this in such lines, as

"They flash upon that inward eye,
Which is the bliss of solitude!"

in what words shall we describe the joy of retrospection, when the images and virtuous actions of a whole well-spent life, pass before that conscience which is indeed the inward eye: which is indeed "the bliss of solitude?" Assuredly we seem to sink most abruptly, not to say burlesquely, and almost as in a medley, from this couplet to—

"And then my heart with pleasure fills,

And dances with the daffodils." Vol. I. p. 328.

The second instance is from vol. II. page 12, where the poet having gone out for a day's tour of pleasure, meets early in the morning with a knot of Gipsies, who had pitched their blanket-tents and straw-beds, together with their children and asses, in some field by the road- side. At the close of the day on his return our tourist found them in the same place. "Twelve hours," says he,

"Twelve hours, twelve bounteous hours are gone, while I
Have been a traveller under open sky,
Much witnessing of change and cheer,
Yet as I left I find them here!"

Whereat the poet, without seeming to reflect that the poor tawny wanderers might probably have been tramping for weeks together through road and lane, over moor and mountain, and consequently must have been right glad to rest themselves, their children and cattle, for one whole day; and overlooking the obvious truth, that such repose might be quite as necessary for them, as a walk of the same continuance was pleasing or healthful for the more fortunate poet; expresses his indignation in a series of lines, the diction and imagery of which would have been rather above, than below the mark, had they been applied to the immense empire of China improgressive for thirty centuries:

"The weary Sun betook himself to rest:—
—Then issued Vesper from the fulgent west,
Outshining, like a visible God,
The glorious path in which he trod.

And now, ascending, after one dark hour,
And one night's diminution of her power,
Behold the mighty Moon! this way
She looks, as if at them—but they
Regard not her:—oh, better wrong and strife,
Better vain deeds or evil than such life!
The silent Heavens have goings on
The stars have tasks!—but these have none!"

The last instance of this defect,(for I know no other than these already cited) is from the Ode, page 351, vol. II., where, speaking of a child, "a six years' Darling of a pigmy size," he thus addresses him:

"Thou best Philosopher, who yet dost keep
Thy heritage, thou Eye among the blind,
That, deaf and silent, read'st the eternal deep,
Haunted for ever by the Eternal Mind,—
Mighty Prophet! Seer blest!
On whom those truths do rest,
Which we are toiling all our lives to find!
Thou, over whom thy Immortality
Broods like the Day, a Master o'er a Slave,
A Present which is not to be put by!"

Now here, not to stop at the daring spirit of metaphor which connects the epithets "deaf and silent," with the apostrophized eye: or (if we are to refer it to the preceding word, "Philosopher"), the faulty and equivocal syntax of the passage; and without examining the propriety of making a "Master brood o'er a Slave," or "the Day" brood at all; we will merely ask, what does all this mean? In what sense is a child of that age a Philosopher? In what sense does he read "the eternal deep?" In what sense is he declared to be "for ever haunted" by the Supreme Being? or so inspired as to deserve the splendid titles of a Mighty Prophet, a blessed Seer? By reflection? by knowledge? by conscious intuition? or by any form or modification of consciousness? These would be tidings indeed; but such as would pre-suppose an immediate revelation to the inspired communicator, and require miracles to authenticate his inspiration. Children at this age give us no such information of themselves; and at what time were we dipped in the Lethe, which has produced such utter oblivion of a state so godlike? There are many of us that still possess some remembrances, more or less distinct, respecting themselves at six years old; pity that the worthless straws only should float, while treasures, compared with which all the mines of Golconda and Mexico were but straws, should be absorbed by some unknown gulf into some unknown abyss.

But if this be too wild and exorbitant to be suspected as having been the poet's meaning; if these mysterious gifts, faculties, and operations, are not accompanied with consciousness; who else is conscious of them? or how can it be called the child, if it be no part of the child's conscious being? For aught I know, the thinking Spirit within me may be substantially one with the principle of life, and of vital operation. For aught I know, it might be employed as a secondary agent in the marvellous organization and organic movements of my body.

But, surely, it would be strange language to say, that I construct my heart! or that I propel the finer influences through my nerves! or that I compress my brain, and draw the curtains of sleep round my own eyes! Spinoza and Behmen were, on different systems, both Pantheists; and among the ancients there were philosophers, teachers of the EN KAI PAN, who not only taught that God was All, but that this All constituted God. Yet not even these would confound the part, as a part, with the whole, as the whole. Nay, in no system is the distinction between the individual and God, between the Modification, and the one only Substance, more sharply drawn, than in that of Spinoza. Jacobi indeed relates of Lessing, that, after a conversation with him at the house of the Poet,

Gleim, (the Tyrtaeus and Anacreon of the German Parnassus,) in which conversation Lessing had avowed privately to Jacobi his reluctance to admit any personal existence of the Supreme Being, or the possibility of personality except in a finite Intellect, and while they were sitting at table, a shower of rain came on unexpectedly. Gleim expressed his regret at the circumstance, because they had meant to drink their wine in the garden: upon which Lessing in one of his half-earnest, half-joking moods, nodded to Jacobi, and said, "It is I, perhaps, that am doing that," i.e. raining!—and Jacobi answered, "or perhaps I;" Gleim contented himself with staring at them both, without asking for any explanation.

So with regard to this passage. In what sense can the magnificent attributes, above quoted, be appropriated to a child, which would not make them equally suitable to a bee, or a dog, or afield of corn: or even to a ship, or to the wind and waves that propel it? The omnipresent Spirit works equally in them, as in the child; and the child is equally unconscious of it as they. It cannot surely be, that the four lines, immediately following, are to contain the explanation?

"To whom the grave
Is but a lonely bed without the sense or sight
Of day or the warm light,
A place of thought where we in waiting lie;"—

Surely, it cannot be that this wonder-rousing apostrophe is but a comment on the little poem, "We are Seven?"—that the whole meaning of the passage is reducible to the assertion, that a child, who by the bye at six years old would have been better instructed in most Christian families, has no other notion of death than that of lying in a dark, cold place? And still, I hope, not as in a place of thought! not the frightful notion of lying awake in his grave! The analogy between death and sleep is too simple, too natural, to render so horrid a belief possible for children; even had they not been in the habit, as all Christian children are, of hearing the latter term used to express the former. But if the child's belief be only, that "he is not dead, but sleepeth:" wherein does it differ from that of his father and mother, or any other adult and instructed person? To form an idea of a thing's becoming nothing; or of nothing becoming a thing; is impossible to all finite beings alike, of whatever age, and however educated or uneducated. Thus it is with splendid paradoxes in general. If the words are taken in the common sense, they convey an absurdity; and if, in contempt of dictionaries and custom, they are so interpreted as to avoid the absurdity, the meaning dwindles into some bald truism. Thus you must at once understand the words contrary to their common import, in order to arrive at any sense; and according to their common import, if you are to receive from them any feeling of sublimity or admiration.

Though the instances of this defect in Mr. Wordsworth's poems are so few, that for themselves it would have been scarcely just to attract the reader's attention toward them; yet I have dwelt on it, and perhaps the more for this very reason. For being so very few, they cannot sensibly detract from the reputation of an author, who is even characterized by the number of profound truths in his writings, which will stand the severest analysis; and yet few as they are, they are exactly those passages which his blind admirers would be most likely, and best able, to imitate. But Wordsworth, where he is indeed Wordsworth, may be mimicked by copyists, he may be plundered by plagiarists; but he cannot be imitated, except by those who are not born to be imitators. For without his depth of feeling and his imaginative power his sense would want its vital warmth and peculiarity; and without his strong sense, his mysticism would become sickly—mere fog, and dimness!

To these defects which, as appears by the extracts, are only occasional, I may oppose, with far less fear of encountering the dissent of any candid and intelligent reader, the following (for the most part correspondent) excellencies. First, an austere purity of language both grammatically and logically; in short a perfect appropriateness of the words to the meaning. Of how high value I deem this, and how particularly estimable I hold the example at the present day, has been already stated: and in part too the reasons on which I ground both the moral and intellectual importance of habituating ourselves to a strict accuracy of expression. It is noticeable, how limited an acquaintance with the masterpieces of art will suffice to form a correct and even a sensitive taste, where none but masterpieces have been seen and admired: while on the other hand, the most correct notions, and the widest acquaintance with the works of excellence of all ages and countries, will not perfectly secure us against the contagious familiarity with the far more numerous offspring of tastelessness or of a perverted taste. If this be the case, as it notoriously is, with the arts of music and painting, much more difficult will it be, to avoid the infection of multiplied and daily examples in the practice of an art, which uses words, and words only, as its instruments. In poetry, in which every line, every phrase, may pass the ordeal of deliberation and deliberate choice, it is possible, and barely possible, to attain that ultimatum which I have ventured to propose as the infallible test of a blameless style; namely: its untranslatableness in words of the same language without injury to the meaning. Be it observed, however, that I include in the meaning of a word not only its correspondent object, but likewise all the associations which it recalls. For language is framed to convey not the object alone but likewise the character, mood and intentions of the person who is representing it. In poetry it is practicable to preserve the diction uncorrupted by the affectations and misappropriations, which promiscuous authorship, and reading not promiscuous only because it is disproportionally most conversant with the compositions of the day, have rendered general. Yet even to the poet, composing in his own province, it is an arduous work: and as the result and pledge of a watchful good sense of fine and luminous distinction, and of complete self-possession, may justly claim all the honour which belongs to an attainment equally difficult and valuable, and the more valuable for being rare. It is at all times the proper food of the understanding; but in an age of corrupt eloquence it is both food and antidote.

In prose I doubt whether it be even possible to preserve our style wholly unalloyed by the vicious phraseology which meets us everywhere, from the sermon to the newspaper, from the harangue of the legislator to the speech from the convivial chair, announcing a toast or sentiment. Our chains rattle, even while we are complaining of them. The poems of Boetius rise high in our estimation when we compare them with those of his contemporaries, as Sidonius Apollinaris, and others. They might even be referred to a purer age, but that the prose, in which they are set, as jewels in a crown of lead or iron, betrays the true age of the writer. Much however may be effected by education. I believe not only from grounds of reason, but from having in great measure assured myself of the fact by actual though limited experience, that, to a youth led from his first boyhood to investigate the meaning of every word and the reason of its choice and position, logic presents itself as an old acquaintance under new names.

On some future occasion, more especially demanding such disquisition, I shall attempt to prove the close connection between veracity and habits of mental accuracy; the beneficial after-effects of verbal precision in the preclusion of fanaticism, which masters the feelings more especially by indistinct watch-words; and to display the advantages which language alone, at least which language with incomparably greater ease and certainty than any other means, presents to the instructor of impressing modes of intellectual energy so constantly, so imperceptibly, and as it were by such elements and atoms, as to secure in due time the formation of a second nature. When we reflect, that the cultivation of the judgment is a positive command of the moral law, since the reason can give the principle alone, and the conscience bears witness only to the motive, while the application and effects must depend on the judgment when we consider, that the greater part of our success and comfort in life depends on distinguishing the similar from the same, that which is peculiar in each thing from that which it has in common with others, so as still to select the most probable, instead of the merely possible or positively unfit, we shall learn to value earnestly and with a practical seriousness a mean, already prepared for us by nature and society, of teaching the young mind to think well and wisely by the same unremembered process and with the same never forgotten results, as those by which it is taught to speak and converse. Now how much warmer the interest is, how much more genial the feelings of reality and practicability, and thence how much stronger the impulses to imitation are, which a contemporary writer, and especially a contemporary poet, excites in youth and commencing manhood, has been treated of in the earlier pages of these sketches. I have only to add, that all the praise which is due to the exertion of such influence for a purpose so important, joined with that which must be claimed for the infrequency of the same excellence in the same perfection, belongs in full right to Mr. Wordsworth. I am far however from denying that we have poets whose general style possesses the same excellence, as Mr. Moore, Lord Byron, Mr. Bowles, and, in all his later and more important works, our laurel-honouring Laureate. But there are none, in whose works I do not appear to myself to find more exceptions, than in those of Wordsworth. Quotations or specimens would here be wholly out of place, and must be left for the critic who doubts and would invalidate the justice of this eulogy so applied.

The second characteristic excellence of Mr. Wordsworth's work is: a correspondent weight and sanity of the Thoughts and Sentiments,—won, not from books; but—from the poet's own meditative observation. They are fresh and have the dew upon them. His muse, at least when in her strength of wing, and when she hovers aloft in her proper element,

Makes audible a linked lay of truth,
Of truth profound a sweet continuous lay,
Not learnt, but native, her own natural notes!

Even throughout his smaller poems there is scarcely one, which is not rendered valuable by some just and original reflection.

See page 25, vol. II.: or the two following passages in one of his humblest compositions.

"O Reader! had you in your mind
Such stores as silent thought can bring,
O gentle Reader! you would find
A tale in every thing;"

and

"I've heard of hearts unkind, kind deeds
With coldness still returning;
Alas! the gratitude of men
Has oftener left me mourning;"

or in a still higher strain the six beautiful quatrains, page 134.

"Thus fares it still in our decay:

And yet the wiser mind
Mourns less for what age takes away
Than what it leaves behind.
The Blackbird in the summer trees,
The Lark upon the hill,
Let loose their carols when they please,
Are quiet when they will.
With Nature never do they wage
A foolish strife; they see
A happy youth, and their old age
Is beautiful and free!
But we are pressed by heavy laws;
And often glad no more,
We wear a face of joy, because
We have been glad of yore.
If there is one, who need bemoan
His kindred laid in earth,
The household hearts that were his own,
It is the man of mirth.
My days, my Friend, are almost gone,
My life has been approved,
And many love me; but by none
Am I enough beloved;"

or the sonnet on Buonaparte, page 202, vol. II. or finally (for a volume would scarce suffice to exhaust the instances,) the last stanza of the poem on the withered Celandine, vol. II. p. 312.

"To be a Prodigal's Favourite—then, worse truth,
A Miser's Pensioner—behold our lot!
O Man! That from thy fair and shining youth
Age might but take the things Youth needed not."

Both in respect of this and of the former excellence, Mr. Wordsworth strikingly resembles Samuel Daniel, one of the golden writers of our golden Elizabethan age, now most causelessly neglected: Samuel Daniel, whose diction bears no mark of time, no distinction of age which has been, and as long as our language shall last, will be so far the language of the to-day and for ever, as that it is more intelligible to us, than the transitory fashions of our own particular age. A similar praise is due to his sentiments. No frequency of perusal can deprive them of their freshness. For though they are brought into the full day-light of every reader's comprehension; yet are they drawn up from depths which few in any age are privileged to visit, into which few in any age have courage or inclination to descend. If Mr. Wordsworth is not equally with Daniel alike intelligible to all readers of average understanding in all passages of his works, the comparative difficulty does not arise from the greater impurity of the ore, but from the nature and uses of the metal. A poem is not necessarily obscure, because it does not aim to be popular. It is enough, if a work be perspicuous to those for whom it is written, and

"Fit audience find, though few."

To the "Ode on the Intimations of Immortality from Recollections of early Childhood" the poet might have prefixed the lines which Dante addresses to one of his own Canzoni—

"Canzone, i' credo, che saranno radi
Colour, che tua ragione intendan bene,
Tanto lor sei faticoso ed alto."
"O lyric song, there will be few, I think,
Who may thy import understand aright:
Thou art for them so arduous and so high!"

But the ode was intended for such readers only as had been accustomed to watch the flux and reflux of their inmost nature, to venture at times into the twilight realms of consciousness, and to feel a deep interest in modes of inmost being, to which they know that the attributes of time and space are inapplicable and alien, but which yet can not be conveyed, save in symbols of time and space. For such readers the sense is sufficiently plain, and they will be as little disposed to charge Mr. Wordsworth with believing the Platonic pre- existence in the ordinary interpretation of the words, as I am to believe, that Plato himself ever meant or taught it.

> Polla oi ut' anko-
> nos okea belae
> endon enti pharetras
> phonanta synetoisin; es
> de to pan hermaeneon
> chatizei; sophos o pol-
> la eidos phua;
> mathontes de labroi
> panglossia, korakes os,
> akranta garueton
> Dios pros ornicha theion.

Third (and wherein he soars far above Daniel) the sinewy strength and originality of single lines and paragraphs: the frequent curiosa felicitas of his diction, of which I need not here give specimens, having anticipated them in a preceding page. This beauty, and as eminently characteristic of Wordsworth's poetry, his rudest assailants have felt themselves compelled to acknowledge and admire.

Fourth; the perfect truth of nature in his images and descriptions as taken immediately from nature, and proving a long and genial intimacy with the very spirit which gives the physiognomic expression to all the works of nature. Like a green field reflected in a calm and perfectly transparent lake, the image is distinguished from the reality only by its greater softness and lustre. Like the moisture or the polish on a pebble, genius neither distorts nor false-colours its objects; but on the contrary brings out many a vein and many a tint, which escape the eye of common observation, thus raising to the rank of gems what had been often kicked away by the hurrying foot of the traveller on the dusty high road of custom.

Let me refer to the whole description of skating, vol. I. page 42 to 47, especially to the lines

> "So through the darkness and the cold we flew,
> And not a voice was idle. with the din
> Meanwhile the precipices rang aloud;
> The leafless trees and every icy crag
> Tinkled like iron; while the distant hills
> Into the tumult sent an alien sound
> Of melancholy, not unnoticed, while the stars,
> Eastward, were sparkling clear, and in the west
> The orange sky of evening died away."

Or to the poem on THE GREEN LINNET, vol. I. page 244. What can be more accurate yet more lovely than the two concluding stanzas?

> "Upon yon tuft of hazel trees,
> That twinkle to the gusty breeze,
> Behold him perched in ecstasies,
> Yet seeming still to hover;
> There! where the flutter of his wings
> Upon his back and body flings
> Shadows and sunny glimmerings,
> That cover him all over.
>
> While thus before my eyes he gleams,
> A Brother of the Leaves he seems;
> When in a moment forth he teems
> His little song in gushes
> As if it pleased him to disdain
> And mock the Form which he did feign
> While he was dancing with the train
> Of Leaves among the bushes."

Or the description of the blue-cap, and of the noontide silence, page 284; or the poem to the cuckoo, page 299; or, lastly, though I might multiply the references to ten times the number, to the poem, so completely Wordsworth's, commencing

"Three years she grew in sun and shower"—

Fifth: a meditative pathos, a union of deep and subtle thought with sensibility; a sympathy with man as man; the sympathy indeed of a contemplator, rather than a fellow-sufferer or co-mate, (spectator, haud particeps) but of a contemplator, from whose view no difference of rank conceals the sameness of the nature; no injuries of wind or weather, or toil, or even of ignorance, wholly disguise the human face divine. The superscription and the image of the Creator still remain legible to him under the dark lines, with which guilt or calamity had cancelled or cross-barred it. Here the Man and the Poet lose and find themselves in each other, the one as glorified, the latter as substantiated.

In this mild and philosophic pathos, Wordsworth appears to me without a compeer. Such as he is: so he writes. See vol. I. page 134 to 136, or that most affecting composition, which no mother, and, if I may judge by my own experience, no parent can read without a tear. Or turn to that genuine lyric, in the former edition, entitled, THE MAD MOTHER, page 174 to 178, of which I cannot refrain from quoting two of the stanzas, both of them for their pathos, and the former for the fine transition in the two concluding lines of the stanza, so expressive of that deranged state, in which, from the increased sensibility, the sufferer's attention is abruptly drawn off by every trifle, and in the same instant plucked back again by the one despotic thought, bringing home with it, by the blending, fusing power of Imagination and Passion, the alien object to which it had been so abruptly diverted, no longer an alien but an ally and an inmate.

"Suck, little babe, oh suck again!
It cools my blood; it cools my brain;
Thy lips, I feel them, baby! They
Draw from my heart the pain away.

Oh! press me with thy little hand;
It loosens something at my chest
About that tight and deadly band

I feel thy little fingers prest.

The breeze I see is in the tree!
It comes to cool my babe and me."
"Thy father cares not for my breast,
'Tis thine, sweet baby, there to rest;
'Tis all thine own!—and if its hue
Be changed, that was so fair to view,
'Tis fair enough for thee, my dove!
My beauty, little child, is flown,
But thou wilt live with me in love;
And what if my poor cheek be brown?
'Tis well for me, thou canst not see
How pale and wan it else would be."

Last, and pre-eminently, I challenge for this poet the gift of Imagination in the highest and strictest sense of the word. In the play of fancy, Wordsworth, to my feelings, is not always graceful, and sometimes recondite. The likeness is occasionally too strange, or demands too peculiar a point of view, or is such as appears the creature of predetermined research, rather than spontaneous presentation. Indeed his fancy seldom displays itself, as mere and unmodified fancy. But in imaginative power, he stands nearest of all modern writers to Shakespeare and Milton; and yet in a kind perfectly unborrowed and his own. To employ his own words, which are at once an instance and an illustration, he does indeed to all thoughts and to all objects—

"———add the gleam,
The light that never was, on sea or land,
The consecration, and the Poet's dream."

I shall select a few examples as most obviously manifesting this faculty; but if I should ever be fortunate enough to render my analysis of Imagination, its origin and characters, thoroughly intelligible to the reader, he will scarcely open on a page of this poet's works without recognising, more or less, the presence and the influences of this faculty. From the poem on the YEW TREES, vol. I. page 303, 304.

"But worthier still of note
Are those fraternal Four of Borrowdale,
Joined in one solemn and capacious grove;
Huge trunks!—and each particular trunk a growth
Of intertwisted fibres serpentine
Up-coiling, and inveterately convolved;
Not uninformed with phantasy, and looks
That threaten the profane;—a pillared shade,
Upon whose grassless floor of red-brown hue,
By sheddings from the pinal umbrage tinged
Perennially—beneath whose sable roof
Of boughs, as if for festal purpose, decked
With unrejoicing berries—ghostly shapes
May meet at noontide; FEAR and trembling HOPE,
SILENCE and FORESIGHT; DEATH, the Skeleton,
And TIME, the Shadow; there to celebrate,
As in a natural temple scattered o'er
With altars undisturbed of mossy stone,
United worship; or in mute repose
To lie, and listen to the mountain flood
Murmuring from Glazamara's inmost caves."

The effect of the old man's figure in the poem of RESOLUTION AND INDEPENDENCE, vol. II. page 33.

"While he was talking thus, the lonely place,
The Old Man's shape, and speech, all troubled me
In my mind's eye I seemed to see him pace
About the weary moors continually,
Wandering about alone and silently."

Or the 8th, 9th, 19th, 26th, 31st, and 33rd, in the collection of miscellaneous sonnets—the sonnet on the subjugation of Switzerland, page 210, or the last ode, from which I especially select the two following stanzas or paragraphs, page 349 to 350.

"Our birth is but a sleep and a forgetting:
The Soul that rises with us, our life's Star,
Hath had elsewhere its setting,
And cometh from afar.

Not in entire forgetfulness,
And not in utter nakedness,
But trailing clouds of glory do we come
From God, who is our home:
Heaven lies about us in our infancy!

Shades of the prison-house begin to close
Upon the growing Boy;
But He beholds the light, and whence it flows,
He sees it in his joy!

The Youth who daily further from the East
Must travel, still is Nature's Priest,
And by the vision splendid
Is on his way attended;

At length the Man perceives it die away, And fade into the light of common day."

And page 352 to 354 of the same ode.

"O joy! that in our embers
Is something that doth live,
That nature yet remembers
What was so fugitive!

The thought of our past years in me doth breed
Perpetual benedictions: not indeed
For that which is most worthy to be blest;
Delight and liberty, the simple creed
Of Childhood, whether busy or at rest,
With new-fledged hope still fluttering in his breast:—

Not for these I raise
The song of thanks and praise;
But for those obstinate questionings
Of sense and outward things,
Fallings from us, vanishings;
Blank misgivings of a Creature
Moving about in worlds not realised,
High instincts, before which our mortal Nature
Did tremble like a guilty Thing surprised!

But for those first affections,
Those shadowy recollections,
Which, be they what they may,
Are yet the fountain light of all our day,
Are yet a master light of all our seeing;

Uphold us—cherish—and have power to make
Our noisy years seem moments in the being
Of the eternal Silence; truths that wake
To perish never;
Which neither listlessness, nor mad endeavour,
Nor Man nor Boy,
Nor all that is at enmity with joy,
Can utterly abolish or destroy!

Hence, in a season of calm weather,
Though inland far we be,
Our Souls have sight of that immortal sea
Which brought us hither;
Can in a moment travel thither,—

And see the children sport upon the shore,
And hear the mighty waters rolling evermore."

And since it would be unfair to conclude with an extract, which, though highly characteristic, must yet, from the nature of the thoughts and the subject, be interesting or perhaps intelligible, to but a limited number of readers; I will add, from the poet's last published work, a passage equally Wordsworthian; of the beauty of which, and of the imaginative power displayed therein, there can be but one opinion, and one feeling. See White Doe, page 5.

"Fast the church-yard fills;—anon
Look again and they all are gone;
The cluster round the porch, and the folk
Who sate in the shade of the Prior's Oak!
And scarcely have they disappeared
Ere the prelusive hymn is heard;—

With one consent the people rejoice,
Filling the church with a lofty voice!

They sing a service which they feel:

For 'tis the sun-rise now of zeal;
And faith and hope are in their prime
In great Eliza's golden time."

"A moment ends the fervent din,
And all is hushed, without and within;
For though the priest, more tranquilly,
Recites the holy liturgy,
The only voice which you can hear
Is the river murmuring near.

—When soft!—the dusky trees between,
And down the path through the open green,
Where is no living thing to be seen;
And through yon gateway, where is found,
Beneath the arch with ivy bound,
Free entrance to the church-yard ground—
And right across the verdant sod,
Towards the very house of God;
Comes gliding in with lovely gleam,
Comes gliding in serene and slow,
Soft and silent as a dream.

A solitary Doe!
White she is as lily of June,
And beauteous as the silver moon
When out of sight the clouds are driven
And she is left alone in heaven!
Or like a ship some gentle day
In sunshine sailing far away
A glittering ship that hath the plain
Of ocean for her own domain."

* * * * * *

"What harmonious pensive changes
Wait upon her as she ranges
Round and through this Pile of state
Overthrown and desolate!
Now a step or two her way

Is through space of open day,
Where the enamoured sunny light
Brightens her that was so bright;
Now doth a delicate shadow fall,
Falls upon her like a breath,
From some lofty arch or wall,
As she passes underneath."

The following analogy will, I am apprehensive, appear dim and fantastic, but in reading Bartram's Travels I could not help transcribing the following lines as a sort of allegory, or connected simile and metaphor of Wordsworth's intellect and genius.—"The soil is a deep, rich, dark mould, on a deep stratum of tenacious clay; and that on a foundation of rocks, which often break through both strata, lifting their backs above the surface. The trees which chiefly grow here are the gigantic, black oak; magnolia grandi-flora; fraximus excelsior; platane; and a few stately tulip trees." What Mr. Wordsworth will produce, it is not for me to prophesy but I could pronounce with the liveliest convictions what he is capable of producing. It is the FIRST GENUINE PHILOSOPHIC POEM.

The preceding criticism will not, I am aware, avail to overcome the prejudices of those, who have made it a business to attack and ridicule Mr. Wordsworth's compositions.

Truth and prudence might be imaged as concentric circles. The poet may perhaps have passed beyond the latter, but he has confined himself far within the bounds of the former, in designating these critics, as "too petulant to be passive to a genuine poet, and too feeble to grapple with him;——men of palsied imaginations, in whose minds all healthy action is languid;——who, therefore, feed as the many direct them, or with the many are greedy after vicious provocatives."

So much for the detractors from Wordsworth's merits. On the other hand, much as I might wish for their fuller sympathy, I dare not flatter myself, that the freedom with which I have declared my opinions concerning both his theory and his defects, most of which are more or less connected with his theory, either as cause or effect, will be satisfactory or pleasing to all the poet's admirers and advocates. More indiscriminate than mine their admiration may be: deeper and more sincere it cannot be. But I have advanced no opinion either for praise or censure, other than as texts introductory to the reasons which compel me to form it. Above all, I was fully convinced that such a criticism was not only wanted; but that, if executed with adequate ability, it must conduce, in no mean degree, to Mr. Wordsworth's reputation. His fame belongs to another age, and can neither be accelerated nor retarded. How small the proportion of the defects are to the beauties, I have repeatedly declared; and that no one of them originates in deficiency of poetic genius.

Had they been more and greater, I should still, as a friend to his literary character in the present age, consider an analytic display of them as pure gain; if only it removed, as surely to all reflecting minds even the foregoing analysis must have removed, the strange mistake, so slightly grounded, yet so widely and industriously propagated, of Mr. Wordsworth's turn for simplicity! I am not half as much irritated by hearing his enemies abuse him for vulgarity of style, subject, and conception, as I am disgusted with the gilded side of the same meaning, as displayed by some affected admirers, with whom he is, forsooth, a "sweet, simple poet!" and so natural, that little master Charles and his younger sister are so charmed with them, that they play at "Goody Blake," or at "Johnny and Betty Foy!"

Were the collection of poems, published with these biographical sketches, important enough, (which I am not vain enough to believe,) to deserve such a distinction; even as I have done, so would I be done unto.

For more than eighteen months have the volume of Poems, entitled SIBYLLINE LEAVES, and the present volume, up to this page, been printed, and ready for publication. But, ere I speak of myself in the tones, which are alone natural to me under the circumstances of late years, I would fain present myself to the Reader as I was in the first dawn of my literary life:

When Hope grew round me, like the climbing vine,
And fruits, and foliage, not my own, seem'd mine!

For this purpose I have selected from the letters, which I wrote home from Germany, those which appeared likely to be most interesting, and at the same time most pertinent to the title of this work.

/7*inalienable rights" and advocating moral duties, Coleridge saw the best avenue for social change to be within the existing traditional society. The events in France demonstrated that abstract freedoms which were not curtailed by moral restraints result in a social collapse. The reason of the individual is subjugated to the passion of the mob.

In 1798 France invaded republican Switzerland and Coleridge lost any remaining sympathy for France and, for that matter, the principles of the Revolution. "France: An Ode" was written at this time; originally titled a" Recantation" the poem traces the poet's initial exultation at the beginning of the Revolution, his mixture of apprehension and hope as the events in Europe unfold, with the invasion of Switzerland Coleridge denounces France and recants his earlier convictions, and the poem concludes with a reflection on the ideal of freedom.

Freedom, Coleridge believes, cannot be attained in governed society and is realised by the Individual through a sublime union with nature and God. Coleridge's political philosophy becomes increasingly similar to the conservatism of Burke and to a Neo-Platonic tradition. Coleridge's conservatism did not prevent him from attacking social injustices (he would late be a strong supporter of Peel's Factory Bill which would improve working conditions, in particular for children) and he would maintain that good government must be moral government. Coleridge's political philosophy was influential; much of Great Britain's nineteenth-century conservatism tempered with social reform finds its basis in the thought of this one time "radical."

Chapter 7

Biographia Literaria: Summary

THE NATURE OF POETIC DICTION

Little of what I have here written concerns myself personally; the narrative is designed chiefly to introduce my principles of politics, religion, and poetry. But my special purpose is to decide what is the true nature of poetic diction, and to define the real poetic character of the works of Mr. Wordsworth, whose writings have been the subject of so much controversy.

At school I had the advantage of a very sensible though severe master. I learned from him that poetry, even that of the loftiest odes, had a logic of its own as severe as that of science, and more difficult, because more subtle. In the truly great poets, he would say, there is a reason assignable, not only for every word, but for the position of every word. In our English compositions he showed no mercy to phrase, metaphor, or image, where the same sense might have been conveyed with equal force and dignity in plainer words. In fancy, I can almost hear him now exclaiming: "Harp? Lyre? Pen and ink, boy, you mean!" Nay, certain introductions, similes, and examples were placed by name on a list of interdiction.

I had just entered my seventeenth year when the sonnets of Mr. Bowles were made known to me, and the genial influence of his poetry, so tender, yet so manly, so natural and real, yet so dignified and harmonious, recalled me from a premature bewilderment in metaphysics and theology. Well was it for me, perhaps, if I had never relapsed into the same mental disease.

The poetry of Pope and his followers, a school of French poetry invigorated by English understanding, which had predominated from the last century, consisted of prose thoughts translated into poetic language. I was led to the conjecture that this style had been kept up by, if it did not wholly arise from, the custom of writing Latin verses. I began to defend the use of natural language, such as "I will remember thee," instead of "Thy image on her wing, Before my fancy's eye shall memory bring;" and adduced, as examples of simplicity, the diction of Greek poets, and of our elder English poets, from Chaucer to Milton. I arrived at two critical aphorisms, as the criteria of poetic style: first, that not the poem which we have read with the greatest pleasure but that to which we return with the greatest pleasure possesses the genuine power; and, second, that whatever lines can be translated into other words of the same language, without diminution of their significance, are so far vicious in their diction.

One great distinction between even the characteristic faults of our elder poets and the false beauties of the moderns is this. In the former, from Donne to Cowley, we find the most fantastic out-of-the-way thoughts, but the most pure and genuine mother English; in the latter, the most obvious thoughts, in language the most fantastic and arbitrary. Our faulty elder poets sacrificed the passion, and passionate flow of poetry, to the subtleties of intellect and to the starts of wit; the moderns to the glare and glitter of a perpetual yet broken and heterogeneous imagery. The one sacrificed the heart to the head, the other both heart and head to drapery.

IN PRAISE OF SOUTHEY

Reflect on the variety and extent of his acquirements! He stands second to no man, either as a historian or as a bibliographer; and when I regard him as a popular essayist I look in vain for any writer who has conveyed so much information, from so many and such recondite sources, with as many just and original reflections, in a style so lively yet so uniformly classical and perspicuous; no one, in short, who has combined so much wisdom with so much wit; so much truth and knowledge with so much life and fancy.

Still more striking to those who are familiar with the general habits of genius will appear the poet's matchless industry and perseverance in his pursuits, the worthiness and dignity of those pursuits, his generous submission to tasks of transitory interest. But as Southey possesses, and is not possessed by, his genius, even so is he the master even of his virtues. The regular and methodical tenor of his daily labours, which might be envied by the mere man of business, loses all semblance of formality in the dignified simplicity of his manners, in the spring and healthful cheerfulness of his spirit. Always employed, his friends find him always at leisure.

No less punctual in trifles than steadfast in the performance of highest duties, he inflicts none of those small pains and discomforts which irregular men scatter about them, and which in the aggregate so often become formidable obstacles both to happiness and utility. He bestows all the pleasures, and inspires all that ease of mind on those around him, which perfect consistency and absolute reliability cannot but bestow. I know few men who so well deserve the character which an ancient attributes to Marcus Cato—namely, that he was likest virtue, inasmuch as he seemed to act aright, not in obedience to any law or outward motive, but by the necessity of a happy nature which could not act otherwise.

As a son, brother, husband, father, master, friend, he moves with firm yet light steps, alike unostentatious and alike exemplary. As a writer, he has uniformly made his talents subservient to the best interests of humanity, of public virtue, and domestic piety; his cause has ever been the cause of pure religion and of liberty, of national independence and of national illumination.

When future critics shall weigh out his guerdon of praise and censure, it will be Southey the poet only that will supply them with the scanty materials for the latter. They will not fail to record that as no man was ever a more constant friend, never had poet more friends and honorees among the good of all parties, and that quacks in education, quacks in politics, and quacks in criticism, were his only enemies.

WORDSWORTH'S EARLY POEMS

During the last year of my residence at Cambridge I became acquainted with Mr. Wordsworth's first publication, entitled "Descriptive Sketches," and seldom, if ever, was the emergence of an original poetic genius above the literary horizon more evidently announced. In the whole poem there is a harshness and acerbity, combined with words and images all aglow, which might recall gorgeous blossoms rising out of a hard and thorny rind and shell, within which the rich fruit was elaborating. The language was not only peculiar and strong, but at times knotty and contorted, as by its own impatient strength. It seldom, therefore, justified the complaint of obscurity.

I was in my twenty-fourth year when I had the happiness of knowing Mr. Wordsworth personally, and by that time the occasional obscurities which had arisen from an imperfect control over the resources of his native language had almost wholly disappeared, together with that worse defect of arbitrary and illogical phrases, at once arbitrary and fantastic, which alloy the earlier poems of the truest genius. There was only evident the union of deep feeling with profound thought; and the original gift of spreading the tone, the atmosphere, and with it the depth and height of the ideal world, around forms, incidents, and situations of which, for the common view, custom had bedimmed all the luster, had dried up the sparkle and the dewdrops.

To find no contradiction in the union of old and new, to contemplate the Ancient of Days and all His works With feelings as fresh as if all had then sprung forth at the first creative fiat, characterizes the mind that feels the riddle of the world, and may help to unravel it. To carry on the feelings of childhood into the powers of manhood, to combine the child's sense of wonder and novelty with the appearances which every day for perhaps forty years had rendered familiar—this is the character and privilege of genius. And it is the prime merit of genius, and it's most unequivocal mode of manifestation, so to represent familiar objects as to awaken in the minds of others that freshness of sensation which is the constant accompaniment of mental, no less than of bodily, convalescence.

This excellence, which constitutes the character of Mr. Wordsworth's mind, I no sooner felt than I sought to understand. Repeated meditations led me to suspect that fancy and imagination were two distinct and widely different faculties, instead of being, according to the general belief, the lower and higher degree of one and the same power. Milton had a highly imaginative, Cowley a very fanciful, mind. This division between fancy and imagination is no less grounded in nature than that of delirium from mania; or of Otway's

Lutes, laurels, seas of milk, and ships amber,
from Shakespeare's
What! Have his daughters brought him to this pass?

THE PHILOSOPHICAL CRITIC

As materialism has been generally taught, it is utterly unintelligible, and owes all its proselytes to the propensity, so common among men, to mistake distinct images for clear conceptions, and, *vice versâ*, to reject as inconceivable whatever from its own nature is unimaginable. If God grant health and permission, this subject will be treated of systematically in a work which I have many years been preparing on the Productive Logos, human and divine, with, and as an introduction to, a full commentary on the Gospel of St. John.

To make myself intelligible, so far as my present subject, the imagination, requires, it will be sufficient briefly to observe: That all association demands and presupposes the existence of the thoughts and images to be associated. The hypothesis of an external world exactly correspondent to those images or modifications of our own being, which alone—according to this system—we actually behold, is as thorough idealism as Berkeley's, inasmuch as it equally removes all reality and immediateness of perception, and places us in a dream-world of phantoms and specters, the inexplicable swarm and equivocal generation of motion in our own brains. That this hypothesis neither involves the explanation nor precludes the necessity of a mechanism and co-adequate forces in the percipient, which, at the more than magic touch of the impulse from without, creates anew for himself the correspondent object. The formation of a copy is not solved by the mere pre-existence of an original; the copyist of Rafael's "Transfiguration" must repeat more or less perfectly the process of Rafael.

The imagination, therefore, is essentially creative. I consider imagination either as primary or secondary. The primary imagination I hold to be the living power and prime agent of all human perception, and as a repetition in the finite mind of the eternal act of creation in the infinite I AM.

The secondary I consider as an echo of the former; it dissolves, diffuses, dissipates, in order to re-create; or where this process is rendered impossible, yet still, at all events, it struggles to idealize and to unify. It is essentially vital, even as all objects are essentially fixed and dead.

Fancy, on the contrary, has no other counters to play with but fixities and definite. The fancy is no other than a mode of memory emancipated from the order of time and space, and blended with, and modified by, choice. But, equally with the ordinary memory, it must receive its materials ready made, from the law of association.

WHAT IS A POEM?

During the first year that Mr. Wordsworth and I were neighbors our conversations turned frequently on the two cardinal points of poetry—the power of exciting the sympathy of the reader by a faithful adherence to the truth of Nature, and the power of giving the interest of novelty by the modifying colours of imagination. The sudden charm which accidents of light and shade, moonlight or sunset, diffuse over a familiar landscape appeared to represent the practicability of combining both.

The thought suggested itself that a series of poems might be composed of two sorts. In the one the incidents and agents were to be, in part at least, supernatural; and the excellence aimed at was to consist in the interesting of the affections by the dramatic truth of such emotions as would naturally accompany such situations. For the second class, subjects were to be chosen from ordinary life; the characters and incidents were to be such as will be found in every village and its vicinity where there is a meditative and feeling mind to seek them.

In this idea originated the plan of the "Lyrical Ballads," in which my endeavors were to be directed to persons and characters supernatural, or at least romantic. Mr. Wordsworth, on the other hand, was to attempt to give the charm of novelty to things of every day, and to excite a feeling analogous to the supernatural by awakening the mind's attention from the lethargy of custom, and directing it to the loveliness and the wonders of the world before us—an inexhaustible treasure, but for which, in consequence of the film of familiarity and selfish solicitude, we have eyes, yet see not, and hearts that neither feel nor understand.

With this view I wrote the "Ancient Mariner," and was preparing, among other poems, the "Dark Ladie" and "Christabel." But the number of Mr. Wordsworth's poems was so much greater that my compositions appeared rather an interpolation of heterogeneous matter.

With many parts of Mr. Wordsworth's preface to the "Lyrical Ballads," in which he defines his poetic creed, I have never concurred, and I think it expedient to declare in what points I coincide with his opinions, and in what points I differ.

A poem contains the same elements as a prose composition; the difference, therefore, must consist in a different combination of them, in consequence of a different object proposed. The mere addition of metre does not in itself entitle a work to the name of poem, for nothing can permanently please which does not contain in itself the reason why it is so and not otherwise. Our definition of a poem may be thus worded. "A poem is that species of composition which is opposed to works of science, by proposing for its immediate object pleasure, not truth; and from all other species (having this object in common with it) it is discriminated by proposing to itself such delight from the whole as is compatible with a distinct gratification from each component part."

For, in a legitimate poem, the parts must mutually support and explain each other; all in their proportion harmonis harmonizing and supporting the purpose and known influences of, metrical arrangement.

A CRITICISM OF WORDSWORTH

Let me enumerate the prominent defects, and then the excellences, of Mr. Wordsworth's published poems. The first characteristic, though only an occasional defect, is the inconstancy of style; the sudden and unprepared transitions from lines or sentences of peculiar felicity to a style not only unimpassioned, but undistinguished. He sinks too often, too abruptly, into the language of prose. The second defect is certain matter-of-factness in some of his poems, consisting in a labourious minuteness and fidelity in the representations of objects, and in the insertion of accidental circumstances, such as is superfluous in poetry.

Thirdly, there is in certain poems an undue predilection for the dramatic form; and in these cases either the thoughts or diction are different from those of the poet, so that there arises an incongruity of style, or they are the same and indistinguishable, and then it presents a species of ventriloquism. The fourth class includes prolixity, repetition, and an eddying instead of progression of thought. His fifth defect is the employment of thoughts and images too great for the subject; an approximation to what might be called mental bombast, as distinguished from verbal.

To these occasional defects I may oppose the following excellences. First, an austere purity of language grammatically and logically; in short, a perfect appropriateness of the words to the meaning. Secondly, a correspondent weight and sanity of the thoughts and sentiments, won not from books, but from the poet's own meditative observation. They are fresh, and have the dew upon them. Third, the sinewy strength and originality of single lines and paragraphs; the frequent curious felicity of his diction. Fourth, the perfect truth of Nature in his images and descriptions as taken immediately from Nature, and proving a long and genial intimacy with the very spirit which gives the expression to all the works of nature. Like a green field reflected in a calm and perfectly transparent lake, the image is distinguished from the reality only by its greater softness and luster.

Fifth, a meditative pathos, a union of deep and subtle thought with sensibility; a sympathy with man as man; the sympathy of a contemplator, from whose view no difference of rank conceals the sameness of the nature; no injuries of wind or weather, of toil, or even of ignorance, wholly disguise the human face divine. The superscription and the image of the Creator still remain legible to him under the dark lines with which guilt or calamity had cancelled or cross-barred it. In this mild and philosophic pathos, Wordsworth appears to me without a compeer.

Lastly, and pre-eminently, I challenge for this poet the gift of imagination in the highest and strictest sense of the word. In the play of fancy, Wordsworth, to my feelings, is not always graceful, and is sometimes recondite. But in imaginative power he stands nearest of all modern writers to Shakespeare and Milton; and yet in a kind perfectly unborrowed and his own. To employ his own words, he does indeed to all thoughts and to all objects

Add the gleam, The light that never was on sea or land, The consecration, and the poet's dream.

Chapter 8

Study Questions

Q1. Coleridge's Biographia Literaria discusses the Evidence for Christianity. Comment.

Or

Q. Coleridge's presentation of his own crisis of faith is only part of the much larger undertaking of Biographia Literaria. Do you agree?

Or

Q. Does Coleridge draws upon the long Christian tradition of commentary on the nature of faith to clarify his understanding of faith?

Of all the perplexities besetting the Victorian mind, there were few as pervasive as the problem of evidence for Christianity. Both physical science and empiricist philosophy contributed to the erosion of any proof for Christianity beyond the inner experience of the believer. Because the response of religious apologists was so diverse, the individual believer had to find his own way through the controversies on both sides to establish his own mature, examined belief. The path was a difficult one: as Walter Houghton so clearly shows, even the century's greatest religious apologists suffered religious doubts.

Basil Willey's histories of religious thought in the nineteenth century present this shift from external to internal evidence as properly correcting a mistaken understanding of religious faith. That may be so, but generating "inner evidence" is no easy matter. The loss of external evidence for Christianity terribly isolates the believer who loses touch with the adequately vivid experience of God—as all believers do, at times. Furthermore, this dichotomy between inner, subjective, emotional evidence, on the one hand, and external, sensory or objective evidence on the other is a splintering of self: the Christian seems destined to this bifurcation as the price of maintaining formal belief. One who refuses this division must reconcile the apparently incompatible ontologies of religion and science, or be left with no coherent ontology at all—with a world in which nothing has clear meaning, nor certain value, nor fixed and reliable identity. The "evidence" problem for nineteenth-century Christians, seen from this perspective, is a stage on the way to recognizably contemporary problems of self.

Samuel Taylor Coleridge was "sweepingly effective in creating a new apologetics" for Christianity based on the higher criticism of the Bible. In such works as the Aids to Reflection (1825), he presented ideas which had "a profound effect... on the English-speaking theological tradition." We must turn to the Biographia Literaria (1817), however, if we wish to observe how the "evidence problem" challenges the integrity of the self, and how this challenge can be met. In the Biographia, Coleridge traces his own crisis of belief and its resolution. This resolution turns on his recognition that our direct knowledge of a world of real objects, like our direct knowledge of God, is a product of faith and cannot be established through logic. The reality of a scientist's findings, then, rests on the same final ground as a believer's testimony to the existence of God.

Like Carlyle, Newman, and Arnold, Coleridge later devises a programme to supply a variety of external evidence: public authority testifying to the validity of spiritual truths and values. In each of these programmes, the spiritual leader is one who has greatest insight into both spiritual values and "things as they are." Such public authority establishes the difference between genuine inner evidence and mere self-delusion, and thus bridges the destructive gap between private, emotional belief, and public, intellectual fact. In tracing Coleridge's crisis of belief, as presented in Biographia Literaria, we will see how his reconciliation of the competing ontologies of science and religion paradoxically enforces both the value of contemplation as the individual's best guide to moral truth, and the authority of organized religion as a crucial support for the unity of the self.

Coleridge's presentation of his own crisis of faith is only part of the much larger undertaking of Biographia Literaria. In this work he traces his principles in politics, religion, and philosophy back to a single set of principles concerning the nature of the mind. He does so by writing (and sometimes rewriting) his intellectual autobiography as the growth of a critic's mind: the pattern of his experiences is presented as leading him step-by-step to an understanding of the nature and significance of imagination. The centrally important experience he recounts is his recognition of the ontological significance of religious faith.

Tracing Coleridge's account of the stages of his recognition may begin with his clearest statement of the interrelation of the sensory and supra-sensory realms of experience. In chapter twelve he offers a complex geographical metaphor to explain that the transcendental is known directly, not inferred from the sensory:

> There is a philosophic (and inasmuch as it is actualized by an effort of freedom, an artificial) consciousness, which lies beneath or (as it were) behind the spontaneous consciousness natural to all reflecting beings. As the elder Romans distinguished their northern provinces into Cis-Alpine and Trans-Alpine, so we may divide all the objects of human consciousness into those on this side, and those on the other side of the spontaneous consciousness; citra et trans conscientiam communem. The latter is exclusively the domain of PURE philosophy, which is therefore properly entitled transcendental.... The first range of hills, that encircles the

scanty vale of human life, is the horizon for the majority of its inhabitants.... But in all ages there have been a few, who measuring and sounding the rivers of the vale at the feet of their furthest inaccessible falls have learned, that the sources must be far higher and far inward; a few, who even in the level streams have detected elements, which neither the vale itself nor the surrounding mountains contained or could supply. There are "trace elements" in the (so to speak) stream of ordinary consciousness; these elements do not originate in the "valley" itself, in the physical world as known through the five senses, although they exist in the mind alongside sense-data. The philosophic self-scrutiny necessary to discover these transcendental elements is the principal method of Coleridge's enquiry into the relation between transcendental and sensory knowledge; this contemplative self-scrutiny is an adequate philosophic method because both kinds of knowledge are present in the ordinary consciousness of every person.

Coleridge emphasizes that certain knowledge of the transcendental elements in consciousness is intuitive and immediate. Quoting Plotinus, he says, "'we ought... to watch in quiet till it suddenly shines upon us; preparing ourselves for the blessed spectacle as the eye waits patiently for the rising sun'" (BL, I, 167). Coleridge has previously described this sort of intuitive and immediate knowledge as the spontaneous activity of the mind: in such knowledge the mind is neither passive (as in sensory knowing) nor absolutely active and self-directing, as in syllogistic logic. In the Biographia Literaria, he closely examines several theories purporting to explain the spontaneous activity of the mind, because this level of knowing is the secondary imagination. Determining the nature of imagination is necessary, Coleridge explains, for the proper conduct of his analysis of Wordsworth's poetry later in the Biographia. Coleridge attributes both the aesthetic power and moral value of Wordsworth's poetry to Wordsworth's highly developed consciousness of the transcendental elements in his own mind.

Coleridge presumes the possibility of direct intuition of transcendental realities: his question is how, not whether. In accordance with his highly stylized autobiographical form, the facts of his own experiences are simply givens. There is for him no doubt concerning these intuitions, and yet—as we shall see—the ground he establishes to validate such intuitions is a very fragile one. Coleridge's confidence in his transcendental knowledge is matched by a confidence in the beneficence of religious doubt and philosophic quandary. Several times he describes his confused failure to discover the nature of spontaneous intuition; each time the confrontation with doubt is followed by a major step toward knowledge. Ultimately, his progressive questionings, frustrations, and doubts lead him to recognize that religious faith is the pre-eminent example of spontaneous (imaginative) intuition.

The first of Coleridge's three confrontations with failure is described in chapter eight. The preceding four chapters have simultaneously evaluated associationism and materialism as theories of the spontaneous, and recounted the studies and meditations of his early manhood. In chapter eight he presents himself as stymied, and uses the occasion of that frustration to formulate the problem abstractly. At issue specifically is the fact that materialism, dualism, and associationism all fail to provide an adequate epistemology as the foundation of a theory of spontaneous mental activity. And so Coleridge asks a central question about the nature of knowing in general:

> But it is not either the nature of man, or the duty of the philosopher to despair concerning any important problem until, as in the squaring of the circle, the impossibility of a solution has been demonstrated. How the esse, assumed as originally distinct from the scire, can ever unite itself with it; how being can transform itself into a knowing, becomes conceivable on only one condition; namely, if it can be shown that the vis representativa, or the Sentient, is itself a species of being; i.e. either as a property or attribute, or as an hypostasis or self-subsistence. The former is, indeed, the assumption of materialism; a system which could not but be patronized by the philosopher, if only it actually performed what it promises. (BL, I, 89-90)

As Coleridge would certainly recognize, any careful question establishes the boundaries within which adequate answers can be found. The correct answer to this formulation of the question must explain knowing as some form of "hypostasis or self-subsistence."

But to establish the boundaries of an adequate theory is not to discover a specific successful theory. In chapter nine Coleridge describes himself as again frustrated—unable to discover a specific explanation of "how being can transform itself into a knowing." He describes this frustration in Kantean terms:

> After I had successively studied in the schools of Locke, Berkeley, Leibnitz, and Hartley, and could find in neither of them an abiding place for my reason, I began to ask myself; is a system of philosophy, as different from mere history and historic classification, possible? If possible, what are its necessary conditions? I was for a while disposed to answer the first question in the negative, and to admit that the sole practicable employment for the human mind was to observe, to collect, and to classify. But I soon felt, that human nature itself fought up against this wilful resignation of intellect. (BL, I, 93)

Coleridge explains that the Critique of Pure Reason reorients philosophy as the science of "the antecedents that must be presupposed in order to render experience itself possible," but Kant's system still does not explain the nature of spontaneous knowing. Still more study finally suggests fruitful lines of enquiry. Reading in the Neoplatonists and mystics, he says, "contributed to prepare my mind for the reception and welcoming of the 'Cogito quia sum, et sum quia Cogito'; a philosophy of seeming hardihood, but certainly the most ancient, and therefore presumptively the most natural" (BL, I, 95).

The quasi-Cartesian "I think because I am, and I am because I think" is a particular hypothesis to explain the hypostasis or self-subsistence of being and knowing. Coleridge adopts Fichte's position that our being is an act (the act of knowing); like the other first-generation post-Kanteans, he proceeds to investigate the most basic act of our being. For Coleridge, the most basic act is the act of faith, but he represents himself as not yet having reached this recognition. These further studies in German and Neoplatonic philosophy seem to confirm the correctness of his general understanding of the boundaries of an adequate epistemology, but the positive form of a philosophy is still not available. 6

Coleridge again describes his own deepening confusion and uncertainty, and again his meditations on the fact of doubt and failure lead him to a crucial recognition. The clearest possible recognition of his failure, and consequently of his own isolation from a comprehensible, shared reality, is followed immediately by the first step toward a definite theory. I will cite this passage from chapter ten at length, so as to include Coleridge's dramatization of his own state:

> I retired to a cottage in Somersetshire at the foot of Quantock, and devoted my thoughts and studies to the foundations of religion and morals. Here I found myself all afloat. Doubts rushed in; broke upon me "from the foundations of the great deep," and fell "from the windows of heaven." The fontal truths of natural religion and the books of Revelation alike contributed to the flood; and it was long ere my ark touched on an Ararat and rested. The idea of the Supreme Being appeared to me as necessarily implied in all particular modes of being... but I was not wholly satisfied. I began then to ask myself, what proof I had of the outward existence of anything? Of this sheet of paper for instance, as a thing in itself, separate from the phenomenon or image in my perception. I saw, that in the nature of things such proof is impossible.... (BL, I, 132-33; last italics mine)

I leave Coleridge mid-sentence to point out the ways in which he sharply controls our understanding of his period of doubt. We know almost from the very beginning that this crisis is successfully resolved. The ark image suggests that his trials were themselves a kind of salvation, a fortunate rescue from a worse fate. Coleridge represents periods of doubt as a natural, fruitful, and recurrent aspect of his intellectual and religious maturing. In context, the statement, "I saw, that in the nature of things such proof is impossible," is not the record of a terrifying encounter with meaningless uncertainty, but rather the recognition of a necessary state of affairs—a state perhaps puzzling, unpleasant, or unexpected, but ultimately comprehensible. The situation may have been terrifying at the time, of course; but that is not the way in which Coleridge presents it to his readers. We know that Mount Ararat is ahead.

Coleridge represents himself as proceeding to recognize that certainty has its basis in the nature of the mind, not in the logical consistency of formal systems: "I saw, that in the nature of things such proof is impossible: and that of all modes of being, that are not the objects of the senses, the existence is assumed by the construction of the mind itself, by the absence of all motive to doubt it, not from any absolute contradiction in the supposition to the contrary" (BL, I, 133). The class "all modes of being, that are not objects of the senses" includes not only "this sheet of paper, a thing in itself, separate from the phenomenon or image," but also the immediate intuition of transcendental realities (as described in the Cis- and Trans-Alpine passage, above, pp. 3-4). Pre-eminent among transcendental realities, of course, is God. The "constitution of the mind itself" supplies "the antecedents which render experience itself possible."

By assimilating issues in epistemology and ontology to issues in religious faith, Coleridge can draw upon the long Christian tradition of commentary on the nature of faith to clarify his understanding of faith as the major "antecedent which renders experience possible." He does so by reformulating the solution just cited as the particular answer to a particular question about the nature of God:

For a very long time, indeed, I could not reconcile personality with infinity; and my head was with Spinoza, though my whole heart remained with Paul and John. Yet there had dawned on me, even before I had met with the Critique of the Pure Reason, a certain guiding light. If the mere intellect could make no certain discovery of a holy and intelligent first cause, it might yet supply a demonstration, that no legitimate argument could be drawn from the intellect against its truth. And what is this more than St. Paul's assertion, that by wisdom (more properly translated by the powers of reasoning) no man ever arrived at the knowledge of God?... I bec[a]me convinced, that religion, as both the cornerstone and the keystone of morality, must have a moral origin; so far at least, that the evidence of its doctrine could not, like the truths of abstract science, be wholly independent of the will.... It could not be intellectually more evident without becoming morally less effective; without counteracting its own end by sacrificing the life of faith to the cold mechanism of a worthless because compulsory assent.

The power of faith, then, is both cognitive and volitional. It is both knowing and willing. The knowledge of God is neither a self-compelled logical assent, nor an empirically-compelled observation. It is free, a knowing that arises spontaneously rather than as the result of inner or outer compulsion.

Ultimately, all knowledge, beyond the immediate notices of the senses, is also dependent upon faith. Empiricism, as a method, presumes that there is a world correspondent to sense data; that presumption has the same basis as the presumption that God exists: "the constitution of the mind itself, by the absence of all motive to doubt it."

It is easy to see here why Coleridge describes Kant's philosophy as one which "took possession of me as with a giant's hand": Kant attended to the character of the mind itself, because that character prescribed the limits and forms of all possible knowledge. Coleridge imitates Kant in this attention to the constitutive activity of the mind, but does so to very different ends. He adopts Kant's position that, although logic cannot establish the fundamental tenets of religion, conscience testifies to the validity of belief in these tenets. But he differs from Kant in asserting that through faith we have direct knowledge of both things in themselves, and the ideas of Reason (God, freedom, and immortality). In extending the "domain" of faith to include immediate knowledge of things in themselves, Coleridge invests conscience with extraordinary philosophical significance. He also claims that the validity of both religion and science depends upon the "inner evidence" supplied by faith and conscience.

Yet this Kantean shift in the ground of evidence for Christianity, commonplace in religious writings later in the century, leaves the believer in precarious circumstances: the "motive to doubt" can be supplied by the sufferings which are an inevitable part of human experience. Just as sufferings can challenge religious faith, social change can disorient conscience. And the loss of religious faith and coherent conscience then isolates the individual in a meaningless universe. Sustaining the culture's transcendental values and beliefs is for these reasons a functional basis for maintaining the coherence of everyday human experience.

In chapter twelve Coleridge presents his own explanation of the spontaneous activity of the mind. In many ways, of course, it is not his own at all, but Schelling's. Yet, while translating for paragraphs at a time, Coleridge is using the excerpts to ends very much his own. Two of the differences between Schelling's text and Coleridge's text are of concern here. The first is that Coleridge moderates Schelling's radical idealism by setting these passages into another context. Part of that new context is a three-fold division of philosophy.

The first branch is natural philosophy, the study of being (BL, I, 175-76). The second is transcendental philosophy, the study of knowing (BL, 1, 177-79). That much is also in Schelling's text. Coleridge goes on, however, to describe a third branch: total philosophy, the "result or equitorial point" of the other two, in which "we begin with the I KNOW MYSELF in order to end with the absolute I AM. We proceed from the SELF in order to lose and find all self in God" (BL, 1, 186). Neither natural philosophy nor transcendental philosophy can establish a formal ontology; neither, by itself, can offer a closed or completed philosophic system.

The second relevant departure from Schelling follows from this three-part division of philosophies. Coleridge asserts with Schelling that the being of the mind is knowing, but he goes further to assert that the ground of being is God. Knowing is self-grounded in philosophic consciousness, but being is not self-grounded—except for God, "I am what I am," in whom knowing and being are "ab initlo, identical and coinherent" (BL, I, 94). We cannot infer from what we know to what is. The movement from one assertion to the other, which we make all the time, is not a logical inference but an act of faith. Attempts to infer, according to Coleridge, are based on a profound misunderstanding of the immediacy of our knowledge of God and of things. Coleridge's changes transform the radical idealism of Schelling's description of the creative power of self-consciousness itself into a description of the creative power of God as manifest in man.

In the famous ten theses, Coleridge explains how this divinity is manifest in man by analyzing self-consciousness. In tracing through the details of this analysis, we will more clearly understand Coleridge's position concerning the nature and function of faith. The first four theses explain that the first principle of transcendental philosophy must be a single principle, and can be neither a subject (i.e., self or intelligence "conceived of as exclusively representative" [BL, I, 174]), nor an object (i.e., "nature as exclusively represented; [and] without consciousness" [BL, I, 174]).

This first principle, Coleridge explains in thesis V, "is to be found therefore neither in object nor subject taken separately, and consequently, as no other third is conceivable, it must be found in identity of both" (BL, I, 182). Theses VI explains the identity of this principle: "This principle, and so characterised, manifests itself in the SUM or I AM; which I shall hereafter indiscriminately express by the words spirit, self, and self-consciousness. In this, and in this alone, object and subject, being and knowing are identical, each involving, and supposing the other. In other words, it is a subject which becomes a subject by the act of constructing itself objectively to itself; but which never is an object except for itself, and only so far as by the very same act it becomes a subject" (BL, I, 183). Coleridge proceeds to explain that, although the spirit or self is the grounds of its own knowledge of itself, it is not the grounds of the being of the self. The ground of being is God, the absolute I AM ("Jehovah") in whom the "ground of existence, and the ground of the knowledge of existence, are absolutely identical" (BL, I, 183).

Q2. Discuss Coleridge's interrelation of imagination, spontaneous knowing, and faith, in thesis VII.

Or

Q. Coleridge states that all genuine ideas involve and apparent contradiction, and can be conveyed only by symbols. Do you agree?

It has been shown, that a spirit is that, which is its own object, yet not originally an object, but an absolute subject for which all, itself included, may become an object [Thesis VI]. It must therefore be an ACT; for every object is, as an object, dead, fixed, itself incapable of any action, and necessarily finite. Again the spirit, (originally the identity of object and subject) must in some sense dissolve this identity, in order to become conscious of it; fit alter et idem. But this implies an act, and it follows therefore that intelligence or self-consciousness is impossible, except by and in a will. The self-conscious spirit therefore is a will; and freedom must be assumed as a ground of philosophy, and can never be deduced from it.

Spirit is the union of self-as-subject with self-as-object. In order to know one's own mind—to become a "self-conscious spirit"—it is necessary to dissolve this union. This dissolving is an encounter with pure knowing. It is an encounter with will itself, as the power and act of knowing, distinct from things known. 11 It is the discovery that the mind itself is ultimately active, not, as Locke had said, passive.

This encounter with will—the pure spirit—is the origin of the stupendous power of secondary imagination. All knowing is a knowing of. Primary imagination is the knowing of objects; secondary imagination is the knowing of the knowing of objects. But in order to achieve this knowing of knowing, secondary imagination must "dissolve, diffuse, and dissipate" the synthesis of knower and known so as to "recreate" the union, conscious now of the pure spirit, thc pure power of knowing, the manifestation of the absolute I AM who is God. And so the "recreated" thing-known is different: translucent in it is the divine. The outstanding truth-value of things known and expressed through the power of a highly conscious (i.e., secondary or philosophic) imagination is the central feature of Coleridge's literary theory. The basis of this claim is the fact that the secondary operation of imagination involves an immediate intuition of the divine. Religious faith, then, is a profoundly imaginative act; so, too, the powerfully imaginative poet is a profound moral teacher.

It may help to summarize before continuing. All certitude of any knowledge beyond that of the immediate notices of the senses is "assumed by a logical necessity arising from the constitution of the mind itself, by the absence of all motive to doubt it, not from any absolute contradiction in the supposition to the contrary" (BL, I, 133). The transcendental analysis of this constitution discovers that the mind is an act, and this act is knowing. This act can be represented by the words, "I am"; in absolute form, this act is the Christian God Jehovah, the "great eternal I AM." The power of knowing, then, is "an echo in the finite of the infinite I AM"; consciousness of this power (i.e., of the spirit itself) is, then, consciousness of the absolute in its pure but relative form, of the divine in its human form.

That is paradoxical, of course; but Coleridge states that all genuine ideas involve and apparent contradiction, and can be conveyed only by symbols, which will be intelligible only to those who possess the philosophic, self-conscious imagination (BL, I, 100, 167). This contradiction is manfest in art by an intense synthesis of apparently opposite things: familiarity with awe, sameness and difference, individual and representative. The self-consciousness of a spirit—the ability to know the act of knowing itself—is access to the infinite, the divine, the absolute; when the dissolved union of knower and known is "recreated," the polarity of human and divine, of sensory and divine, is more clearly manifest because it is consciously intuited. The transcendental is translucent in the sensory.

Coleridge's desire to understand Wordsworth's ability to depict this translucence is presented as his motive for the enquiry culminating in the theory of the secondary imagination. In the Biographia, Wordsworth is a figure for the genius who is at once a poet and a profound philosopher. The aesthetic power of geniune poetry allows a genius to exert effective moral leadership by unifying "deep feeling" with "profound thought."

John Stuart Mill's account of his nervous collapse suggests the importance of such leadership, and the value of external support in the struggle to unify feelings and ideas. "Analytic habits," Mill explains, "... tend to weaken those [associations] which are, to speak familiarly, a mere matter of feelings. [Such habits] are therefore (I thought) favourable to prudence and clear sightedness, but a perpetual worm at the root both of the passions and virtues." Mill's "inveterate habit" of "precocious and premature analysis" renders him a man without any feelings whatever, experiencing only "'a drowsy, stifled, unimpassioned grief.'" Reading Wordsworth reveals to him the healing power of "tranquil contemplation." Such contemplation cultivates the feelings, he explains, so that "there [is] nothing to dread from the most confirmed habit of analysis." Feelings and ideas are harmonized; each complements the other.

Coleridge draws brilliantly upon the skeptical tendencies of British empiricism to argue that our belief in this solidly familiar world of things is only a belief, not a logical conclusion nor a firmly established fact. If we admit the validity of this belief in things, we have (at least logically) admitted the validity of a belief in God. But although he appears to base his philosophy on the feelings of the individual, in fact the existence of a community of like believers is profoundly important for Coleridge: unless everyone believes in a real world immediately known, and agrees that this belief has no formal ground, his defense of religious faith would be impossible. His whole system depends upon "the man of common sense."

The literally autobiographical portions of the Biographia testify repeatedly to the spiritual support Coleridge derives from different figures whose writings help him in ways analogous to Wordsworth's helping Mill. The community of believers is also crucial pragmatically, as a support for the faith of any individual. A full appreciation of the ontological significance of belief makes it intellectually and emotionally possible to accept both science and religion—as long as you are not alienated from a secure community of believers. In many ways, this community becomes for Coleridge the major external prop for the meaning of experience—any experience—and so Coleridge, like other nineteenth-century thinkers, highly values those institutions which support traditional cultural unity.

In the face of rapid social change during the nineteenth century, cultural unity itself begins to erode. Matthew Arnold, Thomas Carlyle, John Henry Cardinal Newman, and the later Coleridge all respond to this erosion by proposing some means of support for the community of believers. In the Biographia (1817), Coleridge describes "poems and philosophic disquisitions" as capable of rescuing "truths of all others the most awful" from "the impotence caused by the very circumstance of their universal admission," although he also laments that the prevalence of anonymous criticism and superficial reading often obscures this power. But later, in On the Constitution of the Church and State (1830), Coleridge proposes state support for a permanent class of "clerisy" to facilitate the rescue. Some clerisy will be philosophers; others will be teachers whose task, in every parish of the nation, will be to aid in "the harmonious development of those qualities and faculties that characterize our humanity," in the belief that "individuals who have directed their meditations and their studies to the nobler characters of our nature... will be led by the supernatural in themselves to the contemplation of a power which is likewise super-human." Such poetry as Wordsworth's cannot in fact exert effective moral leadership on its own.

Matthew Arnold's "critics" are necessary even for poets, whose task is presenting and expounding the truths first discovered by critics. Like Carlyle's Hero, Arnold's critic is one of an elite who perceive the true order of things: "The mass of mankind will never have any ardent zeal for seeing things as they are; very inadequate ideas will always satisfy them. On these inadequate ideas reposes, and must repose, the general practice of the world. That is as much as saying that whoever sets himself to see things as they are will find himself one of a very small circle; but it is only by this small circle resolutely doing its own work that adequate ideas will ever get current at all." Critical dedication to "the best that is known and thought in the world" can prevent the loss of spiritual values to the Philistines, "who believe most that our greatness and welfare are proved by our being very rich, and who most give their lives and thoughts to becoming very rich." Unlike Carlyle's Hero, however, the critic is "to leave alone all questions of practical consequences and applications." "Adequate ideas," and centrally "the idea of perfection as an inward condition of the mind and spirit" will win their own way.

Like Coleridge's clerisy or Arnold's critic, Thomas Carlyle's Hero is "he who lives in the inward sphere of things, in the True, Divine and Eternal, which exists always, unseen to most, under the Temporary, Trivial.... " Unlike the clerisy and the critics, however, the Hero is not simply to teach and to offer example, but also to lead—he is to combine the functions of Church and State, to eschew Arnoldian "disinterestedness." The "mass of mankind" must obey and thereby escape the terror accompanying their own fruitless quests:

> It has ever been held the highest wisdom for a man not [me]rely to submit to Necessity—Necessity will make him

submit—but to know and believe well that the stern thing which Necessity had ordered was the wisest, the best, the thing wanted there. To cease his frantic pretension of scanning this great God's-world in his small fraction of a brain; to know that it had, verily, though deep beyond his soundings, a Just Law, that the soul of it was Good;—that his part in it was to conform to the Law of the Whole, and in devout silence to follow that; not questioning it, obeying it as unquestionable. I say, this is yet the only true morality known.... it is properly the soul of Christianity."

Any truth accessible only through contemplative insight into transcendental realities will be in fact inaccessible to a great many people. Carlyle explains that "the confusing wreck of things crumbling and even crashing and tumbling all round us" will come to rest on the "everlasting adamant" of Hero-worship. 18 The feelings of the masses can be trusted even though the majority proves largely incapable of intelligent meditation on the origin and significance of their feelings. Carlyle's authoritarianism follows naturally from his emphasis on the internal, emotive, and intuitive; his vision of the divinity active within us effectively equates obedience with the highest allegiance to the best aspects of self. Ultimately, Coleridge defines faith by means of a very similar equation.'

John Henry Cardinal Newman advocates absolute authority for related reasons: the individual who would defy the significance of "clothes," of the mere "show of things," is then faced with a confusing disharmony between inner and outer realities. He confesses himself profoundly disturbed by the lack of public confirmation of his own beliefs:

Starting then with the being of a God (which, as I have said, is as certain to me as the certainty of my own existence, though when I try to put the grounds of that certainty into logical shape I find a difficulty in doing so in mood and figure to my satisfaction), I look out of myself into the world of men, and there I see a sight which fills me with unspeakable distress. The world seems simply to give the lie to that great truth, of which my whole being is so full; and the effect upon me is, in consequence, as a matter of necessity, as confusing as if it denied that I am in existence myself. If I looked into a mirror, and did not see my face, I should have the sort of feeling which actually comes upon me, when I look out into this living busy world, and see no reflexion of its creator.

Newman interprets this state of affairs as evidence for the infallibility of the Roman Catholic Church. The teaching authority of the Church is "a direct, immediate, active, and prompt means of withstanding the difficulty" presented by "the energy of human scepticism"; it is "a provision, adapted by the mercy of the Creator,... to restrain that freedom of thought, which of course in itself is one of the greatest of our natural gifts, and to rescue it from its own suicidal excesses." Religious authority, like Hero-worship, is a bulwark against chaos.

Each of these writers presents himself as knowing the truth which his "social programme" is to promulgate. Newman somehow restrained the "suicidal excesses" of his own thought even prior to his conversion; similarly, Carlyle is in some sort Heroic himself, penetrating to the "inward sphere" even while lamenting the lack of Heroism in his own age. Matthew Arnold's commitment to perfection and his stock of "adequate ideas" are prior to the emergence of the critical class he advocates; Coleridge had no benefit of permanent clerisy in exploring the transcendental realm. Each addresses a reader who also cherishes transcendental values. The problem for all of them is what Carlyle calls "the mass of men." These writers are threatened not by an absurd universe—the more modern dilemma—but by the rapid dissolution of the cultural unity necessary to sustain a community of believers.

But cultural unity cannot be decreed by heroes, critics, popes, or clerisy. It arises. What we see arising in the nineteenth century is a culture characterized by bitterly conflicting ontologies, by profound disagreements on how to discover the principles by which one ought to live and think and believe. When the evidence of the senses and the testimony of the heart are experienced as contradictory, as they were and are experienced by many, then highly abstract issues in philosophy acquire a painful immediacy. All coherence goes, not simply from the external world, but from the self as well. The failure of these programmes—and others like them—contributes to the evolution of the permanently fractured self.

Q3. Discuss Coleridge's Theory of Language in relation to his Biographia Literaria.

Or

Q. Precision, pleasure, truth: the complexity of each idea, and the complexities of their interrelations, lies near to the heart of Coleridge's critical genius.Comment

Coleridge regularly advises that the best way to resolve an argument is to define the term on which the disagreement depends. "Words," he asserts, "are living powers, not merely articulated air." This implicit connection between language and truth derives from his theory of language; this linguistics, in turn, relies upon a divinity who guarantees the coherent interplay of mind, word, and thing. Tracing this ascent from word to God reveals how Coleridge can celebrate the great moral force of literature without subordinating both poets and critics to a moral censor. Contrary to the claims of one tradition, Coleridge's philosophy does not set limits for the free play of imagination in literature.

Before climbing this ascent, however, I had best survey his basic definitions of "word" and "grammar," because his scattered reflections on language have never been studied in the context of his mature philosophy. Coleridge's philosophy of language, like his philosophy generally, takes our immediate knowledge of real things as an axiom. 3 According to his definition in Aids to Reflection, words reveal the creative, active mind as it distinguishes between real things and mere artifacts of sensory receptors:

Now when a person speaking to us of any particular object or appearance refers it by means of some common character to a known class (which he does in giving it a name), we say, that we understand him; that is, we understand his words. The name of a thing, in the original sense of the word name (nomen, ïïýìåíïí, ôï, intelligible, id quod intelligitur) expresses that which is understood in an appearance, that which we place (or make to stand) under it, as the condition of its real existence, and in proof that it is not an accident of the senses, or affectation of the individual, not a phantom or apparition, that is, an appearance which is only an appearance.

The act of naming asserts that the thing named exists in a reality shared by speaker and auditor. Coleridge calls naming "the condition of real existence" because the speaker effectively distinguishes between real and chimerical when he gives something a name: language does not supply names for entities we have neither sensed nor imagined. Language expresses and records our knowledge through words, which signify not ideas, nor things, but the relation between idea and perceived object.

I can sharpen our focus on Coleridge's definition of "word" by sketching its context. His assertion of the mind's active role in establishing the meanings of words contrasts sharply with the dominant Lockean tradition in linguistics. Throughout the third book, "Of words," in his An Essay concerning Human Understanding (1690), Locke maintains that words signify ideas. Since ideas arise only from experience of things (or reflections on such experience), words refer to objects only indirectly. In this contention, Locke himself 'differs sharply from the dominant linguistic tradition in his own day. The contrast can be simplified as follows: for Locke, words signify ideas [of objects]; for John Wilkins and other seventeenth-century linguists, words signify objects. In his An Essay Toward a Real Character, and a Philosophical Language (London: S. Gellibrand, 1668), Wilkins undertakes a monumental task: "the great foundation of the thing here designed [is]a regular enumeration and description of all those things and notions, to which marks or names ought to be assigned according to their respective natures". Wilkins hopes to remedy the confusion of tongues and advance the cause of the Royal Society by inventing a language (his "real character") in which there is a completely unequivocal one-to-one correspondence between signs and signifieds. (Despite losing his manuscript in the Great Fire, Wilkins completed this enumeration, and invented a language based on Hebrew.) Coleridge's definition of "word" as the relation between idea and object places him intermediate between the positions represented by Locke and Wilkins, and in a line that Ernst Cassirer traces through Heraclitus, Plato, Berkeley, Herder, and von Humboldt.

Coleridge's definition of "word" represents language as participating intimately in the complex relation between mind and world: the process of naming and the process of knowing (in the strict sense) are represented as a single process. As the paragraph cited above continues, Coleridge develops the definition in two directions. First, as "evidence," he cites the frequent identity in the Bible of nomen (name) and numen ("invisible power and presence"). This identity of name and power hints at Coleridge's conception of the metaphysical significance of language. His claim here has obvious affinities with such "Platonic" theories as that of James Harris. Yet Harris contends that words refer not to "external particulars, nor yet... particular ideas" but rather to "general ideas." These are "a kind of superior objects; a new race of perceptions... each one of which may be found entire and whole in the separate individuals of an infinite and fleeting multitude, without departing from the unity and permanence of its own nature." For Coleridge, the metaphysical significance of language depends not on the connection between words and signified objects (or universals), but rather on the mental activity that underlies language.

We will return to this metaphysical perspective later. For now, the more important direction is psychological. The objects of understanding (a power always distinguished by Coleridge from the intuitive reason) are strictly linguistic:

Thus, in all instances, it is words, names, or, if images, yet images used as words or names, that are the only and exclusive subjects of understanding. In no instance do we understand a thing in itself; but only the name to which it is referred... No one would say he understands red or blue. He sees the colour, and had seen it before in a vast number and variety of objects; and he understands the word red, as referring his fancy or memory to this his collective experience. Sensation is predominantly a physical act; understanding is predominantly an intellectual one. We do not know things in themselves: we feel or smell or touch them. In a characteristically syncretic use of Kant, Coleridge presents language as the principal vehicle for the interaction of knowing mind and shared, concrete reality:

> If this be so, and so it most assuredly is—if the proper functions of the understanding be that of generalizing the notices received from the senses in order to the construction of names: of referring particular notices (that is, impressions or sensations) to their proper names; and, vice versa, names to their correspondent class or kind of notices—then it follows of necessity, that the understanding is truly and accurately defined in the words of Leighton and Kant, a faculty judging according to sense.

Perceptual physiologists study sense-data; philosophers study language because it reveals the workings of the mind.

Granted these definitions, Coleridge can in part determine the accuracy of any statement by appeal to literally common sense, by asking whether this formulation actually reflects our previous experience of the reality thus asserted. Such a test underlies several themes in Coleridge's commentary on Wordsworth. In one place he accuses Wordsworth of "prolixity" and "bombast" when Wordsworth moves too far outside the usual experience of the objects and situations that are presented in a poem: his language loses clarity as it loses touch with "such knowledge and value of the objects described, as can be fairly anticipated of men in general, even of the most cultivated classes" (BL, II, 109-1 5). But elsewhere, Coleridge praises Wordsworth as one likely to write "the FIRST GENUINE PHILOSOPHICAL POEM" (BL, II, 129): the Prelude's account "Of the foundations and the building up /

Of a Human Spirit" draws powerfully on the capacity of language to represent the relation between mind and world ("To William Wordsworth").

As Coleridge sees it, then, language expresses the contents and activity of consciousness. In the manuscript "Logic," Coleridge explains that "Formal Grammar" "reflects the forms of the human Mind, and gradually familiarizes the half-conscious boy with the frame and constitution of his own Intellect." 8 This "frame and constitution" is logic: "it is plain that Logic[,] in as much as it presents the universal and necessary rules of the Understanding, must in these rules present likewise the criterion of truth, that is, of formal truth, or truth relative to the constitution or constituent forms, laws and rules of the thinking faculty". In the "Opus Maximum" manuscript, Coleridge clarifies his special interpretation of the common eighteenth-century equation between logic and grammar: "In fact the science of grammar is but logic in its first exemplification or rather its first product... i.e., thoughts in connexion or connected language". Logic defines both the rules of correct understanding and the rules of correct word-use; as formalized in grammar, logic is the power of language to express relations.

This power generates the philosophical significance of language, and hence of poetry. Coleridge's description of part four of the "Logic" begins to formulate this significance: "the etymological history of the Word (Logos) from which the Science, that treats of Words in relation to connected Thoughts, derives its technical Name—and the several Successive meanings of the word from the visual image, its simplest and primary significance, to its last and highest sense in the Christian Theology".Although language itself does not constitute reality, it expresses the constituent forms of the understanding: the power to make relations, and hence to begin to discover divinity active in the world.

Traditionally, poetry is the highest or best or richest use of language. From this linguistic perspective, the critic can claim that the outstanding qualities of poetry are qualities of language: the heights that poets can reach are defined by the limits of language, because even the power of imagination requires a medium for its expression. Coleridge makes this ordinary idea central: poetry is the most precise use of words. "It would be scarcely more difficult to push a stone out from the pyramids with the bare hand than to alter a word, or the position of a word, in Milton or Shakespeare (in their most important works at least), without making the author say something else, or something worse, than he does say" (BL, I, 15). Coleridge explains that as a schoolboy, "I learnt from ["Bowyer"] that Poetry, even that of the loftiest and, seemingly, that of the wildest odes, had a logic of its own, as severe as that of science; and more difficult, because more subtle, more complex. and dependent upon more and more fugitive causes. In the truly great poets, he would say, there is a reason assignable, not only for every word, but for the position of every word" (BL, I, 4). John Wilson thought this claim about the logic of poetry "too wilfully absurd and extravagant to have entered into the head of an honest man, whose time must have been wholly occupied with the instruction.of children." 10 Yet logic is the heart of the matter, because logic is not syllogisms but the forms, laws, and rules of the thinking faculty itself: poetry achieves its precision by exactly reflecting the order and activity of the mind. Our pleasure in a poem flows from our repetition of that activity in or through the act of reading itself: "The reader should be carried forward, not merely or chiefly by the mechanical impulse of curiosity, or by a restless desire to arrive at the final solution; but by the pleasureable activity of mind excited by the attractions of the journey itself" (BL, II, 11).

Precision, pleasure, truth: the complexity of each idea, and the complexities of their interrelations, lie near to the heart of Coleridge's critical genius. Even this brief survey of his reflections on language reveals that chapter fourteen's distinction between poetry and science cannot be the simple Enlightenment commonplace it has long seemed to be. The poet's "immediate object is pleasure not truth, but pleasure of a specific kind. Yes, we delight primarily in the aptness of an expression, not its contents. But the nature of words and the nature of grammar guarantee that the utterly apt expression will truly reveal the relations among God, man, and a shared reality. Lear was not a real king, perhaps; but to discredit or to ignore the play's truth on that ground is akin to discrediting Mendel's conclusions because his peas are not all peas. One attains truth about the laws governing physical reality by directly testing one's ideas. One attains truth about the laws governing intellectual or spiritual realities indirectly, by aiming at precision, by relying on the Logos.

Such pleasurably precise language conveys moral truth because precisely used words accurately recreate the perceptual union of speaker and object: "I include in the meaning of a word not only its correspondent object, but likewise all the associations which it recalls. For language is framed to convey not the object alone, hut likewise the character, mood and intentions of the person who is representing it" (BL, II, 1 I 5-16). 11 Reading a precisely written text, then, generates in the reader an awareness which is akin to his own self-consciousness: he simultaneously perceives the author's consciousness, the described reality, and the union of these two. Such a text conveys not just a shared reality, but the act of perception: a subject and an object in active union. It follows that the most self-conscious author writes the most precise texts: one improves writing by reflection on the activity of one's mind, not by merely observing the subject-matter more closely. It also follows that the study of such texts is an excellent way of studying both consciousness itself and the world-as-known. And either way, one will discover the handiwork of God.

Pursuing the psychological direction has only brought us back around to the metaphysical—and to an old and thorny philosophic problem. What is the relation between speaker and object that a word represents? More broadly stated, what is the relation between mind and world? And what makes a true statement possible? Coleridge tries to solve these problems with a philosophy based on the triune Christian God, but his linguistics does not perform a standing broad jump into this solution. He works it out, painstakingly, in the various expositions of his concept of Method.

Coleridge takes the Greek origins of "Method" seriously: Method is a path or transit to knowledge; it prescribes the procedure for fruitful enquiry and (simultaneously) for adequate discourse. For reasons that will become clear as we go along, the philosophical roots of Coleridge's linguistics are to be found in the Essays on Method in The Friend, and in the history of method that structures the Philosophical Lectures.

One crucial, fundamental fact is easily stated: Method and language are both processes involving relations:

METHOD... becomes natural to the mind which has been accustomed to contemplate not things only, or for their own sake alone, but likewise and chiefly the relations of things, either their relations to each other, or to the observer, or to the state and apprehension of the hearers. To enumerate and analyse these relations, with the conditions under which alone they are discoverable, is to teach the science of Method.

As the science of relations, Method is also the science of words (or of thought), subsuming under itself both logic and grammar. The major relation that Method seeks is that between "ideas" and "laws." These are correlative terms, strictly defined: a natural law (e.g., the law of gravity) is the objective counterpart of an idea or intuition arising from reflection on the appropriate data. The counterpart of the law is not the data or observations it "explains," but the act of mind whereby this data is identified and ordered.

Correct method discovers the correlation of idea and law in its many particular forms, and the dual reference of words represents it. Hence, in explaining the relation of ideas and laws, Coleridge defines the "content" of language, or the form of the total reality which language names. What emerges, gradually, is the claim that language reveals the psychological laws for which the correlative idea is the Logos, the Word of God (for whom word, idea, and law are not correlative but identical). Coleridge credits Pythagoras with the fundamental insight: "the very powers which in men reflect and contemplate, are in their essence the same as those powers which in nature produce the objects contemplated". These powers were "by the Pythagoreans and Anaxagoras called the Nous (the Logos or the Word of Philo and St. John)". The Philosophical Lectures develop this insight through analyses of such figures as Aristotle and Bacon, who study these powers as manifest in the natural world, and those such as Plato, who study them as manifest in the mind.

Language is one of these manifestations in the mind. Plato "direct[s] his inquiries chiefly to those objective truths that exist in and for the intellect alone, the images and representatives of which we construct for ourselves by figure, number, and word". Mathematics had long been taken as a model for absolute certitude; the dramatic correspondence between the pure mathematical system and the observable world had always had metaphysical significance. Coleridge echoes the claim that words, like figures and numbers, are part of a perfect system which nonetheless reflects the form of an imperfect and changeable world. It is in its capacity to represent a (logical, grammatical) system of relations that language is analogous to mathematics.

Words are to consciousness what geometrical figures are to space, or numbers to time. Language symbolically represents both the relation of mind to world (the correlation of ideas and laws) and the relation of human knowledge to divine knowledge (logic and the Logos). Language differs from geometry in part because language changes and develops, while geometry does not (or would not have seemed to, for Coleridge). But this difference is minor. The development of language reflects the development of consciousness; had Coleridge recognized that the properties of space are still evolving (in his sense), then he would have seen that geometry must evolve with them.

The Philosophical Lectures trace the development of consciousness as evident in language: the history of philosophy records our gradually accumulating recognitions as they are evident in the history of words. Hence, Coleridge continually insists on "de-synonymising," for this is the process by which language develops and records the growth of consciousness: "desynonymizing words... is the process of language. As society introduces new relations it introduces new distinctions, and either new words... or different pronunciations. Now the duty of a philosopher is to aid and complete this process as his subject demands". Although language is at any one point a perfect system, it is always changing because consciousness is always changing.

The history of words is a history of the mind of man, Coleridge explains; like many of his contemporaries, he believes that language reveals the character of the race.Because accurate language itself reliably guides us to truth, many of Coleridge's arguments appeal to usage. The most famous of these may be his response to Word worth's claim to have imitated "a selection of the real language of men," or his claim that "Between the language of prose and that of metrical composition, there neither is, nor can be any essential difference" (BL, II, 28-68). But such appeals are throughout Coleridge's prose. We saw this earlier: he establishes his view of understanding by citing our use of "understand" as a verb distinct from "see" or "hear."

His defense of his "true and original realism" usually appeals to usage at least in part. For instance, immediate knowledge of independently real objects is denied only by "philosophers of the schools... [Who] live and move in a crowd of phrases and notions from which human nature has long ago vanished" (BL, I, 179). Or in The Friend, he contends that "so universally has this conviction leavened the very substance of all discourse, that there is no language on earth in which a man can abjure it as a prejudice, without employing terms and conjunctions that suppose its reality...". Examples could be multiplied, because Coleridge takes the strategy quite seriously. It is for him no mere rhetorical device, but an important and theoretically grounded means for resolving arguments and advancing human knowledge.

Coleridge's theory of language also permeates his judgments about contemporaries. The intellectual dimness of anonymous critics accounts for their inability to use words more distinctly; the consequences of this inability underlies their envious malevolence (BL, I, 25-29). His opposition to Jacobinism, and to various things French, matches an opposition to the Gallic habit of unconnected, epigrammatic periods. On the other hand, Edmund Burke's power as a "scientific statesman; and therefore a seer" arises from his habitual precision of expression (BL, I, 125). Once again, examples are everywhere at hand: since the development of intelligence rests on close attention to the meanings of words, the quality of expression reveals the quality of thought. Hence it is that "No man was ever yet a great pot, without being at the same time a profound philosopher" (BL, II, 19). In the worst poets, by contrast, "it is difficult to determine whether... the sense of the diction be the more absurd" (BL, I 27n).

These practical applications of his theory of language clearly reflect Coleridge's confidence both in our ability to know directly, without linguistic mediation, and in our ability to judge the adequacy of a verbal formulation. Although linguists today would not seriously consider this claim that language, like geometry, is a perfect system that nonetheless accords with an imperfect world, its net result—that arguments about the truth of a proposition must come down to arguments about the proper use of words—has a distinctly modern ring. Yet Coleridge would take quick issue with the notion that words refer only to other words, and not to realities. He would say, I suspect, that dissolving either the connection or the distinction between word and object named is the same school-error as dissolving the connection or the distinction between sensation and object sensed: it breeds chimerical problems.

Coleridge's confidence in the harmony of creation and the powers of the mind does not contradict his many statements about the importance of intellectual discipline. Mankind requires patient study of the science of Method to discover and to express accurately the correlation of ideas and laws.

Yet for God (as I said earlier), word, idea, and law are not correlative but identical. God insures and enables the harmony of mind and world that Method discovers and language reveals. The divine fiat is at once word, idea, and creation itself. Early and late in his career, Coleridge asserts that the world is "the language of God." It is an old metaphor that Coleridge's linguistics invests with particular richness. Our knowledge of God and our knowledge of the world are very closely related, but not identical. As Coleridge says in "The Destiny of Nations: A Vision," we know God by an act of interpretation of the world-text:

> For all that meets the bodily sense I deem
> Symbolical, one mighty alphabet
> For infant minds.

A good "reader" can see God everywhere present in the world, as we ordinarily perceive something of the character of an author behind any text. Just as a text presupposes an author, the coherence of the world presupposes a creator.

The first step toward seeing God in the world is to perceive its order—to learn its grammar. The system of relations comprising that order is God's immanence in the world; the reflection and meditation necessary to discover relations reveal' the necessity of postulating a God to account for the correspondence between idea and law. We all enjoy reading the texts written by friends; knowing the friend, one sees his immanence in the text far more easily. Knowing God directly through faith similarly affects the ease and clarity with which we see God in the world. Through faith in Christ—the Logos—we "speak" directly to God, and directly hear him. Without Christ, God remains only a "necessary postulate," the presumed author of an anonymous text, but not someone with whom we converse. The "language of God" metaphor gracefully represents the world-view Coleridge struggled to realise in a formal philosophic system.

As it has been widely recognized recently, the mind is no more passive in reading than in perceiving. A text, like a tree, is created as it is perceived and yet exists (at least according to Coleridge) as a stable object which can be known in the rigorous sense of that word. The dynamic process of "reading" the "world-text," like the dynamic process of reading generally, reflects the fundamentally symbolic nature of both cosmos and language. As J. Robert Barth explains in Coleridge and the Symbolic Imagination, "We believe in the symbol as symbolic, and find ourselves enriched by it. Thus enriched, we are able to commit ourselves more fully to the symbolic reality, and are able to perceive it more fully. Through this new perception, we are again enriched." 16 Coleridge's theory of symbol reaches its fullest articulation within his religious thought, but its literary origin is evident.

Q4. Why does Coleridge assert the priority of poems as a medium of poetry? What can the language of a poem achieve that the language of prose cannot? Why is a poem most likely to achieve "'truth operative, and by effects continually alive'" (BL, II, 102)

Explain the context of above lines.

Truth becomes operative or effective only as it is felt, only as it arouses a response from the passions as well as the intellect. Coleridge draws on his theory of polarity to provide a dynamic (rather than associationism) psychological mechanism for the traditional link between metrical, figurative language and the expression of passion:

The origin of metre... I would trace to the balance in the mind effected by that spontaneous effort which strives to hold in check the workings of passion... This salutary antagonism is assisted by the very state, which it counteracts.... This balance of antagonists becomes organized into metre... by a supervening act of the will and judgment [.]... As the elements of metre owe their existence to a state of increased excitement, so the metre itself should be accompanied by the natural language of excitement. There must be not only a partnership, but a union; interpenetration of passion and of will [.]... This union can be manifested only in a frequency of forms and figures of speech (originally the offspring of passion, but now the adopted children of power)....[There is] a previous and well understood, though tacit, compact between the poet and his reader, that the latter is entitled to expert, and the former bound to supply, this species and degree of pleasurable excitement.

Figure and metre express the poet's passion and arouse the reader. As the poet "brings the whole soul of man into activity," so the poem addresses both the reader's intellect and his feelings in ways that prose cannot. A poem, Coleridge explains, is "the art of communicating whatever we wish to communicate so as both to express and to produce excitement... for the purpose of immediate pleasure."

In its sustained and pleasurable excitement, the poem meets the requirements for Methodical discourse more fully than any other genre. The definition of "poem" in chapter fourteen of Biographia Literaria specifies these criteria in their literary forms (BL, II, 10-12). Correct method demands unity; the parts of a poem must "mutually support and explain each other; all in their proportion harmonizing with, and supporting [,] the purpose and known influence of metrical arrangement." Yet this unity may not be static: it must be progressive or dynamic. One function of metre is to excite "perpetual and distinct attention to each part"; although the parts of a poem are closely interrelated, the reader attends to each part in its own right because of "the pleasurable activity of mind excited by the attractions of the [reading-] journey itself." By virtue of this attention, the reader experiences both the progression from one part to the next, and the unity of the whole. Awareness of the individuality of parts is sustained by the same principle as awareness of their unity: the pleasurable excitement of reading. A poem is distinct from other deliberately pleasant uses of language because only poetic language can offer "such delight from the whole, as is compatible with a distinct gratification from each component part."

In a poem, the Methodical correlation of idea and law shifts, but only slightly. Ideas correlate not with laws (which formulate the order of entire "data sets"), but with representative particulars. These particulars are created by the poet—not observed, nor abstracted from observation. Poets reconcile an idea with its image, its reflection in the world as humanly known. Hence, the "opposite or discordant qualities" reconciled by the synthetic imagination are the universality of ideas and the idiosyncrasy of concrete particulars: the poet's images create a world in which ideas are translucent—not transcendental. Such a world can be created without metre, Coleridge acknowledges; but only by substituting some (unnamed) means of sustaining attention as metre sustains it.

The critical criteria derived from this poetics examine how well a poem is written: exacting word-choice, prosodic grace, figurative power, structural integrity. Coleridge's theory of language advances the claim that texts which measure up will offer significant moral truth, but his theory of language on this point separates itself from his theory of poetry and criticism. "An undeviating poet in the strict sense of the term is an impossibility," Coleridge states; but it does not therefore follow that devotion qualifies any writer of verse as a poet in this strict sense (COS, 89). Coleridge's criticism of Wordsworth reflects this crucial distinction. Parts of the "Excursion" may "do one's heart good," but they are ineffective poetically (BL, II, 104-07). Wordsworth's urge to be a moral philosopher should work itself out in "sermons or moral essays" rather than in poems. This distinction is a delicate one, I know; that delicacy can best be demonstrated by the evident truth and the consistency of the following statement: The value of literature is moral; the distinctive qualities of literature are linguistic.

It would seem, at this point, as if language can do anything. Yet Coleridge was fully aware of the limitations of words. As Cassirer points out, such awareness usually accompanies linguistic theories that describe words as representing relations rather than merely ideas or things. Language cannot adequately express every possible aspect of human experience; even the greatest poets can only speak "What may be told, to the understanding mind / Revealable"

("To William Wordsworth"). Experiences that do not arise in relation to some shared reality—whether sensory or psychological—can make only indirect use of words. 18 The signified relation will be incomplete for the reader if he cannot identify the "shared" reality forming one pole of the relation. (The reader's experience of textual incoherence may of course be his own fault: hence the emphasis on true taste as one manifestation of genius.) Poets—or poems—who take consciousness itself as a subject-matter will encounter the limits of expression as often as they reach genuinely unique aspects of consciousness. Such uniqueness, whatever its origins (or validity), isolates speaker from audience.

To "modes of inmost being," Coleridge explains, "the attributes of time and space are inapplicable and alien, but [these modes] yet cannot be conveyed save in symbols of time and space" (BL, II, 120). The specifically literary excitement of reading a poem may evoke the reader's intuitive apprehension of these modes, but the reader cannot accept what he does not somehow understand for himself. Neither can the writer believe in an audience for statements about experiences he regards as entirely sui generis. As George Watson observes, the Romantic poets were particularly challenged by the need to find or create the audience for whom their styles would be effective.

Despite the limitations of language, Coleridge claims that poets speak a great moral truth. This truth is not theology, nor ethics, nor science. It is truth about the mind. The poet's self-consciousness makes it possible for him to draw into unity both an object and a human response to that object: in poems, the signified is an object as humanly known and valued. Reading engenders consciousness of another's consciousness in action; poems reveal the synthesis of fully human subject and real object which is the activity of consciousness. Coleridge's linguistics accounts for the creation of this humanly coherent universe, for it are words—not sensation—that place the mind in relation to a reality outside itself. By naming, we distinguish between me and not-me, and through the genial power of secondary imagination we both ponder and express this distinction. Thus, "art... is the mediatress between, and reconciler of, nature and man.... Art itself might be defined as of a middle quality between a thought and a thing."

Coleridge's theory of language makes it possible to speak about both self and other simultaneously. So does Shelley's. He describes poetic language as one that both "marks the before unapprehended relations of things and perpetuates their apprehension" and that is "a more direct representation of the actions and passions of our internal being, and is susceptible of more various and delicate combination than colour, form, or motion." And Wordsworth describes language in the same dual way: language is "an incarnation of the thought... [not] only clothing for it," and yet "the best part of language" originally derives from "the beautiful and permanent forms of nature." What an artist conceives as the limits of his medium must influence his work: the truth that a poet attains is only such truth as his language can express. The extraordinary interrelatedness of all things so often celebrated in Coleridge's poetry and his prose proclaims exactly that idea inherent in his linguistics: the One Life within us and abroad.

Q5. What is the Function of Autobiography in Biographia Literaria?

Or

Q. Coleridge's compositions are designed to make the reader engage a particular problem or issue in ways that will lead him to the conclusions that Coleridge has already reached. Discuss

Biographia Literaria has never been taken very seriously as an autobiography because; as Coleridge himself explains "the least of what I have written concerns me personally." Personal history is put aside for chapters at a time as Coleridge analyses associationism, or Wordsworth's "Preface" to Lyrical Ballads. The book's discontinuities have baffled and infuriated generations of readers, whose ambivalence Symons captures so adeptly: "Biographia Literaria is the greatest book of criticism in English, and one of the most annoying in any language." 1 As a result, the book is most commonly studied only in excerpts: biographers, critics, and philosophers each select fragments from what is judged an essentially fragmented whole. These excerpters may also suspect that, as Laurence Lock ridge suggests, "To venture into Coleridge's prose is dangerous business"—a threat to one's sanity no less than to one's reserves of energy. 2 But accept the autobiographical character of the Biographia, and soon its obscurity begins to resolve into an intelligible, sophisticated, difficult design. With the Prelude before him as an example, Coleridge defines his idea of imagination as the growth of a critic's mind. Many of the most puzzling features of his text derive from his fusion of autobiography and argument.

Yet it is a difficult book. At first glance, there is ample evidence that Biographia Literaria is a fragmented disaster whose difficulties can neither be resolved nor understood: the "missing" transcendental construction in chapter thirteen; the incorporations from Schelling; its origin as a preface to Sibylline Leaves. But this evidence shrivels if examined in strong light. The infamous chapter thirteen, for example, culminates an extensive pattern of reference to the intellectual powers of Englishmen; it is an elaborately planned appeal to the philosophic reader. Philosophic readers have been appropriately disappointed: the strategy succeeds at least in part. But such readers err in judging this chapter a neurotic break or a failure of nerve, or a change in plan literally unexpected by its author. There is substantial evidence to the contrary. 3 In a parallel way, the Biography's origin as a preface reflects no reprehensible spontaneity on Coleridge's part: one finds plans for the Biographia in letters and notebook entries dating back at least to the autumn of 1803. 4 The plagiarisms from Schelling have been evaluated in general by Thomas McFarland and in painstaking detail by Elinor Stoneman Shaffer, both of whom conclude that the literal appearance of plagiarism is misleading. 5 In the light of recent scholarship, this traditionally prima-facie evidence loses its impressive appearance.

But the reputation of Biographia Literaria has also rested on the experience of many attentive and informed readers. For a text so often described as unreadable, it has been read more often and valued more highly than quite makes sense. The paradox is revealing: there is no frustration quite the equal of intuiting a coherence that refuses to emerge into the full daylight of objectifying comprehension. There are, in fact, many brief descriptions of the Biographia's general thematic unity. Shawcross is exemplary. He attributes "the miscellaneous character of the book" to the poor state of Coleridge's "health and spirits," but goes on to say: "It is with this end in view ['the desire... to state clearly, and defend adequately, his own poetic creed'] that, in the autobiographical portion of the book, he describes the growth of his own literary convictions; that, in the philosophical, he seeks to refer them to first principles; and that, in the criticism of Wordsworth's poetry and poetic theory, he emphasizes the differences which, as he imagines, exist between Wordsworth and himself" (BL, I, chi). Coleridge's complaint seems to the point: "Now surely a [work] the contents and purposes of which are capable of being faithfully and completely enumerated in a sentence of 7 or 8 lines, and where all the points treated of tend to a common result, cannot justly be regarded as a motley Patch-work, or a Farrago of heterogeneous Effusions!" (LS, 114n). 6 General thematic unities are seldom denied. Yet it is one thing for an attentive reader to perceive the relations among the topics Coleridge discusses; it is something altogether different to perceive that Coleridge so manages his discourse as to define exactly how "all points treated of tend to a common result." A sympathetic reader can link the parts to a postulated common result, but this does not prove that Biographia Literaria, as a discourse, generally succeeds in establishing these relations through various formal and rhetorical strategies. Such strategies comprise what I call "design": the blueprint of the whole regarded both as a governing structure and as the intent or governing idea implicit in and enacted by this structure. Biographia Literaria possesses a design, whose central principles it is my purpose here to explain.

The generations of scholars and critics succeeding Shawcross have explicated Coleridge's "literary convictions" and his "first principles" to reveal a thinker known to relatively few in 1907: a Coleridge who is erudite, philosophically acute, and humanly profound. As we have more and more fully seen how his intricacy of mind engages complex human questions, it becomes less possible to believe that so great a thinker could have been so fundamentally incompetent a writer. Common sense questions whether such extraordinary powers of concentration and synthesis could have been so entirely suspended when he sat down to compose. He himself insisted that genius and command of language vary together. His books are not perfectly written—whose are?—but their difficulty resides primarily in the complexity of his ideas, and in the complexity of design these ideas require for their intelligible presentation. Coleridge knew he would be charged with obscurity; he often tried both to defend himself, and to preclude the charge through elaborate explanations of his principles in writing. Understanding these principles alleviates much of the confusion and frustration that so many readers experience.

Coleridge's desire to make his readers think, to make them engage genuine ideas, underlies the design of Biographia Literaria. It also accounts in part for the book's reputation as excessively difficult reading. In what he regarded as "the finest passage in the Friend," Coleridge acknowledges the problems he creates for his readers.

Alas! Legitimate reasoning is impossible without severe thinking, and thinking is neither an easy nor an amusing employment. The reader, who would follow a close reasoned to the summit and absolute principle of any one important subject, has chosen a Chamois-hunter for his guide. Our guide [Coleridge himself, as The Friend] will, indeed, take us the shortest way, will save us many a wearisome and perilous wandering, and warn us of many a mock road that had formerly led himself to the brink of chasms and precipices, or at best in an idle circle to the spot from whence he started. But he cannot carry us on his shoulders: we must strain our own sinews, as he has strained his; and make firm footing on the smooth rock for ourselves, by the blood of toil from our own feet.

The image of such sticky, bloody feet may be lurid, but it has very often seemed to me entirely apt. Owen Barfield grants that the relation between subject and object is no doubt the pons asinorum of Coleridge's philosophic endeavor, but then argues that "the concept, and perhaps the experience, of thinking as an act, or as an 'act and energy,' are the toll-gate in the middle of the bridge, the barrier that has to be opened before we can get across." 8 Barfield demonstrates how thoroughly this central concept influences all of Coleridge's thought; my major concern is the way in which it shapes his composition.

Coleridge's compositions are designed to make the reader engage a particular problem or issue in ways that will lead him to the conclusions that Coleridge has already reached. He wants to make us think things through for ourselves, under his tutelage. To the extent that his particular interests are all versions of a predominant interest in thinking itself, one can say that he writes in ways designed to help us think about thinking. That is no small ambition. Further challenges to the reader emerge from the fact that Coleridge seldom accommodates to lesser energies or lesser talents than his own. He may lead us away from precipices, but he does not hesitate to lead us up rough and steep paths if these take us most directly to our destination.

Some of the reader's troubles derive from Coleridge's lack of skill in the fine art of enticing tired minds to further and further effort. But often the reader stumbles because the way is genuinely and irreducibly difficult. As Sara Coleridge notes, the original thinker cannot rely on "known ways and smooth well-beaten tracks": he forces his readers into unaccustomed mental exercise. Both contemporary and modern readers have echoed this image of a difficult path to describe the effort Coleridge's discourse requires. The image is particularly apt:

as Coleridge often observed, the Greek word we translate as "method" translates literally as "way" or "path" or "mode of transit." The "Essays on Method" in The Friend claim that valid method demands powerful imagination. So does reading the Biographia. As Bishop C. Hunt, Jr., observes, "What we might call the 'dramatic' element in philosophy, the process of search and its written reenactment, assumes a larger significance. Much of Coleridge's best writing can be read as a kind of dramatic monologue in prose, a mimetic representation of the mind in the act of thinking something through." Thinking along with Coleridge as he thinks something through demands more than energy and learning. It requires that we read his prose with the same use of the same skills we engage when we read his poetry.

When Coleridge asserts that he wants his readers to think, he means that we must develop and exercise the ability to observe our own minds. We must acquire the self-consciousness that is secondary imagination's most basic act. His clearest statement of this requirement is the distinction between thinking and attending in Aids to Reflection:

> It is a matter of great difficulty, and requires no ordinary skill and address, to fix the attention of men on the world within them, to induce them to study the processes and superintend the works which they are themselves carrying on in their own minds; in short, to awaken in them both the faculty of thought* and the inclination to exercise it. For alas! The largest part of mankind is nowhere greater strangers than at home.
>
> Distinction between thought and attention.—By thought is here meant the voluntary reproduction in our minds of those states of consciousness, or... of those inward experiences, to which, as to his best and most authentic documents, the teacher of moral or religious truth refers us. In attention we keep the mind passive: in thought, we rouse it into activity. In the former, we submit to an impression—we keep the mind steady, in order to receive the stamp. In the latter, we seek to imitate the artist, while we ourselves make a copy or duplicate

of his work. We may learn arithmetic, or the elements of geometry, by continued attention alone; but self-knowledge, or an insight into the laws and constitution of the human mind and the grounds of religion and true morality, in addition to the effort of attention requires the energy of thought. He who would explicate creativity itself requires a thinking audience no less than he who would explicate "moral or religious truth." Whether the critic's "inward experiences" are those of reading or of writing, his reader needs the imaginative power of self-consciousness as a prior condition to understanding imagination itself in rigorous theoretical terms. "The primary facts essential to the intelligibility of my principles I can prove to others only as far as I can prevail on them to retire into themselves and make their own minds the objects of their steadfast attention"

Alone and unbalanced, this requirement provides nothing less than a license for solipsism. Coleridge's marginalia on Schelling document his response to such nonsense. His many explanations of the relation between ideas (the content or object of thinking) and experience reveal how his method excludes the irresponsible and the eccentric. Ideas and laws are correlative terms, strictly defined. An idea is a subjectively-originating set of relations exactly echoed by relations observable in experience.

An idea whose counterpart is a law of the natural world can be "objectively" or physically demonstrated. One who understands will be compelled to assent. An idea whose counterpart is a law of the mind cannot be physically demonstrated, because it has a psychic not physical referent. Furthermore, assent cannot be logically compelled because the spirit itself is essentially free: it cannot be coerced into generating the confirming mental experience. Nonetheless, "At the annunciation of principles, of ideas, the soul of man awakes, and starts up, as an exile in a far distant land at the unexpected sounds of his native language, when after long years of absence, and almost of oblivion, he is suddenly addressed in his own mother-tongue". The imaginative person intuitively and immediately grasps the truth of a valid idea.

Experience confirms—although it cannot demonstrate—the validity of ideas about non-physical realities. For instance, experience illustrates but does not prove the existence of God: "Assume the existence of God,—and then the harmony and fitness of the physical creation may be shown to correspond with and support such an assumption;—but to set about proving the existence of a God by such means is a mere circle, a delusion. It can be no proof to a good reasoned...". Historians face the same situation as theologians: "If you ask me how I can know that this idea—my own invention—is the truth, by which the phenomena of history are to be explained, I answer, in the same way exactly that you know that your eyes were made to see with; and that is, because you do see with them....This idéa, not only like a kaleidoscope, shall reduce all the miscellaneous fragments into order, but shall also minister strength, and knowledge, and light..." As Biographia Literaria explains in detail, the same is true of literary critics. They must illustrate their ideas by particular reference to texts, while yet remembering that criticism is not an empirical science.

Coleridge's intent to make his readers think, to make them engage ideas, accounts for the oft-lamented "digressive" texture of his works, especially the Biographia. In The Friend, he cites Plato approvingly: "'It is difficult, excellent friend! To make any comprehensive truth completely intelligible, unless we avail ourselves of an example. Otherwise we may as in a dream, seem to know all, and then as it were, awakening find that we know nothing'". His "examples" seem digressive in part because they are lengthy and in part because he obviously enjoys them for their own sake; but primarily they seem so because they form no part of an induction. They relate not to each other, but to the ideas they illustrate. They are not particulars from which he generalizes and concludes according to the logical principles governing the use of evidence. The rational and imaginative reader who tries (consciously or unconsciously) to synthesize the anecdotes into a proper induction will be driven to distraction.

Coleridge's digressive surface creates hazards for the well-trained academic reader, but it is easy enough to discern intelligible motives. According to Coleridge, strictly objective observation, abstraction, and generalization are a waste of time, because the number of potentially relevant particulars is nearly infinite. Without a prior idea or, as J. R. de J. Jackson so aptly paraphrases, a good hunch, "the life of an ante-diluvia patriarch would be expended, in merely polling the votes, and long before he could [have] commence[d] the process of simplification, or have arrived in sight of the law".

Hence, for one who possesses an idea, the role of particulars in a discourse can be largely rhetorical. And yet, for Coleridge this role is not merely rhetorical. Because empirical confirmation stands prominently among the tests for a valid idea, Coleridge's particulars are "illuminations" somewhat as Blake uses that word. They comprise one of the major strategies whereby he tries to prevail upon and help his readers to "retire into themselves." As a consequence, one who reads the Biographia ignoring its "digressions" wastes his time no less surely than the empirical patriarch: these illuminations are crucial to the full intelligibility of Coleridge's principles.

To the problems inherent in the strategy one must add the fact that, as Coleridge himself admitted, he tended to offer too many of these illuminations. "[M]y illustrations swallow up my thesis—I feel too intensely the omnipresence of all in each, platonically speaking...".As Dequincy so shrewdly observed, that excess can confuse Coleridge's audience, and obscure the idea he is trying to illuminate:

Coleridge, to many people, and often I have heard the complaint, seemed to wander; and he seemed then to wander the most, when, in fact, his resistance to the wandering instinct was greatest—viz., when the compass and huge circuit by which his illustrations moved traveled farthest into remote regions before they began to revolve. Long before this coming round had commenced most people had lost him, and naturally enough supposed that he had lost himself.... However, I can assert, upon my long and intimate knowledge of Coleridge's mind, that logic the most severe was as inalienable from his modes of thinking as grammar from his language.

In the most practical of ways, then, the "digressive" texture coherently reflects Coleridge's desire to help his readers think about ideas. Even for the most astute reader, the strategy probably fails at times, partly because it so easily breaks down into the excessive indirectness characteristic of Coleridge, and partly because any reader habituated to sustained abstract argument may be annoyed or unduly distracted by the change of pace. But it will fail less often for a reader who understands in advance what Coleridge is doing, and why.

An example of my own will illustrate the character of Coleridge's illuminations. Shawcross dismisses most of chapter two: "the irritability of men of genius" is "a quite irrelevant topic" (BL, 1, 212). Irrelevant to what? To poetic diction? To autobiography? One who accepts Shaw cross's judgment ignores Coleridge's first major account of the psychological consequences of imagination. The "irritability" issue forges the major link between the controversy over Lyrical Ballads and the theory of imagination. Without a firm grasp of this link—and the principal metaphors that subsequently call it into play—one is apt to miss nearly half of what the Biographia says about imagination. Shaw cross's error is provoked by the conclusion of chapter one: a profusion of anecdotes superficially concerned with Coleridge's delight in literary parody.

Yet on a closer look, the "Higgenbottom" sonnets illustrate that the simple style he advocates can easily descend into the trivial. This story, and the related stories centreed on "The Ancient Mariner," reveals Coleridge as a man blessed with a good-humored, common-sense balance both in his theories and in his personality. Chapter two focuses sharply on this question of balance in personality and in literary style as evident in great poets and anonymous critics; it smoothly and coherently develops the argument about diction introduced in the preceding chapter by tracing qualities of diction to an origin in qualities of mind. The discontinuity that misled Shawcross resides only in the illustrations Coleridge uses: the first chapter draws primarily on memories of his youth and early manhood; the second, on his knowledge of literary history and his encounters with contemporary criticism.

Coleridge's desire to make his readers think explains more than the superficially digressive texture of the book. It explains the principal feature of the design: its fusion of personal history and philosophic argument. To understand this design, one must first recognize that the Biographia's autobiography is art—not chronicle. One must distinguish between Coleridge the author, and "Coleridge" the created narrator, the hero of a story that has a coherent development and formal unity that only art can impose upon a real life. Coleridge the author adapts his own history to perfect it as the vehicle for a philosophic inquiry into the distinction between fancy and imagination. The diversity of his own experience supplies the illustrations that progressively reveal the idea of imagination: the stages of the reader's intuition of this idea correspond to the stages of "Coleridge's" intellectual life. As George Watson observes, Biographia Literaria follows "a plan neither narrative nor logical but a disconcerting combination of the two."

Sara and H. N. Coleridge, and J. Shawcross, have pointed out the differences between this created self and the real man; but the necessarily delicate analysis of these differences should be done only by a psychologically astute biographer. For present purposes what matters most is that Coleridge turns the primary autobiographical act of self-creation into a vehicle for philosophic and literary discourse. This central feature of the Biographia's design in part reflects his commitment to the ideal unity of poetry and philosophy. But in part it also solves major practical problems. The philosophic analysis is not complete, yet it presents itself as capable of formal closure. The strictly literary unity of the autobiography seeks to bridge this gap by eliciting the reader's confidence that closure can be attained. The autobiographical narrative, in turn, is often and severely interrupted by abstract logical arguments. But the created self is a metaphysician from boyhood; he incorporates these arguments—not without strain, at times—as accounts of his scholarly endeavors.

The synthesis of autobiography and philosophy serves another, more crucial purpose as well. It helps Coleridge convince his readers of something he cannot prove logically: that the theory of imagination does not lead to pantheism. The created self is deeply religious and repeatedly concerned with the moral consequences of materialist philosophies. We may judge that his theory is wrong, or formulated badly; but we cannot doubt that it is orthodox in intent. For this person, the pursuit of philosophic questions and the discovery of identity have been a single process. For us, the development of a philosophic inquiry, and the growth of the critic's mind, is a single story. Although for practical reasons it is sometimes convenient to distinguish the text as autobiography from the text as philosophic discourse, ultimately these two aspects are inseparable. They are polar opposites informing the Biographia's design; their unifying or originating power is Coleridge's idea of imagination.

Early in chapter nine, one dense footnote focuses many scattered hints that Biographia Literaria stands in deliberate contrast to the common, contemporary form of philosophic writing in England: "... [The word] discourse [as used in Paradise Lost] does not mean what we now call discoursing; but the discursion of the mind, the processes of generalization and subsumption, of deduction and conclusion.

Thus, Philosophy has hitherto been Discursive; while Geometry is always and essentially Intuitive" (BL, I, 109n). Coleridge saw himself as devising a philosophic work that would be intuitive at least in part, because it is impossible to define "imagination" by discursive methods alone. Geometry is always intuitive, in Coleridge's terms, because the geometer seeks to communicate an idea that finds perfect echo in nature's laws. That is, both the idea of a triangle, and a triangle drawn in sand, will have angles whose sum is one hundred eighty degrees. The triangle in sand is not the law, but the symbol of the idea (whose corresponding law is mathematical). Geometry is unique among fields of inquiry because its formulae accurately and simultaneously represent both the idea in the mind and the law in nature. In other fields, discursive formulations are not so perfect. "An Idea, in the highest sense of that word, cannot be conveyed but by a symbol; and, except in geometry, all symbols of necessity involve an apparent contradiction" (BL, I, 100). Except in geometry, symbols can be explicated discursively only as contradictions in terms: the idea can be conveyed symbolically (through some equivalent of the triangle in sand), but the symbol itself is paradoxical. That is why "a great idea can be taught gradually, that is by considering it as a germ which cannot appear at any one moment in all of its force".In most fields, the "great idea" must be taught gradually if it is to emerge from a discursive text.

Except in geometry, then, symbols communicate ideas more adequately than discursive, logical formulations, because a symbol holds together the contradictions that logic can only break apart. A symbol, Coleridge explains, "Is characterized by a translucence of the Eternal through and in the Temporal. It always partakes of the Reality which it renders intelligible; and while it annunciates the whole, abides itself as a living part in that Unity, of which it is the representative". The symbolic relation between Eternal and Temporal, or between God and Man, cannot be defined through logic; and every symbol participates in this relation. In Biographia Literaria, "imagination" is the title of an idea whose symbolic forms include poetry. If we are to grasp this idea, so as to assent or to refuse assent, then the Biographia cannot limit itself to "deduction and conclusion." These cannot render its idea fully accessible to the inquiring reader. These cannot bring the reader to what J. Robert Barth, S. J., calls a symbolic "encounter" with the idea of imagination—not the theory, but the idea that the theory can only describe paradoxically.

Thus, the created self who is not a pantheist, whose history is not quite, Coleridge's own, cannot be regarded as just a device. Like all good metaphors, the created self is neither a lie, nor an ornament. It is Coleridge's response to Hume's demonstration that closed logical systems cannot adequately describe the character of the mind, or the nature of reality. Any orderly explanation—any human act creating order—is grounded in an act of faith. This is not directly nor necessarily a faith in God, but rather a faith in the possibility of order and knowledge that for many individuals has culminated in religious experience. The modern philosopher, by whatever particular title he or she is known, must offer more than just the logical proofs we have come to distrust as necessarily partial. The philosopher must also evoke our faith in the order he has discovered. He or she must appeal not only to logic, but also to imagination, to our intuitive (rather than sensory) relation to the world around and within us. If something in our souls does not "awake and start up," we distrust the theory even before we have detected its error.

Coleridge responds to Hume's challenge by creating "Coleridge" as a gradually-emerging symbol of the fusion of actual human experience and rigorous philosophic inquiry: questioner and question are subjective and objective poles of the unity that is the examined life. As Barth explains, "the making or perceiving of a symbol is for Coleridge a kind of act of faith. It is meant to evoke a response of the whole person, in faith, hope, and love, it is a commitment of self to someone other than one's self." "Coleridge's" history is designed to elicit our faith in the idea "imagination" even before rigorous proof has been established. We are first to trust the man, and then his theory. The coherence of the man's life, and the validity of the theory, are two forms or manifestations of a single integrity. As Richard Mallette argues, "the narrator's personality...steps forth at every junction to shape and mould our experience.... The total effect...lends to the Biographia an imaginative unity that would otherwise be lost in a work that attempts to survey the horizonless landscapes of literary theory, practical criticism, philosophical disquisition, and personal autobiography."

But put questions of consent aside for now: the theory remains inaccessible until one understands this character "Coleridge." The Biographia's speaker is in part an ironic self-parody by a man who knew himself all too well. The speaker is garrulous, he is eclectic and distractable, he is learned in the "obscure" and the "useless." His manner of telling reflects these qualities: his story turns freely, abruptly, from one thing to another. Only after several readings does one perceive the inexorable, orderly momentum of the whole: the impromptu is never random. The speaker's freely associational leaps are exquisitely calculated to insist, over and over again, that the thinker finds unity within apparent diversity. Minor issues reflect major questions because all significant problems are ultimately interrelated. Gradually one discovers the central concerns that unite and direct these associational shifts.

With that recognition comes another: Coleridge is an exceptionally witty, playful writer. As he develops the contrast between his speaker and anonymous critics, he transvalues the elements of his self-parody: the speaker is eclectic and antiquated only to those enamored of a facile, inconsistent, popularized Lockeanism. His diffident double negatives point emphasis to issues too profound for this degraded group to recognize. His unexpected leaps land him always in the heart of the matter. One who reflects carefully on the abrupt shifts will always find his way to basic questions about fancy and imagination.

The strategy is at once arrogant and entertaining: it is an intriguing style occasionally carried too far. Even the best reader may be occasionally confused, not by the subtlety of the relations per se, but by the unpredictability that the strategy generates. As Jackson explains, "the reader is not permitted to know where he is being taken, or why he is being taken there; by obscuring the end in view, the intricacies of the way are allowed to become confusing and even irritating."I suspect that Coleridge's judgment may have been overwhelmed at times by the potent combination of his anger at anonymous criticism, and his delight with parody. And perhaps, as in any autobiography, fiction blurs with fact: both the author and the speaker are "responsible" for the reader's periodic bewilderment.

Although this "speaker" clearly lacks the full artifice of Browning's speakers, he is far more deliberately a construct than the speakers of most autobiographies. Coleridge's created image may quite aptly resemble himself, but "he" also serves such definite ends so well that analysis requires some means of distinguishing creator from creation. Coleridge's celebrated introspective powers should lead us to expect such delicate complexity in his intellectual autobiography. Richard Haven suggests that Coleridge was "a born psychologist trying to write as a metaphysician," that "Coleridge's philosophy should be seen not as an unsuccessful attempt at a logical analytical system, but, like his poetry, as a projection, an 'elaborated transformed symbol,' of his own psychological experience." Much recent scholarship has stressed Coleridge's extraordinary fidelity to his own moral and intellectual experience, fidelity sustained despite the enormous difficulty of reconciling the diverse elements into an intelligible whole. Autobiography is the natural vehicle for such a mind, because it allows him to present experiences that illuminate major speculative insights, but it does not require formal logical unity. The autobiography of a richly imagined "self" can make arguments Coleridge wants to make, and yet bear up under the strain of the gaps that emerge when these arguments are separated from their autobiographical enactment.

Although Coleridge's later works are generally clearer, and more skillfully persuasive, Biographia Literaria remains the central text for the study of Coleridge's prose. As James Olney explains, in Metaphors of Self: The Meaning of Autobiography,

... a man's life work is his fullest autobiography [.]... When, moreover, a man writes, in addition to his other works, something that is confessedly autobiographical... then we may expect to be able to trace therein that creative impulse that was uniquely his: it will be unavoidably there in manner and style and, since autobiography is precisely an attempt to describe a lifework, in matter and content as well. A man's autobiography is thus like a magnifying lens, focusing and intensifying that same peculiar creative vitality that informs all the volumes of his collected works; it is the symptomatic key to all else that he did and, naturally, to all that he was. Coleridge achieves what Olney describes even more fully than conventional autobiographers: his intellectual autobiography portrays not the man, but the man thinking. In Biographia Literaria one meets face to face the thinker whose methods inform all the other works: he who believes his intuitions and then seeks confirmations; he who attributes to others his own ideas, and uses others' texts without attribution; he whose penetrating syntheses revise the habitual patterns of understanding. Both Coleridge's vitality and his peculiarity are most evident in Biographia Literaria: one who grasps the design of this most rewarding, most frustrating text will more easily follow Coleridge's track anywhere else.

Coleridge's desire to make his readers think about genuine ideas underlies the Biographia's digressive texture; his fusion of autobiography and philosophy serves to illuminate and to validate the idea "imagination." These features of the design are a coherent, intelligible response to problems arising from the unity of ideas and laws. But this does not explain—nor explain away—all the difficulties impeding the Biographia's readers.

The design is also characterized by peculiar or inadequate transitions for which there is often no defense. Prudent authors of difficult arguments take particular care with transitions. Their transitions integrate parts, subordinate parts to whole, and repeatedly orient the reader within sequences of patterns large and small. Such transitions separate form from content by commenting on the form as such; this helps the reader to monitor his comprehension of major structures. Coleridge's argument is exceedingly difficult, but his transitions are hardly prudent. Often they are cryptic, just a sentence or two catapulting us into strange new terrain. More often, they seem to estabish only a whimsical, undisciplined, associational flow. The speaker seems to ramble unbearably, as so many readers have complained.

In part, I grant, Coleridge's transitions are simply awful. They suggest an incredible insensitivity to audience. Perhaps he so quickly penetrated to fundamental issues in his own reading that he failed to perceive the needs of blunter minds. A person as well read and as astute as Coleridge himself might have little trouble recognizing the unifying issues, but the rest of us are too apt to discover the central points only by wandering in circles. In other works, Coleridge seems to realise the useful (albeit mechanical) function of the conventional transition: major divisions commonly begin by commenting on the form as such. These transitions are often clumsy and intrusive because the essential argument usually precludes tidy summary. But they help, if only in assuring the reader that the author is executing a deliberate plan. This is no small matter: without confidence in the ultimate coherence of the whole, one would not expend the effort Coleridge's prose requires.

Yet the famous Coleridgean carelessness does not explain everything. It is also clear that the autobiographical fiction of Biographia Literaria makes it difficult for Coleridge to write transitions that maintain our sense of order, unity, and progression. Had Coleridge continually specified the relations between philosophic and autobiographical movements, and between the parts of these and the idea of imagination, then the autobiographical fiction would have become palpably fake. No real life is so direct, so fortuitously ordered. Coleridge's solution is to orient the reader primarily to the life and times of "Coleridge" rather than to the evolving definition of imagination: as he explains, "I have used the narration chiefly for the purpose of giving a continuity to the work" (BL, I, 1). But this solution has its awkward moments: in the opening lines of chapters nine and fourteen, for instance, the abrupt return to autobiography may disorient even the most careful reader.

His fusion of narration and philosophy also creates problems. The definition of imagination does not unfold in a direct, clear, logical fashion, so the reader's progress and his locale within this definition cannot be sketched briefly. Furthermore, Coleridge cannot easily separate form and content by commenting on the form as such: his dual design enacts its principal idea to a far greater extent than one commonly finds. The form is to make us think; the content is to tell us what thinking is—which is to say, to render us conscious of what we are doing as we ponder the issues Biographia Literaria raises.

Kathleen Wheeler explores this self-reflexivity by analyzing passages that refer both to the theory of imagination and to the experience of reading the text itself. She argues that German Romanticism provides both a motive and a rationale for such writing. So does the tradition of spiritual autobiography. For these passages to function as they must, the work as a whole must systematically lead the reader to reflect on them both objectively, for what they say, and subjectively, for whence they arise. The work does so, I contend, by engaging our sympathies with both the madcap adventures and the scholarly endeavors of its most colourful speaker.

Transitions cannot locate the reader within this process, because there is little reason to assume that all readers of the same chapter are at the same "point" in understanding the idea of imagination. Like the youthful speaker himself, the new reader may not fully appreciate the implications of certain experiences or discoveries. When Coleridge's transitions fail, it is often because he presumes that more is understood at a given point than an actual reader is likely to understand, even after several attentive readings. Many subtle but quite adequate transitions will fail, of course, for the reader who assumes that there can be no unity within the diversity of Biographia Literaria.

Although Coleridge's design impedes conventional transitions, it encourages—and perhaps requires—the unity that metaphors can provide. The cinque-spotted water insect, for instance, belongs to an elaborate pattern of imagistic reference to imaginative synthesis. Light and water recurrently signal the rhetorical power of imaginative works. These metaphors, and others, both signal and generate the complex unity of Biographia Literaria's many discrete issues. They establish its character as an essentially imaginative—not logical—discourse because they simultanously develop the speaker and elucidate his ideas. Some have condemned Coleridge's densely imagistic passages as pious or poetic excrescences in what ought to be sober philosophy. But to ignore these lines is to mutilate both the text and its ideas.

How does one read a text of such complexity? What methods are adequate? Arthur Symons makes the basic point: "one who is ceaselessly attentive will be ceaselessly rewarded." 31 But even reasonably ceaseless attention reaches a point of diminishing return: by creating a form nearly as difficult as his ideas, Coleridge risks losing our interest in both. But recognizing the Biographia's duality, recognizing its mediation between philosophy and narrative, enormously simplifies the reader's task. From the character of the design it follows that each chapter must be read both as a stage in the speaker's intellectual development, and as a stage in the effort "to effect...a settlement of the long continued controversy concerning the true nature of poetic diction; and...to define...the real poetic character of the poet, by whose writings this controversy was first kindled" by demonstrating that fancy and imagination are "two distinct and widely different faculties" (BL, 1, 1-2, 60). Only if each part is read in both ways will all the relations among parts become evident. Without such bifocal vision, the whole remains fragmentary and, at times, rudely incoherent. But distinction is not separation: philosophic and autobiographical aspects provide objective and subjective accounts of a single idea that cannot be fully defined from either perspective alone.

Yes, Biographia Literaria is difficult—but it is not impossible. Its real flaws do not amount to so much when one considers the clarity, the acuity, and the grace that are generally evident. The reader's greatest burden is imposed not by these flaws, but by the complexity of Coleridge's thought.

Coleridge wants his readers to think, and so he writes in ways designed to encourage and to require that effort.

Q6. Discuss Coleridge's art in prose

Or

Q. Critically analyse Coleridge's Biographia Literaria.

Or

Q. Can Coleridge's best writing be read as a kind of dramatic monologue in prose, a mimetic representation?

Coleridge's prose is notoriously hard going. Yet we accommodate to it; we develop some of the conscious and unconscious skills Coleridge demands of his readers. In The Design of 'Biographia Literaria,' I argued that it helps to categorize the kinds of difficulties we have in reading Coleridge's prose. 1 The most substantial problems are those created by the complexity of his ideas. Other problems arise from the ideal of discourse toward which he worked, the ideal of engaging us as whole moral beings. And finally, major problems arise from the habitual ways in which Coleridge managed—and mismanaged—the basic tasks of a writer. Yet reading Coleridge becomes much easier going if we know how he handles transition, emphasis, unity, definitions, and the like. I propose to examine three elements of Coleridge's writerly habits: his definitions, the way he structures or develops arguments, and the way he situates himself historically.

Coleridge's definitions always ground themselves in extensive metaphor patterns. The famous definition of imagination in chapter 13 has been examined and cross-examined for generations, but the metaphors anchoring this definition have had far less attention. Most of these metaphors arise when the Biographia contrasts imaginative people and imaginative works with the character and the work of fanatics. A crucial early point is the definition of fanaticism in chapter 2. The German word for "fanaticism," Coleridge explains, "is derived from the swarming of bees... The passion being in an inverse proportion to the insight; that the more vivid, as this the less distinct; anger is the inevitable consequence" (1:19). This link between violence and blindness repeatedly comes into play as Coleridge describes the controversy over Wordsworth: "the acrimonious passions, with which the controversy has been conducted by the assailants" provide one good estimate of the intelligence and insight of these critics (2:7).

Anonymous criticism perfectly satisfies the early definition of fanaticism: "These facts, and the intellectual energy of the author [Wordsworth], where it was outwardly and even boisterously denied, meeting with sentiments of aversion to his opinions, and of alarm at their consequences, produced an eddy of criticism, which would of itself have borne up the poems by the violence, with which it whirled them round and round" (2:7). Note how the image of swirling upward, tornado-like, repeats the movement of swarming bees: the philosophic critic's activity is later compared to a windmill's (2:88). Anonymous criticism is blasphemous, personal and "popular" (1:41-42; 2:211); philosophical criticism is principled, systematic, and noble (1:44; 2:87-89). True poets and philosophic critics are genial in both senses of that word: geniuses, to the extent that their imagination supplies genuine insight; and genial because their personalities are literally above the petty, personal, and political squabbles of lesser minds.

Anonymous critics admire an equally decadent modern poetry that offers only "the glare and glitter of a perpetual, yet broken and heterogeneous imagery" (1:15). Such glare and glitter differ sharply from the illumination Wordsworth provides: "the original gift of spreading the tone, the atmosphere, and with it the depth and height of the ideal world around forms, incidents, and situations, of which, for the common view, custom had bedimmed all the lustre, had dried up the sparkle and the dew drops" (1:59). Wordsworth's Descriptive Sketches, Coleridge explains, announced "the emergence of an original poetic genius above the literary horizon" (1:56). Citing Wordsworth approvingly, Coleridge asserts that he knows how to

add the gleam,
The light that never was, on sea or land,
The consecration and the poet's dream.

Changed light and cleansing water repeatedly characterize the renewed vision genius provides.

Coleridge characterizes modern literature with images of hollow and false things; genial works are described with images for the imaginative acts they both require and elicit. Moderns are fraudulent:

> In the days of Chaucer and Gower, our language might (with allowance for the imperfections of a simile) be compared to a wilderness of vocal reeds, from which the favourites only of Pan or Apollo could construct even the rude Syrinx; and from this the constructors alone could elicit strains of music. But now, partly by the labours of successive poets, and in part by the more artificial state of society and social intercourse, language, mechanized as it were into a barrel-organ, supplies at once both instrument and tune. Thus even the deaf may play, so as to delight the many.... Hence of all trades, literature at present demands the least talent or information; and of all modes of literature, the manufacturing of poems. The difference indeed between these and the works of genius is not less than between an egg and an egg-shell; yet at a distance they both look alike. (1:25-26)

What once demanded divine favour now can be manufactured—apparently—without the least exercise of skill. Such productions lack the truth and permanence of great literature. Coleridge emphasizes this permanence in his first "critical aphorism" in chapter i: "not the poem which we have read, but that to which we return with greatest pleasure, possesses the genuine power, and claims the name of essential poetry" (1:14). His image for this permanence and value is an act:

> [In "a just poem,"] The reader should be carried forward, not merely or chiefly by the mechanical impulse of curiosity, or by a restless desire to arrive at the final solution; but by the

pleasureable activity of mind excited by the attractions of the journey itself. Like the motion of a serpent, which the Egyptians made the emblem of intellectual power; or like the path of sound through the air; at every step he pauses and half recedes, and from the retrogressive movement collects the force which again carries him onward. (2:11)

This "pleasureable activity" is the working of secondary imagination, earlier imaged by the water-insect:

Most of my readers will have observed a small water-insect on the surface of rivulets... and will have noticed, how the little animal wins its way up against the stream, by alternate pulses of active and passive motion, now resisting the current, and now yielding to it in order to gather strength and a momentary fulcrum for a further propulsion. This is no unapt emblem of the mind's self-experience in the act of thinking.... (In philosophical language, we must denominate this... the Imagination. But in common language, and especially on the subject of poetry, we appropriate the name to a superior degree of the faculty, joined to a superior voluntary controul over it.) (1:85-86)

This alternately progressive and retrogressive movement images the imagination for us just as the mechanism of the barrel-organ or the hollowness of an eggshell images literary fraud. On the one hand we have an image for a producing faculty; on the other, for a useless product. Lacking the productive faculty, moderns provide only a false and mechanical version of the real thing. Their readers are "carried forward" passively, as perhaps on a whirlwind; readers of genuine works travel under their own power, enjoying that activity as such.

Coleridge subsumes all these metaphors, and the realities they name, in two accounts of the poet as a landscape. The false poet is an irritable character because "men, whose dearest wishes are fixed on objects wholly out of their own power, become in all cases more or less impatient and prone to anger.... Even as the flowery sod, which covers a hollow, may be often detected by its shaking and trembling" (1:25). Recall that the

Biographia is to define the trunk and roots of the distinction between fancy and imagination (1:64). The roots of such "shaking and trembling" poetic flowers are not solidly anchored. The careless observer might not recognize the probkm at first; but one need not be much of a gardener to realise how poorly such "flowers" will survive the vicissitudes of an entire season—or the tribulations of the years.

All that is false and perverse and ephemeral about such works is captured by Coleridge's most daring description of anonymous critics as ones "whose intellectual claims to the guardianship of the muses seem, for the greater part, analogous to the physical qualifications which adapt their oriental brethren for the superintendence of the Harem" (1:42). Decadent modern literature and its advocates are but a perversion of mankind's most valuable productive powers: "poetry is the blossom and fragrancy of all human knowledge, human thoughts, human passions, emotions, language" (2:19). Contrast the description of Wordsworth:

> "The soil is a deep, rich, dark mould, on a deep stratum of tenacious clay; and that on a foundation of rocks, which often break through both strata, lifting their backs above the surface. The trees which chiefly grow here are the gigantic black oak; magnolia magni-flora; fraxinus excelsior; platane; and a few stately tulip trees." What Mr. Wordsworth will produce, it is not for me to prophecy; but I could pronounce with the liveliest convictions what he is capable of producing. It is the First Genuine Philosophic Poem. (2:128-29)

This is not to be read as an allegory, wherein specific poetic abilities correspond to various geological layers; it is to contrast with the metaphors describing all that is hollow and ephemeral in modern literature. Even the flower image reappears, in the magnolias and tulip trees. The lines from Milton in chapter 13 also stand in context:

> O Adam, One Almighty is, from whom
> All things proceed, and up to him return,
> If not deprived from good: created all,
> Indued with various forms, various degrees

Of substance, and, in things that live, of life;
But more refin'd, more spirituous and pure,
As nearer to him plac'd, or nearer tending,
Each in their several active spheres assign'd,
Till body up to spirit work, in bounds
Proportion'd to each kind. So from the root
Springs lighter the green stalk, from thence the leaves
More airy; last the bright consummate flower
Spirits odorous breathes. Flowers and their fruit,
Man's nourishment, by gradual scale sublim'd,
To vital spirits aspire: to animal:

To intellectual!—give both life and sense,
Fancy and understanding; whence the soul
Reason receives, and reason is her being,
Discursive or intuitive. Par. Lost. b.V.

The movement from rocks and clay to magnolia magniflora claims that Wordsworth's genius mirrors God's creation. He is the mirror and the lamp, the one whose genius illuminates reality for the rest of us precisely because he exists in such perfect harmony with it.

Throughout the Biographia one finds an ongoing tension between the vivid particular world—"the table itself, which the man of common sense believes himself to see"—and the transforming power of imagination— "'The light that never was, on land or sea'" (1:179, 2:124). The fanatic's inability to sustain both poles of creativity reveals—perversely—how genius functions. These complementary accounts are integrated by metaphors that we ignore or slight at our peril because Coleridge's idea of imagination is most lucidly explained not in the abstraction of the "philosophical chapters" but here, in this rich and lively polemic. Chapters 12 and 13 do little more than summarize abstractly what is elsewhere more clearly stated.

Reading Coleridge's prose comfortably also demands sensitivity to the sometimes eccentric ways in which he structures his arguments. At his best, as Bishop C. Hunt, Jr., so aptly explains, "what we might call the 'dramatic' element in philosophy, the process of search and its written reenactment, assumes a larger significance. Much of Coleridge's best writing can be read as a kind of dramatic monologue in prose, a mimetic representation, like Wordsworth's philosophic poetry, of the mind in the act of thinking something through." 4 This drama may in part arise from the dictating of the Biographia. Most transcribed tape-recordings of conversations are astoundingly incoherent because the transitions and connections are lost. Such connections in Coleridge's prose are feeble beyond reason, given the rigor of his thinking. Consider as well DeQuincey's account of how radically fragmented Coleridge's conversation could be even for those present. And yet DeQuincey also says, "I can assert, upon my long and intimate knowledge of Coleridge's mind, that logic the most severe was as inalienable from his modes of thinking as grammar from his language."

Even when Coleridge seems to turn most distractedly—like the White Rabbit to zip past and disappear—at such times he is probably doing one of a finite number of reasonable things which he (quite unreasonably) does not signal to us in advance. Let me sketch three of these: exploring grounds and presuppositions; defining a new perspective on an old issue; or turning back to an issue now that its grounds are clear and various perspectives have been considered. These strategies supply the "dramatic element" that Hunt described. This is far from a complete list, but for present circumstances it is enough.

Chapter 2 analyses the supposed irritability of men of genius, a subject Shawcross dismisses as "quite irrelevant" (1:212). Yet this chapter first and most richly contrasts the genius and the fanatic. Shawcross is misled by Coleridge's failure to specify the connection between chapters 1 and 2, but the connections are nonetheless there. In chapter 1 Coleridge describes his study of Bowles, and his attempt to understand the basis of genuine literary value—the difference between "the Greek Poets from Homer to Theocritus inclusive; and still more... our elder English poets from Chaucer to Milton" and such moderns as Erasmus Darwin (1:14). He also contrasts his own education with that which produces the kinds of minds that become anonymous critics. The chapter ends with a funny little anecdote concerning literary parodies.

There are two sorts of connection between chapters 1 and 2. Locally, or superficially, Coleridge goes from wondering why anyone would think him angered by a parody to wondering why people always think poets are irritable. This sort of connection might be no more than Coleridge's capacity for being "solicited" away from the virtuous path of his argument by a handsome new notion. But he is not wandering off track: he is delving beneath the state of affairs just described. He explores the basis of the difference between great poetry and modern trash, and correlatively between great criticism and anonymous criticism. The transition functions as if an imagined interlocutor interrupted Coleridge to ask, "Why is this so? Why did that fellow think you would be so angry?" In answering Coleridge refuses to be "solicited:" he takes his interlocutor to the grounds of what he has been describing throughout chapter 1.

Knowing Coleridge's abiding interests helps us follow such transitions because we know where Coleridge is apt to turn to answer such a question. But why are the transitions so poor? Coleridge's use of his notebooks demonstrates how much he relied on set pieces, and yet any set piece would need minute revision to allow Coleridge to explore the grounds he wants while maintaining reasonable unity in his "local" topic. Such revisions are tedious. Rather than submit to such "professional" drudgery, Coleridge unduly relies on metaphor patterns to hold things together. His habit of dictating and the conversational quality of his prose are again relevant: in conversation it is easy to observe how people relate their abiding interests to the topic at hand, and it is easy to follow such integrations. It is for whatever reason far more difficult in prose, and more difficult yet when the abiding interests are as complex as Coleridge's.

Coleridge also loses readers at the beginning of chapter 5. Chapter 4 ends with the proposal that he investigate the seminal grounds of the distinction between fancy and imagination so as to resolve the controversy over Wordsworth and poetic diction. Chapter 5 ties immediately to that by delving under it, to the more comprehensive issue of mental activity and levels of will. The chapter begins, "There have been men in all ages, who have been impelled as by an instinct to propose their own nature as a problem, and who devote their attempts to its solution. The first step was to construct a table of distinctions, which they seem to have formed on the principle of the absence or presence of the Will" (1:65-66). If you were not lost at chapter 2, as of course many are, then the "problem" of our own "nature" might seem a reasonable enough reference to the fanatic/genius contrast. But even those who follow to this point are following tentatively, because what ought to be a crucial connection deserves greater emphasis than Coleridge provides. Because the emphasis is missing, we intuitively downgrade the connection, thereby revising our nascent sense of what the Biographia is "about." Almost any reader, then, is likely to throw up hands in despair as chapter 5 gets underway. What has Mackintosh to do with anything? Is the "men of all ages" business just a historical flourish to introduce him?

Coleridge might have made a coherent transition in several ways. Since he attended Mackintosh's lectures in 1800, he might have represented them as one of the series of "influences" which he describes in the first four chapters. Hartley certainly was a major influence who would fit very nicely in that catalogue. He could also improve the transition with a simple bit of emphasis: specify that he will resolve the controversy and explore the roots of imagination and fancy by considering the levels of will, which men of all ages... etc. But Coleridge's prose is remarkably without any such aids to orientation. We are to see where we are going by looking about us as we progress. We lose our way here because Coleridge assumes the continuity of his discourse and supplies only the facts. To the extent that we are influenced by the powerful tradition that assumes the discontinuity of Coleridge's discourse, we are blind to relationships which are tolerably obvious but not specified.

(And let me note in passing that this chapter opening is a crucial point for discovering or destroying the unity of the Biographia generally, because it is profoundly important to keep in mind the short table of will here provided. Coleridge refers to it, adds to it, argues with other philosophers about details of it, all as if it were written on a blackboard behind him.)

But what is going on with Mackintosh, after all? We who were comfortable with critics and poets are now rightly annoyed. And, of course, Coleridge does this to us all the time. At such points of apparently massive dislocation, Coleridge is introducing a new perspective, or a new set of perspectives on the issue at hand. The new perspective here is philosophy: Coleridge cannot explore the roots of imagination without talking about the nature of the mind itself. Fair enough. This reaching to first questions and fundamental issues is part of why we value Coleridge so much as a thinker.

But he does more than this. He adds to the contrast between true poets and false poets, or that between anonymous critics and philosophic critics. He adds a parallel distinction between false philosophers and true philosophers and a parallel problem to the evil politics of poetry in a pernicious politics of philosophy, which must in modern times be addressed to the multitudes rather than to an intellectual and moral elite. Later he does this again, drawing the same contrast between fanatic political writers and genial ones (i.e., Burke, and also Coleridge himself in the Morning Post). And the politics of philosophy all comes to bear when Coleridge's imaginary friend dissuades him from publishing chapter 13. In short, he is both providing a new perspective—philosophy—and continuing to elaborate the preceding set of issues. His ultimate point is to argue for the cultural importance of secondary imagination, wherever it is manifest. But he does not, as more linear minds might, separate explaining what imagination is from explaining why it is so important. Byron's wicked lines are marvelously apt.

Coleridge's transitions also disorient us when he attempts to close one of his "huge circuits," as he does for instance at the opening of chapter 14. Transitions like these demand a close review of the beginning of that circuit to locate the issues and metaphors that will reappear. Such a comparison of chapters 1 through 4 with 14 to 16 uncovers both new emphases and entirely new issues. Central among these new issues is an argument about the nature of language and the relation between language and consciousness. These are evident in the opening chapters as well, with their concern for purity and precision of diction; but at this point they come richly to the fore.

When Coleridge reaches back like this, we are less seriously disoriented than at other eccentric transitions, because repetition is so rare in his prose that it collects its own emphasis. There is another reason as well. Working as I have with Coleridge's organizing habits has made me scrupulously aware of my own modes of organizing. And at one point I realised—perhaps you will too—that I used such huge circuits in the classroom all the time. A bright student asks a complex question, or reveals a historical or philosophical lacuna that has to be filled. One stops to provide the necessary information or analysis, then takes a deep breath and returns to the original topic at hand, a topic that has now been to some extent transfigured. It is as if the energy of that inhalation is to lift the class with me to see all the transfigurings the new ideas provide.

Coleridge supplies this energy too, or this guidance, in the extraordinary density of his prose at such closings-of-circuits. The connections to the origin of the circuit are so many and so potent that they easily force an entire rereading of the chapters to which they refer, which in turn triggers other rereadings and reconsiderations, in what strikes me as a quintessentially Coleridgean way. Although no doubt a master of the fragment, perhaps even of the aphorism, Coleridge is simultaneously a most sustained and systematic thinker. He expends little energy on the niceties of composing, and especially on the small mechanical tricks of transition and structure; but the essential continuities are so obsessively, overwhelmingly present that either we lose our way in the tangle of connections, or we let the text engage us in a closely directed reflection upon the topic at hand. We, too, then become "minds in the act of thinking something through."

Finally, allow me to sketch an issue which deserves major new study: how Coleridge situates himself historically. We know that Coleridge saw himself not as an original and innovative thinker, but as one of a substantial and ancient community of thinkers working on closely related issues from roughly the same presuppositions. This idea of an intellectual community underlies not only the famous plagiarisms, but also the seldom-examined problem of how Coleridge changes the texts he incorporates. It also underlies both the anachronism and the teleologism of his version of Western intellectual history. Coleridge's idea of history, in short, is elaborate and complex to an extent seldom properly understood and never adequately defined.

Coleridge's idea of history shapes his texts in innumerable ways, three of which are simple enough to be briefly summarized. First, references to the ancient community of thinkers commonly define major suppositions and starting points. For instance, chapter 5's reference to "men in all ages":

> There have been men in all ages, who have been impelled as by an instinct to propose their own nature as a problem, and who devote their attempts to its solution. The first step was to construct a table of distinctions, which they seem to have formed on the principle of the absence or presence of the will. Our various sensations, perceptions, and movements were classed as active or passive, or as media partaking of both.... Our inward experiences were thus arranged in three separate classes, the passive sense, or what the school-men call the merely receptive quality of the mind; the voluntary; and the spontaneous, which holds the middle place between both.

But it is not in human nature to meditate on any mode of action, without enquiring after the law that governs it; and in the explanation of the spontaneous movements of our being, the metaphysician took the lead of the anatomist and natural philosopher. (1:65-66)

Coleridge then argues that perception is not passive (as the tradition seems to suggest). Perception, he argues, is a form or mode of the spontaneous, because "the will and reason are perhaps never wholly suspended" (1:77). This eventually leads to his definition of primary imagination as "the living Power and prime Agent of all human Perception" (1:202). The voluntary quality of the mind Coleridge calls "fancy" (1:87, 202). The faculty of the spontaneous is the imagination, although "in common language, and especially on the subject of poetry, we appropriate the name to a superior degree of the faculty, joined to a superior voluntary controul over it" (1:86).

These distinctions and definitions are not quite the commonplaces Coleridge suggests, and not quite original either. He is on the one hand referring to a rich tradition not widely known by his English contemporaries, and on the other asserting that a rich and ancient tradition leads directly to the argument he wishes to make. The truth of the matter is not wholly in either hand. To discover and define that truth, to understand the argument about perception and imagination that Coleridge makes in Biographia, we must watch carefully what happens when Coleridge invokes "tradition".

Coleridge also situates himself historically by citing from his "ancient community"—often by plagiarizing. Even when these passages are verbatim transcriptions, Coleridge usually changes what he takes by placing it in a new context that inevitably changes how we read it. Given the extent to which he demands a scrupulous attention to his own contexts, he may have written with great awareness of how he was forcing a rereading of what he incorporated. That might be part of why he did not rewrite sufficiently to preclude the charge of plagiarism: perhaps he is quite in control of the tensions thereby created.

But often he does not simply incorporate. Often there are major interpolations, or major redefinitions of key terms preceding the plagiarized passage. These changes are sometimes just ignored, or worse yet condescendingly brushed aside as the "mere" Christianizing of ideas or systems otherwise too bold or too free for what is then characterized as a rigidly orthodox personality. All such settings-aside are monumentally mistaken: these changes commonly reflect or share in the central issues of the argument Coleridge is making. If we are to understand that argument in all its complexity, these changes need to be mapped in just as much detail as the plagiarisms themselves.

I am not a comparative literature scholar; I cannot offer this mapping with the necessary detail and precision. But let me offer a couple of interesting examples. In chapter 12, in the famous "range of hills" passage, Coleridge compares consciousness to a stream. At the conclusion of this passage, he underscores the metaphor: "That the common consciousness itself will furnish proofs by its own direction, that it is connected with master-currents below the surface, I shall merely assume as a postulate pro tempore" (1:167). Later, then, Coleridge incorporates a considerable passage from Schelling that talks about the "direction" of a point in motion. Coleridge is using the passage to say something different from what it says in Schelling, because what for Schelling is mathematics, for Coleridge is metaphor.

Or again, Coleridge appends to thesis VI a connection between the Schellingian "I am" and the traditional, Biblical, divine "sum quia sum" (1:183). It is a mistake, a profound and serious mistake, to blur the difference between Schelling's "I am" and Coleridge's "great eternal I am." Let me explain why. The real gap in the Biographia is not in chapter 13; it is between thesis VI and its Scholium. The essential connection that Coleridge cannot define to his or our satisfaction is the relation between human cognition and the knowledge and power of God. In the Biographia, Coleridge asserts that through faith we have immediate knowledge of both a personal God and a real world of physical objects immediately known. The

Logosophia will explain how this can be so (it is necessarily indemonstrable, given its origin in faith and free will). He draws this thorny issue into the Biographia in order to ground the moral value of the highest exercise of secondary imagination, "the vision and the faculty divine." Coleridge forthrightly acknowledges that his position can never be proven without losing its moral force "It could not become intellectually more evident without becoming morally less effective." Schelling, on the other hand, is performing a sophisticated maneuver in a highly technical kind of epistemology. The central issue for Coleridge is not epistemology but theology. To deny the difference is to become blind to the foundation of Coleridge's argument about the cultural centrality of literature and literary criticism.

Coleridge's idea of history also shapes his texts through his proper use of quotations. Whether separated from his text as headnotes and epigrams, or whether embedded as citations that are properly identified as such, these passages usually summarize and thereby emphasize central aspects of the issue at hand. Because Coleridge's prose provides so few structuring elements, these citations deserve and reward thoughtful attention. Chapter 13 begins with three citations, one from Milton, one from Leibniz, and one from Synesius. Chapters 12 and 13 have been written about more than any other two chapters in the Biographia, yet I have never seen a discussion of these three headnotes.

Milton's lines trace the relation from God, or pure knowing, to creation. This is the subjective pole of philosophy, as defined in chapter 12 (1:176). I quoted these earlier, but they are worth rereading.

> O Adam, One Almighty is, from whom
> All things proceed, and up to him return,
> If not depraved from good: created all
> Such to perfection, one first nature all,
> Indued with various forms, various degrees
> Of substance, and, in things that live, of life;
> But more refined, more spirituous and pure,

As nearer to him plac'd, or nearer tending,
Each in their several active spheres assign'd,
Till body up to spirit work, in bounds
Proportioned to each kind. So from the root
Springs lighter the green stalk, from thence the leaves
More airy: last the bright consummate flower
Spirits odorous breathes. Flowers and their fruit,
Man's nourishment, by gradual scale sublim'd,
To vital spirits aspire: to animal
To intellectual!—give both life and sense,
Fancy and understanding; whence the soul
Reason receives, and reason is her being,
Discursive or intuitive.. Par. Lost. b.V.

The movement from rocks and clay to magnolia magniflora for an English audience. God creates and orders the universe, maintaining both our being and the being of the world around us, and thereby guaranteeing or grounding the possibility of our knowing that world. Human knowing is the most nearly divine of human powers.

There follows a passage from Leibniz that travels in the opposite direction, from matter to mind. This is the objective pole of philosophy, as defined in chapter 12 (1:175).

If indeed corporeal things contained nothing but matter they might truly be said to consist in flux and to have no substance, as the Platonists once rightly recognized.... And so, apart from the purely mathematical and what is subject to the fancy, I have come to the conclusion that certain metaphysical elements perceptible by the mind alone should be admitted, and that some higher and, so to speak, formal principle should be added to the material mass, since all the truths about corporeal things cannot be collected from logistic and geometrical axioms alone, i.e. those concerning great and small, whole and part, shape and position, but others must enter into it, i.e. cause and effect, action and passion, by which the reasons for the order of things are maintained. It does not matter whether we call this principle of things an entelechy or a power so long as we remember that it is intelligibly to be explained only the idea of powers."

The lines from Leibniz recapitulate the major conclusion of chapters 5 through 9: we cannot explain the real world and our knowledge of it by assuming that the mind is passive in perception. The lines say more than this, of course, more that also involves the significance of Kant for the Biographia's argument and for Coleridge's position generally. But the essential thrust here is the inadequacy of materialism as a philosophy, a central and recurrent concern throughout the first volume: "all the truths about corporeal things cannot be collected from logistic and geometric axioms alone."

The lines from Synesius which follow have been variously translated; I follow George Watson.

I worship the hidden order of intellectual things.
The Mean dances and is not still.

And this is the imagination, a spontaneous act, a dancing, which at its basic level is perception, but at its highest level is art. Great poetry grounds itself on close and shrewd perception, on a renewed vision of the beauties around us; but it can do so only because it sees within this material world the translucence of the divine. Coleridge argues so bitterly with Wordsworth's emphasis on observation because it seems that Wordsworth undervalues or fails to recognize the necessary priority of the mind who is observing.

Why does Coleridge do this? Why does he supply citations where we surely expect a firm, lucid summary, emphases duly allotted? No doubt there are layers and categories of reasons why; let me select just one. Coleridge's entire argument about the value of Wordsworth's poetry, about the value of great poetry generally, and therefore about the character of imagination and fancy depends at last on Coleridge's assertion that it is contranatural to doubt the existence of a real world correspondent to sense, and to doubt the existence of some divinity (1:133-36). Grant this, you grant him everything; deny this, and the Biographia offers only a muddled Shellingeanism and some interesting comments on poetry and a good deal of inconsequential rambling. Faith is at once the strongest and the most fragile of bases. Given that it is impossible to solve the metaphysical problem of mind and matter, faith is as good an answer as we are apt to find. And yet a systematic structure built on faith is fragile indeed: the best answer we are likely to find is nonetheless far less certain than anyone would like. The best guide, then, is tradition. I may err, you may err, but if the One Almighty exists, then surely over time the truth will emerge from the ancient community of those who think about such issues with open minds and hearts. Coleridge cites rather than summarizes to bolster his argument, to persuade us that the "unscientific" argument he is making has its own power, its own prestige, its own history.

And maybe he was lazy, or maybe he was crazy, or maybe he hated revising. Maybe he synthesized with such ease that he thought he was being quite clear. It's an unanswerable question. The best we can do, I propose, is to discover Coleridge's eccentricities and understand them. If we understand his habits as a composer of arguments, we will follow those arguments more easily. We will see his place in history more accurately, and we will learn from his genius more fruitfully. He is a difficult writer, but he is not impossible; and above all, his prose works are worth the effort they demand.

Q7. What role does Schelling play in Coleridge's Biographia Literaria?

Or

Q. Coleridge makes use of biographical genre as the framework for his ideas about literature, ethics, and aesthetics. Do you agree?

Walter Benjamin, one of the sharpest critics of the twentieth century, has convincingly argued that the crucial concept in German Romantic criticism is that of reflection. Reflection can be conceived as 'the thought of thought' or as a 'movement' of self-consciousness. In reflection (or speculation) the early German Romantics sought an Archimedic point at which they could articulate the difficult relationship between freedom and necessity, existential finitude and infinite thought. "Romanticism", Walter Benjamin writes, "based its theory of knowledge on the concept of reflection, because this concept guaranteed not only the immediacy of knowledge, but also, and in an equal measure, the peculiar infinity of its process." Generally speaking, this statement could be considered adequate for early German Romanticism, but I feel that the same cannot be said about English Romanticism, or at least not without further qualification.

During the first Romantic generation in Great Britain, the catchword for poetry and criticism, as we all know, was instead that of imagination. Now then, what exactly is the difference between reflection and imagination? To put it in rather simple terms, we could say that there is a sort of relationship of inverted symmetry between them: reflection is a centripetal movement, the thinking subject which turns upon itself; and inversely, imagination is a centrifugal movement, an external projection of forms which were first perceived and then modified by the unconscious memory. Reflection is to imagination what the introvert side of the mind is to the extrovert side. In the case of either poetry or criticism, these two mental attitudes are fused together but usually one of them plays the dominant role. In view of this opposition, we can make a distinction between the self-absorbed spirit and the ecstatic spirit: Wordsworth versus Coleridge, for example. Or between a reflexive, concentrated kind of poetry and a diffuse, enthusiastic kind: Holderlin compared to Shelley, for instance. And also, we might be able to make a distinction between a reflexive and an imaginative brand of criticism. The criticism of Fredric Schlegel, for instance, would belong to the first type, and that of Coleridge (in spite of all its philosophical bias) would belong to the second. The difference between these two critical attitudes summarizes the different bias of German and British criticism from Romanticism to the present day: the former is more theoretical and systematic, the latter more practical and empirical. Here I shall discuss the mutual bearing of both Early English and Early German Romanticism, with particular attention to the crucial role that Coleridge played in transferring German ideas to the English speaking literary community. This argument is far from new. But I shall also attempt to demonstrate how , in his Biographia Literaria , Coleridge, by narrative slight of hand, bracketed off the speculative foundation of his literary hermeneutics, and in so doing, how he set the biographical model as a hidden basis of Anglo-American literary criticism, sharply distinguishing it from German criticism and continental criticism to our days.

The hero of the Biographia Literaria , as we all know, is the ideal poetic character , of which the historical persona Wordsworth is the only privileged mask. Coleridge makes use of biographical genre as the framework for his ideas about literature, ethics, aesthetics, etc. ; in other words, he uses biography to support his critical speculation on world order and the poetic language that expresses it. In reality, he adopts the basic ingredients of Myth-making, insofar as it is a way of understanding the world, i.e. naming things and retracing of their genealogies. What this amounts to is that Coleridge, in an autobiographical mode, fulfills the dream of German Romanticism, that of constructing a mythology of the future, albeit only in fragments and always unfinished, as the last horizon of modern historical consciousness, the last hope of grasping a far too quickly changing world.

Seen from this perspective, the Biographia Literaria can hardly appear as a failure, despite all of its preposterous philosophical claims and conceptual incoherence; and the same can be said of all of Coleridge's immense fragmentary critical production and his entire literary career. Perhaps instead, both the success and the limitations of the Romantic dream to create a new speculative mythology and a narrative of free, imaginative, historical self-consciousness will appear to us through the "fictional" character and destiny of Coleridge himself, as is shown in his Biographia Literaria.

The Romantic-Idealistic project of historical (or mythological) self-founded consciousness is in fact essentially contradictory, but no less meaningful or dramatic therefore in the events of modernity. And this means that its significance can be perhaps better grasped even in its complete reversal, that is in the bankruptcy of historical consciousness and in the whimsical revisionism which characterize this post-modern age, this "terminal moment " of Western literary civilization. This disruption in the logical linear narrative, which is now currently manifested in literary, historical and fictional (not to speak of multimedia) texts, began at the end of the eighteenth century with the Romantic eschatological world-histories and the subsequent idealistic dialectics of history. This sort of heart fibrillation in the historical subject, which has led to present day postmodern apathy of memory and imagination, can be paradoxically seen exemplified in the career of this most imaginative poet and critic, Coleridge.

The Ancient Mariner, his most effective poetic mask, is a compulsory witness to his own personal story and to modern history as a whole: he represents historical self-consciousness caught up in the vortex of its own reflection and to which every inaugural, and therefore unjustifiable, gesture (as the killing of the albatross) must necessarily appear guilty. This modern wanderer, man without a country, consciousness without a fixed centre, can do nothing else except evoke again and again the consequences of that first gratuitous act whose meaning now eludes his understanding, leaving only a compulsion to repetitive story-telling, which can reenact the experience but not retrieve its meaning.

This same experience of the loss of meaning in and throughout history, which started with the Romantics, and was later referred to by Nietzsche as "the historical malady, grew worse and worse with time, until eventually could appear to Stephen Dedalus, the prototype young artist of the early twentieth century, as the "nightmare to try to awake from".

In the representation of the modern self-alienated literary subject an important role is played by Coleridge's Biographia Literaria whose initial nucleus seems to go back to an early biographical project of Coleridge and Wordsworth (1800-02) which consisted of a "theory of biography as a form of poetry and criticism" ; and which in turn mirrored the Jena Romantics' and especially the early Schelling's project of a mythology as the ultimate end (the ideal realization) of philosophy and art. Thus, we could say that the structure the Biographia Literaria inherited from that first early combined effort of the two poets is a "biographical intensification" of both nature and the spirit together.

Here we can find a clear example of the Romantic project to establish a self-sufficient historical-biographical subject and of its failure as a result (if nothing else) of the contradictions inherent in autobiography as a literary genre which involves two radically different metaphors: those being the world as a book and the world as an organism ; the tension between these two metaphors foreshadows the conflictual space of Western historical consciousness in its last phase, insofar as it is the combined effect of literary historiography and biotechnological fiction ; this same conflict has been echoed throughout the twentieth century in the paradoxical convergence of the philosophies of life and the hermeneutics of writing.

We all know that Wordsworth is the hero of the Biographia Literaria , but in addition to him there is another important, although less visible, protagonist, and this is Schelling. His influence on Coleridge was a good deal more important than that of other German philosophers and men of letters he came into more or less direct contact with, and this I believe had a decisive impact on the format and meaning of the Biographia Literaria.

In the introduction to his Philosophy of Art (1803-04) Schelling in fact writes that the "doctrine of art constitutes, within the boundaries of philosophy, a more restricted sphere in which, with greater immediacy, we can contemplate the eternal, in a so-to-speak visible figure". And he adds that in the philosophy of art we contemplate "first of all, not art as such, as a particular thing in itself, but [...] the universe in the form of art [...] as a representation of the infinite"; just as philosophy, he continues, "manifests the absolute in the archetype, so art manifests it in the image which is a copy of it". The privileged place that art holds in Schelling's thought during his Jena years, is quite well-defined in his System of Transcendental Idealism , where we can discern a line of thought that leads straight to the regions of mythopoeia. It was precisely this sort of essentially art-oriented philosophy that attracted the visionary poet and aspiring philosopher Coleridge.

Among the general principles of Schelling's philosophy of art, there are some of particular interest for our purpose: above all, there is the concept of the infinite and various affirmations of God in all things, what Schelling calls "the in-formation [or imagination: Einbildung] of his infinite ideality in reality as such" and which makes up eternal nature. Schelling also states that the in-formation of the ideal in the real, or the form of being affirming itself as a whole, is equal to matter ; ideality, on the contrary, is the affirming principle that dissolves all fixity, and is like light ; whereas the living organism constitutes a kind of synthesis, or rather an indifference , between these two, objective and subjective, poles. The declination of the ancient Greek metaphysics of light comes about here in the shape of the organism (and is driven by the organic metaphor). Something similar can be said of Coleridge's "primary imagination", which is the virtue of ideal light belonging to nature and corresponding to the Einbildung of Schelling.

Organism is to nature as a work of art is to the whole human spirit. It embodies the essential indifference (or initial communion) of all possible distinctions: of infinite and finite, of abstract and concrete, of theory and practice; "this indifference", writes Schelling- "is represented in the ideal world through art. In fact, in itself art is neither mere acting nor mere knowing, but an acting wholly imbued with science, or, vice-versa, a knowing that has become wholly acting". We find these principles echoed in the English Romanticism manifesto, the Preface to the Lyrical Ballads , which announces the roles that Coleridge and Wordsworth will respectively play in this work in a reenactment of the eternal comedy of the universal and the specific, and which Coleridge will bring back up in his autobiography. In the project of the lyrical ballads, writes Coleridge, "it was agreed that my endeavours should be directed to persons and characters supernatural or at least romantic; yet so as to transfer from our inward nature a human interest and a semblance of truth sufficient to procure for these shadows of imagination that willing suspension of disbelief for the moment, which constitutes poetic faith.

Mr. Wordsworth, on the other hand, was to propose to himself as his object, to give the charm of novelty to things of every day, and to excite a feeling analogous to the supernatural, by awakening the mind's attention to the lethargy of custom, and directing it to the loveliness and the wonders of the world before us". The spirit and tone of this re-evocation that Coleridge makes in regards to the ideal roles of the poet, which he and Wordsworth had intended to play in the Lyrical Ballads, contain an essential feature of Romantic poetics, that being a continuous conversation between finite and infinite which we see systematically displayed in Schelling's philosophy of art.

"The precise meaning of the excellent German word Einbildungskraft [poetic imagination]," Schelling goes on to say, "is the power of uni-formation (Ineinsbildung), on which in reality all creation is based; [it...] is the power of individuation, that is, the creative power". This is most likely what Coleridge calls "esemplastic power", or secondary imagination , which is the principle of art. Schelling, during the first part of his career, which is the part that interests us here, considered the universe as an absolute work of art, and with regard to which the individual work of art makes up a second nature (heterocosmos): "with this principle", he announces, "the construction of the general idea of art has been accomplished. Art, in fact, is shown to be the real representation of the forms of things as they are in themselves, and thus of the forms of the archetypes." We can certainly notice here that Bildung also means "education, transmission of knowledge", similar to the way the word paideia does in Greek and so, the concept of Einbildungskraft has not only to do with poetics, but also with ethics and politics; which involve the functions of the preacher and poet-prophet so dear to the hearts of the English Romantic poets, starting with Coleridge and Wordsworth. Coleridge's entire body of work (both poetry and criticism) could even be seen as an immense series of glosses on this German word " Einbildungskraft" , which has no exact equivalent in English. In this perspective, we can perceive Coleridge as an epigonic rhapsode intent on reuniting the scattered limbs of our literary civilization under the heading of creative imagination; this effort stood at the heart of Romanticism as a mode of subjective impassioned historical conscience, whose shortcomings eventually resulted in the rise of Modernism as the cult of impersonality and the pathos of the artistic form which exorcises the nightmare of history.

In order to understand Romantic poetics and also its influence on the twentieth century, Schelling's open and dramatic idealism is, in my view, of greater help than Hegel's dialectics and aesthetics. And for Coleridge in particular Schelling was a powerful influence in helping him develop both critical ideas and poetic images. In fact, no aesthetics with such comparable mythological horizons is to be found in the legacy of Kant, Fichte or Hegel. And it was this sort of aesthetics that theoretically minded poets like Coleridge badly needed.

In Schelling we can also find the source of another of the most well known of Coleridge's discriminations: that between fancy and imagination. Schelling in fact defines "the imagination as what the productions of art are conceived and shaped in; but fancy is what contemplates them from the outside, which, as it were, projects them out and in this sense also represents them [...] and thus fancy is the intellectual intuition of art." But several important distinctions in Coleridge's literary criticism - signally the one mentioned here above and the one between primary and secondary imagination - are in fact more or less exact replicas of Schelling's propositions. This is not to say that Coleridge is a plagiarist, which is not my aim here to demonstrate, but it is matter of fact.

Let us start now at the beginning of the Biographia Literaria and follow its development in some detail, in order to clarify the whole issue. At the beginning of his Biographia Literaria , Coleridge in fact insists on the vicarious role he intends to assign to narration as opposed to speculation and the statement of values. He is quite explicit on this point: "it will be found that the least of what I have written concerns me personally. I have used the narration chiefly for the purpose of giving a continuity to the work, in part for the sake of the miscellaneous reflections suggested to me by particular events, but still more as introductory to a statement of my principles in Politics, Religion, and Philosophy, and an application of the rules, deduced from philosophical principles, to poetry and criticism. But of the objects, which I proposed to myself, it was not the least important to effect, as far as possible, a settlement of the long continued controversy concerning the true nature of poetic diction; and at the same time to define with the utmost impartiality the real poetic character of the poet, by whose writings this controversy was first kindled, and has been since fuelled and fanned." As a matter of fact, the poet he is speaking of is Wordsworth, the avowed hero of the Biographia Literaria. But in its opening passage Coleridge has already posed to us the entire question of narration and reflection, a relationship which, outside the philosophical realm, creates a space for the modern essayist genre. Here, Coleridge also announces what his basic genre and topic are, namely biography and the poetic language. From this introductory passage we can already infer what the ideal terms will be wherein Coleridge's entire work is going to develop: the tale of a single intellectual life as a token of the development of the universal logos.

The peculiar nature of the poetic character (as instanced by Wordsworth's persona) is presented as the meeting place of thought and feeling, of the natural and the ideal, the objective and the subjective, which is perfectly in line with Schelling's thought. What most struck Coleridge at his first encounter with Wordsworth's poetry was in fact avowedly "the union of deep feeling with profound thought; the fine balance of truth in observing, with the imaginative faculty in modifying the objects observed ; and above all the original gift of spreading the tone, the atmosphere, and with it the depth and height of the ideal world around forms, incidents, and situations, of which, for the common view, custom had bedimmed all the lustre, had dried up the sparkles and the dew drops." Wordsworth stands for the ideal poet and we can notice here the typical biographical procedure of Coleridge's criticism building up the ideal character and poetic language around the concrete figure of his friend.

In the whole first part of his "autobiography" (chapters V-IX), Coleridge, unsatisfied with English philosophical empiricism and psychological associationism from Locke through David Hartley, explains how he began to question himself, in an exquisitely Kantian style, about the possibilities of a critical philosophy and the a priori conditions of experience and how eventually he turned to the newly-founded German idealism, particularly the Platonic branches of it, which he found most to his liking. Coleridge was therefore asking himself if "a system of philosophy, as different from mere history and historical classification" (IX, 71) were to be possible: a question that would fascinate and obsess him throughout his life. Let us then follow a little further the lead of his autobiography, in an attempt to discover the connection between thought and narration, not only at a thematic but also at a structural level. It seems to me that the various ways in which narrative form and conceptual system are here related form the nucleus of Coleridge's criticism as a whole. But this relationship, if we look closely, is circular, going from the empirical chronicle of personal events to their underlying rationale, which in turn is brought back to its historical (or mythological) foundation ; this remains forever unspeakable and waited for, in the way quite common to all the providential universal histories of the late German Enlightenment and early Romantic periods. Their typical route is from personal story to logical system, and then back to universal myth. For example, according to Kant, Schiller and other late 18 th century thinkers, natural man after the Fall, in his role in the universal pattern of history, must patiently work for the final Revelation of his character and true ethical state, even though these are forever to come. Coleridge is not inventing anything new here in regards to the German Romantics' eschatological pattern of history, but he does bring it all back around to the foundational element of biography.

The rather excessive recurrence of the spiritual organic metaphor in Coleridge's texts has often been emphasized (Abrams 1971, pp.95ff), perhaps a little bit less so has the recurrence of its counterpart, the equally important "mechanic" metaphor of the "letter": in fact, Coleridge takes the literacy of Romantic universal histories and of the idealistic philosophy of history quite literally. On the one hand, he gives all the workings of the mind and imagination a growing plant metaphor, so that he deserves I. A. Richard's witty remark that with Colerigde, knowledge becomes growledge ; on the other hand, however, Coleridge also takes the idealistic spiritual history (Geistgeschichte), foreshadowing the coming of a final golden age, back to its narrative and literary basis (the genre of literary biography). So he drastically deflates and personalizes the universal spirit of German philosophy, offering his own life as a concrete token of a general quest for the role of poetry and of the ideal poetic character in our culture. Coleridge thus performs a sort of chemical decomposition of the autobiographical self that lies at the heart of the Romantic project of man's aesthetic and political education, which in the end should lead to a happy vision of the complete human character.

Auto - bio - graphy: if we take the etymological roots of this genre name at their face value, we can trace a few basic features of the Romantic world view: the idea of a reality founded on the reflexive knowledge of the "I think"; the predominance of organic metaphors in thought and expression; a pervasive literacy that haunts both the poetic and the philosophic mind, and more so when they try to contemplate an original prelapsarian state of nature or a final ethical state of man in an ever deferred future.

Q8. Coleridge's Biographia Literaria is the attempt to trace a pattern in the development of British poetry and philosophy. Comment

Or

Q. Discuss the role of two protagonists in the Biographia Literaria: Wordsworth and Schelling.

Coleridge's Biographia Literaria is the attempt to trace a pattern in the development of British poetry and philosophy, and to found a system of critical thought by reflecting on a single "poetic" life. In fact this effort perfectly mirrors (in the biographical perspective) Schelling's metaphysics aiming to unite spirit and nature in an artistically orientated world history. The place that both Coleridge and Schelling give to poetry as the combined end of history and philosophy is identical; but in the case of the former the emphasis is biographical, whereas it is speculative in the latter. However, if we compare them, we are left with the impression of "a terrible symmetry" between the two projects: the system of transcendental idealism and the literary biography. And it is here that we should begin a correct evaluation of Coleridge's criticism. If by contrast the beautiful architecture of Schelling's conceptual system helps us to see the clumsiness and shortcomings of Coleridge's speculations, then the narrative plot of the biography brings to light the precarious ground of the idealistic system ; its entire being from beginning to end, as it were, fictional.

Let us look then at some stages of Coleridge's poetical-philosophical Bildungsroman, in search of its constitutive aporias, starting with the question of the possibility of philosophical history: "I was for a while disposed", he writes "to answer the [...] question in the negative, and to admit that the sole practicable employment of the human mind was to observe, to collect, and to classify." At the beginning of his intellectual career Coleridge, in the wake of British 18 th century empiricism, was dubious about the possibility of a deductive philosophical system, and yet he felt a kind of repugnance "against this willful resignation of the intellect";

then gradually he came to the conclusion that sensism and empiricism inevitably lead to the radical skepticism of Hume, so that Coleridge eventually turned towards the newly emerging German Idealism. During this account of his philosophical education, while he is speaking of his interest in the German mystic Jacob Boehme, Coleridge at a certain point confesses that he is using the exact words of a "contemporary writer of the continent" (referring in fact to a text of Schelling's from 1806), but he assures us that the ideas there expressed were something that he had independently thought of long before. Later on he actually meets Schelling face to face, where he writes: in Schelling "I first found a genial coincidence with much that I had toiled out for myself, and a powerful assistance in what I had yet to do.".

Now and again in his autobiography, Coleridge comes out with passionate defenses against any possible accusations of plagiarism: "indeed all the main and fundamental ideas, were born and matured in my mind before I had ever seen a single page of the German Philosopher; and I might indeed affirm with truth, before the more important works of Schelling had been written, or at least made public". Coleridge attributes the occasional similarities between him and Schelling to the fact that both of them belong to the same philosophical tradition stretching from the Neo-Platonist and the mystics to Kant; but then he vehemently protests against wishing to "enter in a rivalry with Schelling for the honors so unequivocally his right" as being one of the founding fathers of German Idealism. Coleridge declares that he will instead be content with making Schelling understandable to his fellow countrymen and using him as best he can.

Thus he concedes that, in whatever way his works be found the same as or similar to the works of Schelling, the worth should by all means "be attributed" to the latter; provided that he, Coleridge, not be accused of "ungenerous concealment or intentional plagiarism" for any possible lack of precise reference to the German philosopher; and that instead this "general acknowledgment" of his would suffice once and for all. And, in fact, he is convinced that the truth is "a divine ventriloquist" and therefore it is of little importance to him "from whose mouth the sounds are supposed to proceed, if only the words are audible and intelligible." By examining Coleridge's whole argument we could easily conclude that the defensive strategy here and elsewhere employed denotes a certain "anxiety of influence" regarding Schelling, and that it almost amounts to an avowal of the heavy debt Coleridge has contracted with the German thinker. But were we to stop at such an ascertainment, even though it would be completely correct to do so, the question of the role of Coleridge as mouth-piece of German Idealism in English Literature would not yet be posed in its whole scope.

In his autobiography, the chapter on Coleridge's philosophical education is followed by another, the tenth, "of digression and anecdotes, as an interlude preceding that one on the nature and genesis of the Imagination or Plastic Power", which indeed begin with an impressive statement: "'Esemplastic'. The word is not Johnson's, nor have I met with it elsewhere. I constructed it myself from the Greek words, eis en plattein , to shape into one ; because, having to convey a new sense, I thought that a new term would both aid the recollection of my meaning, and prevent its being confounded with the usual import of the word, imagination." All very well, but the word is also a splendid English translation of the term " Ineinsbildung " which is used by Schelling to denote one of the key concepts of his " Philosophy of Art ", so this time we cannot grant Coleridge our "willing suspension of disbelief". All the following chapters in the biography, up to chapter XIII, are then a series of digressions and deferments of the long-awaited and never before heard explanation of how the creative imagination works, which, alas, we shall never be given.

At a certain point, however, Coleridge declares himself ready to discuss "the nature and genesis of imagination" and here he immediately stakes a distance from his friend and rival Wordsworth who, in a recent preface to his Poems from 1815, wrote - contrary to the beliefs of Coleridge - that fancy and imagination can both be traced back to the "aggregative and associative" capacity.

And so here we come to the stumbling block, the well-known central chapter (the XIII) of the Biographia Literaria that deals with "the imagination, or esemplastic power"), and which Coleridge introduces placing two quotations side by side, one from Milton, the other from Leibniz (both about the unity and transcendence of being), almost as though he wanted to appease himself to his two tutelary gods, the poet and the philosopher, for the arduous task awaiting him. For the moment Wordsworth must exit the stage to which he will make a triumphant return in the following chapter. Now Coleridge has to move across the dangerous ground of metaphysics, so he lets the "transcendental philosopher" have his word, which sounds ominous indeed: "grant me a nature having two contrary forces, the one who tends to expand infinitely, while the other strives to apprehend or find itself in this infinity, and I will cause the world of intelligences with the whole system of their representations to rise up before you."

The antithetical nature he is speaking of and the metaphysical dualism he is giving voice to are the same as those we find in the young Schelling (especially during his Jena years), whose philosophical system is in fact held up on the principles of polarity and analogy, the complementary possibilities of nature and spirit, and the dialectic of the unlimited and the limited. The shadow of Schelling is lying behind the two antithetical forces from which Coleridge hopes to deduce the workings of the creative imagination.

There are in fact two protagonists in the Biographia Literaria: Wordsworth and Schelling. One is allowed to come to foreground almost in flesh and blood but the other lies hidden behind the scenes, projecting his powerful shadow on the whole work. What I mean here is that the development of Wordsworth's poetic language, laid out in the Biographia Literaria, amounts to a concrete narrative manifestation of Schelling's system of thought which on principle is waiting for an artistic fulfillment. Between the concrete and the abstract, the specific and the general, stands the poetic subject (author, theme and language), the real protagonist of the

Biographia Literaria. The growth of the poet's mind can in fact be seen as represented by the intersection of several opposites: universal/particular; thought/expression; imagination/fancy; Schelling/Wordsworth.

The Biographia Literaria is constructed on a whole converging series of exemplary and unsystematic approximations around the unattainable centre where the ideal character of poet-philosopher should reside. But this centre is shifting and mobilized, an empty space, a transcendental metaphor with an untouchable spiritual tenor, instead of which aptly appears a typical vehicle of literary communication: the providential letter of a friend of Coleridge's, a sort of fundamental writing that stands in place of the long waited for deduction of creative imagination; this narrative expedient constitutes a surprising and very effective example of what much later the French philosopher Jacques Derrida would call écriture: a sort of ontological pre - text that melds both history and biography as side effects of an omnivorous textuality.

In some respects Coleridge, this half-successful poet and philosopher, is way ahead of the outlooks and outcomes of our late modernity when he offers us the quintessence of the Romantic mind trying to trace the by now hopelessly literary, modern historical consciousness back to the springs of Greek and Jewish mythology. Like many of Coleridge's unfinished projects, the Romantic dream of an ethical state and of a religious-humanistic education was condemned to fail from the start because it made up part of the more powerful Enlightenment project to dominate and exploit nature by technical-scientific means. Romanticism represents perhaps the last great convulsion within the project of modernity as a whole that is the paradoxical attempt to bring all technical and literary achievements of our civilization back to their natural and mythical sources.

If we now return to the Biographia Literaria, we find Coleridge intent at his supreme trial, the deduction of the workings of the imagination from the original dyad (the infinite and the limit) of Platonic and Schellingian origin; but his speculative powers now fail him, and he is compelled to introduce a dues ex littera in order to disentangle himself from, if not philosophically, at least normatively, the net that he has caught himself up in. In fact, as an unexpected gift of providence he receives a letter from a wise friend who prudently advises him to put off his much-awaited demonstration of creative imagination until a better time.

His fidus Ecathes , endowed with "practical judgment [...] taste and sensibility", confesses to Coleridge that the same puzzling impression left on him by the imagination chapter could also be left on other readers. The effect of its novelty, his friend writes, was so strong as to create in him a sense of bewilderment, followed by a shock of recognition ; he felt as if he had been left all alone in a Gothic cathedral, in an uncanny play of light and shadow, and, with a shiver of terror, he had come upon the portraits and busts of great men he knew, but who now appeared to him with almost alien expressions and different proportions to those he was used to."In short", he writes in the letter, "what I had supposed substances were thinned away into shadows, while everywhere shadows were deepened into substances".

The scenario is no doubt Gothic, and yet we ought to be able to recognize here a revision of Plato's myth of the Cave. And just to place the whole story in a Neoplatonic setting, Coleridge's friend confesses to the poet that he found the essay on the imagination obscure and suggestive like an "Orphic tale". Nevertheless, he swears, he looks forward to the "publication of the great work on constructive philosophy", in a future more propitious occasion. With regard to the effect it could have on the readers of the Biographia Literaria, Coleridge's friend however strongly discourages the poet from publishing the chapter on imagination, and advises him to save it for the "announced treatises on the Logos or communicative intellect in man and deity".

Nothing more than this, and yet nothing less either. But his friend also adds some other more practical considerations regarding reader expectation (after all, the title does not indicate a treatise on metaphysics), and the length and the excessive cost of the text, which all sound totally convincing.

At this point of Coleridge's biography, however, it appears that the existence of the philosophical deduction of imagination has been taken for granted, as if this fundamental hidden essay had already been written. Referred to since the beginning as a future event yet to happen, this act of writing has by now already taken place. We are thus to face this conspicuous absence at the very core of the Biographia Literaria which as a result still gives both conceptual and narrative impulse to the whole work.

This functional empty slot in the biographical narrative allows for all the imaginative and speculative shifts in the Biographia Literaria, as well as (ideally) in the whole of Coleridge's criticism and poetry. Starting with his getting out of debt to Schelling and to the conceptual foundation of his own criticism, Coleridge thus manages to solve his problems for the moment, can finally return to the declared hero of the Biographia Literaria, the ideal poet Wordsworth, and finally accomplish his narration.

This deferment, removal and substitution of the deduction of creative imagination should not surprise us much however, when even in the economy of Kant's three Critics the place of the imagination between the island of the intellect and the open sea of the practical pure reason is just as problematic. Kant has left his heirs to deal with this problem. In fact, imagination is the creative principle, not only of Romantic poetry but also of idealistic philosophies of history and of Romantic universal historiography as a whole. But the actual basis of all of them (poetry, philosophy and history) is the literacy of our Western civilization, which starts with the story of the Fall of Man in the Holy Scriptures. At the roots of all our hermeneutic efforts there lies still the old question of the letter of Mosaic Law in its problematic but lively relation with the spirit of providential history.

Coleridge wisely followed the advice of his friend, and left us with this curious child of his own mind, the Biographia

Literaria , which was to influence the whole of English literary criticism, and even to define the range of its possible branches and languages from the 1800's down to the present day. Having spared us the conceptual deduction of the universe, Coleridge leaves us with a milder surrogate: literary criticism. He only grants his reader the naked definition of imagination and then divides it, still meticulously following Schelling's distinction between Einbildung and Ineinsbildung , into primary and secondary (natural and artistic) creative power, in one of the most famous passages in English literary criticism:

The Imagination then I consider either as primary, or secondary. The primary Imagination I hold to be the living power and prime agent of all human perception, and as a repetition in the finite mind of the eternal act of creation in the infinite I am. The secondary Imagination I consider as an echo of the former, co-existing with the conscious will, yet still as identical with the primary in the kind of its agency, and differing only in degree, and in the mode of its operation. It dissolves, diffuses, and dissipates, in order to create: or where this process is rendered impossible, yet still at all events it struggles to idealize and to unify. It is essentially vital, even as all objects (as objects) are essentially fixed and dead.

Then he compares imagination to fancy, again sticking to Schelling's terminology:

Fancy, on the contrary, has no other counters to play with, but fixities and definitions. The fancy is indeed no other than a mode of memory emancipated from the order of time and space; while it is blended with, and modified by that empirical phenomenon of the will, which we express by the word Choice. But equally with the ordinary memory the Fancy must receive its materials ready made from the law of association.

So here, fancy is defined in a language which recalls both the tradition of English eighteenth century associations from Locke to Hartley, and Schelling's definition of Phantasie in his Philosophy of Art. After this conceptual tour de force , Coleridge returns to more earthly occupations, the critical analysis of poetic language in general, and more specifically that of Wordsworth, which is the most clearly-defined subject of the Biographia Literaria. Coleridge will devote almost all the remaining chapters of his book to this topic, which is something I will not discuss here. Finally he closes his work by defending himself against accusations of being a potential heretic and "devoted to metaphysics", and with a full-scale act of adoration of the "great I AM "which is also "the filial Word" , the auto-bio - graphical subject which lies at the heart of the idealistic philosophies of history and of the poetics of Romanticism.

In the Biographia Literaria, Coleridge paradoxically begins by bracketing off this autobiographical subject - explicitly making it known that he does not want to write about himself but about the ideal poet- and ends with an act of adoration of the infinite "I am" and of "the filial Word that re-affirmed it from eternity to eternity, whose choral echo is the universe." In the middle of his text we find a significant absence of rational foundation of imagination and of the poetics of history, these being substituted by a providential letter. In Coleridge's Biographia, all at once we uncover the conceptual disorder of its author, his uncommon critical insight, his occasional guilty conscience and his moral enthusiasm; but, above all, we find a moving testimony of the ideal poetic character who has taken upon himself the arduous task of becoming the subject of his own history. Well beyond its influence on Anglo-American literary criticism, which at present appears to be exhausted, this book leaves us with the continuing problem of the emergence of a testimonial (poet-logical) voice in historiography, a problem which we can perhaps now better understand from our privileged viewpoint of the crisis of Western literary civilization.

As various critics (Benveniste, Barthes, Foucault, Derrida, and H. White among others) have recently observed, in the twentieth century the act of writing has become both radically intransitive and pervasive and it has, as it were, withdrawn from the world and closed itself up. But this comes about not as a result of some previously hidden, inborn virtue of language which only now, in its final apocalypse, reveals the intrinsic textuality of the world as the ineluctable fate of the West; the meaning and function of literature become instead a real question in the twentieth century as the effect of the growing influence of the mass-media over the printed page. The hypotheses of the absolute textuality of the world are only symptoms, rather than diagnoses, of our predicament in the global village, in the age of the "world become image".

From this turning point of literary civilization, we are likely to see the subject of Romantic history in a much clearer light than before and in all its epoch-making impact. The absolute I think, being the transcendental foundation of history, appears now in its intrinsic literary essence as that which has long since actually been in Western culture: the absolute I write, the subject of all written enunciation. This subject was variously declined and inflected by the polyphony of the emerging media of the twentieth century until it finally appeared to the reflective minds of our thinkers as the preternatural power of language or text that writes us. In the twentieth century, Coleridge's friend (his deus ex litera) eventually became impersonal and the act of writing went from being transitive to being intransitive. But it is precisely this crucial shift in emphasis from 'subject-maker of writing' to 'object-vehicle of writing', being a distinctive feature of late modernity, which is portrayed as a narrative stratagem in Coleridge's Biographia Literaria: it deeply informs and supports Coleridge's work and sets the ideal horizon line for the last revolution of the modern literary subject, before its presumable transformation into something else.

Chapter 9

Critical Essays

COLERIDGE'S THEORY OF CRITICISM

In treating of Coleridge as literary critic, there is no alternative but to speak either very briefly or at considerable length. The latter is here impossible. All that can be done, therefore, is to indicate the main avenues which his criticism opened out.

The only written monument of his critical work is that contained in Biographia Literaria (1815–17), and in a short series of articles contributed to Farley's Bristol Journal a year or two earlier (1814). All else has to be gleaned from the very imperfect reports of his lectures, recorded by Collier, Crabb Robinson and others. These lectures, of which there were, in all, some dozen courses, were delivered, partly in London partly at Bristol, between the years 1808 and 1819. Their avowed subjects, apart from a course on the history of philosophy (1818–19), were, mainly, the drama in general, or Shakespeare and Milton. But Coleridge was never the man to be bound down by a syllabus; and his audience had, on occasion, to bear, as best they could, a defense of school-flogging, an attack on "the Lancastrian system of education" and other such irrelevancies, when they had come to hear a discourse on Romeo and Juliet. Yet, in spite of these glaring faults, the lectures were seldom worthy both of their subject and of their author. And, with the written pieces, they form a body of work such as makes an epoch in the history of

English—it would hardly be too much to say, of European—criticism.

Coleridge concerns himself not only with the practice of criticism, but, also—perhaps, by preference—with its theory. On both sides, he offers the sharpest contrast with the critics of the century, and, not least, of the generation, preceding. The Wartons and Hurd, no doubt, stand apart from the men of their day. In sentiment, they rebel against the canons of the Augustans; and, so far, they are at one with Coleridge. But they were content to defend their instinctive judgments on purely literary grounds, and made no attempt to justify them on more general principles. Indeed, they seem never to have suspected that their revolt against the established taste in poetry carried with it a revolt against the established system in philosophy. Coleridge, on the other hand, was philosopher just as much as poet. He lived in the full tide of a philosophical, no less than a poetic, revival. He was himself among the leading figures in both. He had, therefore, on both sides, a far richer store of material to draw from than had been open to the earlier rebels. And it was the first instinct of his nature to weave, or force, every side of his experience into a consistent whole

At the first step, he rules out the assumption, which, from Horace onwards, had wrought such havoc in criticism, that the object of poetry is to instruct; or, as a less extreme form of the heresy had asserted, to make men morally better. That this may be an effect of poetry—of much that is noblest in poetry—he is not in the least concerned to deny. That however, is no more than an incidental result. And the true end, or function, of poetry is to give immediate pleasure: pleasure, he explains in a somewhat disconcerting addition, "through the medium of beauty."

This may not carry us very far. But, at least, it serves to warn us off from the wrong road, and to set our feet at the beginning of the right one. More than this: by further additions and modifications, Coleridge so expands his original doctrine as to bring us considerably further on the path. In the first place, the assertion that the pleasure which imaginative art aims at giving is wrought "through the medium of beauty," however much it may check the logical flow of the argument, at least serves to enforce the truth, already laid down by Aristotle, that imaginative pleasure differs in kind from all other forms of pleasure: nay, that one form of imaginative pleasure differs in kind from all other forms of imaginative pleasure: that given by poetry, for instance, from that given by sculpture or painting; that given by the drama from that given by lyric or by epic. In the second place, his own analysis of that which constitutes "beauty" is so illuminating; his own exposition of the conditions necessary to poetic pleasure is so subtle, as to bring us a great deal further on the road than, at the first moment, we may have been aware. The former throws a flood of light upon the points in which the various arts differ from each other, as well as upon those they have in common. The latter—enforced, as it is, by a criticism of Shakespeare's early poetic work, and reinforced by an equally delicate criticism of the charm attaching to the consummate presentment of "common form" in poetry, particularly by the Italian poets of the later renascence—is one of the most satisfying things ever written in this kind. In applying the principles which he had already laid down in theory, the author succeeds both in defining them more closely and in extending them more widely; in the very statement of his theory, he contrives to offer a model of the method which critics should aim at following in practice.

Of the rest of his work in practical criticism, no account can be offered. It must suffice to mention his criticism of Wordsworth in Biographia, and that of Shakespeare, as dramatist, in various courses of his lectures. The former, in itself, is a fine and discriminating piece of work. But it is more than doubtful whether Coleridge was the man to have undertaken it. He was aware that the slightly astringent touch, which he felt justice demanded, would give offence to his brother poet. And, considering the relation between the two men—a relation once of the warmest friendship, now of strained forbearance—it would have been more gracious to keep silence. Indeed, so far as the criticism deals with Wordsworth's theory of "poetic diction," it cannot but strike the reader as carping; not to mention the appearance of treachery involved in attacking a theory for which he himself was commonly held, and, probably, with some justice, to be, in part, responsible. As critic of Shakespeare's dramatic genius, his part is less ambiguous, though even this is complicated by questions of unacknowledged debts to Schlegel.

He was the first English writer to insist that every work of art—in this instance, every play—is, by its very nature, an organic whole; and that, if this is harder to discern in the complicated structure of Shakespearean and much other modern drama, it is because, at least in the nobler examples, such plays are not less, but more, vitally articulated; not less, but more, spontaneous and organic. Structure, scenic effect, poetry, character—all are shown to spring from the same common root in the spirit of the poet; each to enhance the imaginative effect which, instinctively, he had in view. And he enforces this, not as a mere abstract doctrine—though it lies at the core of his theory of beauty—but by an exposition of individual masterpieces which, for subtlety and suggestiveness, had certainly, if we except Goethe's masterly criticism of Hamlet, never been approached. It remains true that, having done so much, he might justly have been expected to do even more; and that nothing but his own nerveless ness, at once the cause and effect of the opium habit, could have prevented him from doing it.

If, in literary criticism, there has sometimes been a disposition to exaggerate the value of the work actually accomplished by Coleridge, in philosophy, the tendency has almost always been to give him less than his due; certainly, as to what he achieved in the way of writing; too often, even as to his intrinsic capacity. Yet, his importance in the history of English philosophy is not to be denied. It is neither more nor less than to have stood against the current which, for the last century, had swept everything before it; to have assailed the mechanical philosophy which, from the time of Locke, had firmly entrenched itself in this country and in France; and, however much he may have been overborne by the prejudices of the moment, at least to have paved the way for their ultimate exposure and defeat. Even at the moment, in the high tide of Bentham's influence, his labours were by no means in vain. As writer—still more, in his talk and in his personal influence—he served for a rallying point to all who felt, if they could not explain to themselves, the inadequacy of the prevailing system: the one man who was capable of laying bare its fallacies, the one man who was able to give a reasoned account of the larger faith after which they were blindly groping. The evidence of this is to be found in the lives of such men as Arnold and Maurice; or, more compactly, in the generous essay of Mill and the brilliant, but not too generous, chapter devoted to the subject in Carlyle's Life of Sterling

Coleridge as Philosopher

In philosophy, as he himself would have been the first to acknowledge, he was building on the foundations laid by Kant and, to a less degree, by Fiche and Schelling. At what time he became acquainted with the writings of Kant, is a disputed point. He himself seems to place it in 1800; and, though he was constitutionally inaccurate about all matters of fact, it is hard to see why this date, the period immediately following his return from Germany, should not be accepted. The question is hardly one of supreme importance. For, despite some unlucky borrowings from Schelling (alas! unacknowledged), he was in no sense a mere adapter, still less a mere copyist, from the Germans. He worked, as all philosophers must work, on hints furnished by his predecessors; and that is all.

His aim was to show the necessity of replacing the mechanical interpretation of life and nature, which he found in possession of the field, by one consistently spiritual, indeed religious. And he carries out this purpose over the whole field of experience: in metaphysics and philosophy; in ethics and politics; not to mention his application of the same principle to imaginative creation, as briefly indicated in the preceding section. In metaphysics, his work is probably less satisfactory than in any other branch of his vast subject. And that, partly because he is here more ready than elsewhere to follow the hazardous guidance of Schelling; partly because the temptation to press speculative truth into the service of a particular religious creed was more than he was able wholly to resist. Hence, with all his subtlety, he does not succeed in driving home the essentially creative action of the mind in the process of knowledge—and that, after all, is the main point at issue—at all as clearly as Kant had done before him.

And, by his use of the distinction between the "reason" and the "understanding"—a distinction originally due to Kant—for the purpose of bolstering up opinions originally derived from a wholly different source, he opens the door to all kinds of fallacies and perversions. With Kant, the distinction between the reason and the understanding has a purely restrictive purpose. Its effect is to deny to the former anything more than a "regulative" or suggestive function in the ordering of knowledge; and to claim from the latter, which, from its nature, must always go hand in hand with a sensible intuition, the sole title to the discovery of truth. In other words, it is a distinction which leads straight to what have since come to be known as agnostic conclusions.

To Coleridge, it serves a purpose exactly the reverse. So far from separating the spheres of the two faculties, he sweeps away all barriers between them. He allows to the one an apparently unlimited power of re-affirming what the other had found it necessary to deny; and thus exposes himself to Carlyle's sarcasm that he had discovered "the sublime secret of believing by the reason what the understanding had been obliged to fling out as incredible."

It would be grossly unfair to say that this exhausts the teaching of Coleridge in the region of metaphysics. His criticism of the mechanical system—and, in particular, of the theory of association, as elaborated by Hume and Hartley—would, in itself, suffice to overthrow any such assertion. But it can hardly be denied that this is the side of his doctrine on which he himself laid the heaviest stress; nor, again, that it is the side upon which he is most open to attack.

In the kindred field of psychology, his results are both sounder in themselves and more absolutely his own. His records of the working of the mind, especially under abnormal or morbid conditions, are extraordinarily minute and subtle. It would hardly be too much to say that he is the founder of what has since become a distinct and most fruitful branch of philosophy: the study of experimental psychology. And this, which is fully known only to those who are familiar with Anima Poet, is, perhaps, his most original contribution to philosophy.

In ethics, he is more upon the beaten track. But it was a track almost unknown to Englishmen of his day. And it is his lasting service, at the moment when the utilitarian scheme of things swept all before it, to have proclaimed the utter insufficiency of any doctrine which did not start from the postulate of duty. Here, once more, he bases his teaching upon that of Kant. But he enters a just protest, as Schiller had done before him, against the hard saying that the highest goodness is that which tramples upon the natural instincts of the heart. And, throughout his exposition, as given in Aids to Reflection, he shows (as, from his personal experience, he well might) a sense of human frailty—a sense, that is, of one of the two main elements of the problem—which the noble stoicism of Kant had been too apt to treat as matter for nothing but shame and contempt.

Few, probably, now think of Coleridge in connection with political philosophy. Yet, there is no subject to which, throughout life, he gave more time and thought; from the days of Conciones ad populum and The Watchman (1795–6) to those of The Friend (1809–10; 1818), or of The Constitution of Church and State (1830). Coleridge habitually spoke of himself as the heir of Burke. And that constitutes at once the strength and the weakness of his position as political philosopher. More systematic, but with far less of imaginative and historic insight than his master, he inherited, in fact, both the loves and the hates of Reflections and Letters on a Regicide Peace.

On the negative side, he is the fiery foe of the rights of man, of Jacobinism, of the sovereignty of the people. And he makes no effort to disentangle the truth which—under a crude form, no doubt—found expression in watchwords which, in his early manhood, had shaken Europe to her depths and had in no sense lost their power when he died. To the end, he was unable to see that no state, which does not draw its will from the whole body of its members, can be regarded as fully organized or developed; and that this was the ideal which the French revolution, perhaps before the time was ripe, certainly through many crimes and blunders, was striving to make good. Against this ideal, he had nothing to propose but that of a government, based upon the will of the propertied classes only, and imposing itself upon the rest of the community from above.

The result is that, at the present day, his theory seems ludicrously out of date: far more so than that of the Jacobins, or of Le Contract social, which he does his best to cover with ridicule and contempt. So childish, indeed, was his fear of Jacobinism, so keen his scent for the faintest breath of its approach that, when Erskine brought in a bill, the first of its kind, for the prevention of cruelty to animals (1809), he denounced it, in his largest capitals, as "the strongest instance of legislative Jacobinism." It was bad enough that rights should be demanded for men; to concede them to animals was iniquitous and absurd.

In spite of these follies, it is right to acknowledge that his criticism of Jacobinism and of Le Contract social, however little we may agree with it, reveals powers beyond the reach of any man living in England at the time; probably, if we except Hegel, beyond the reach of any man in Europe. Yet, as with all thinkers worthy of the name, it is in expounding the positive side of his doctrine that his powers are seen at their brightest and most convincing. The core of his creed, as of Burke's, lay in the conviction that the civic life of man is the offspring not of deliberate calculation, "the cautious balancing of comparative advantages," but of instincts, often working unknown to himself, which are rooted in the deepest fibers of his nature. He is assured that the state, so far from being a cunning piece of mechanism, put together at the will of individuals and to be taken to pieces at their pleasure, is something larger and more enduring than the individuals who compose it.

He knows that, in a very real sense, it has a life of its own: a life which, at countless points, controls, no less than it is controlled by, theirs. He believes that the moral, as well as the material, existence of men is largely determined by the civic order into which they are born. And he infers that, if this order be roughly shaken, the moral, as well as the material, well-being of those who belong to it is grievously imperiled. These are the vital principles which lie behind all that he wrote on political matters, and which find their best expression, characteristically barbed by a bitter attack on Hume, in an eloquent passage of one of his Lay Sermons.

COLERIDGE AND THE EXPLOSION OF VOICE

Coleridge is so often described in terms which are akin to the word, "explosive," and by all accounts he was at times an unusually dynamic, charismatic and unpredictable person. His writings themselves could also be termed "explosive" merely from their physical form; a fragmented mass, some pieces finished but most not, much of his writing subject to procrastination or eventual change of mind.

Today I want to address a moment in his life which produced, as Richard Holmes has characterized it, an explosion of his poetic talent—autumn 1799, when he first met Sara Hutchinson, and wrote, amongst other poems, the ballad, "Love." In addressing this moment, I want to suggest that the voice of Coleridge at this time was explosive, vital and new, but only when set against the "ancient" balladic tradition with which he engaged. Whilst accepting the dynamism and the unpredictability of Coleridge, I want to show that his acceptance of a formal mode allowed him to find his own particular, romantic voice; for, as Stephen Parrish has pointed out, "for Coleridge, the passion was obscured unless the poet spoke in his own voice." The ballad revival of the eighteenth century supplied Romantic writers with an archive of voices from the past, a past which many seemed to idealize as a time of true feeling, when Nature not only had its place but was also imbued with a raw power. Particularly in the late 1790s, Coleridge worked within such a tradition, and in so doing, found his own voice from the minstrelsy of the past.

I want to begin by illustrating the literary environment in which Coleridge found himself at the end of the eighteenth century. Ancient ballad and song culture was being revived throughout Europe from the early eighteenth century onwards, possibly beginning with the "Ossian" fragments in Scotland. Although most British commentators were skeptical of the authenticity of Ossian, as Hugh Trevor-Roper reports, they were feted in other parts of Europe; and Germany in particular. The title of this conference is "The National Graduate Romanticism Conference"; the proximity of "Romantic" and "National" in this tag is fortuitous, since it is important to realise the close relationship between the ballad revival and a sense of nationhood. In Johann Herder's famous essay on Ossian, the place of the song or ballad as a kind of national cultural archive is made plain. He refers to the ballads as "the gnomic song of the nation," and continues, in letter form, to his "friend":

What I wanted to do was remind you that Ossian's poems are songs, songs of the people, folk-songs, the songs of an unsophisticated people living close to the senses, songs which have been long handed down by oral tradition.

Herder locks into the fashionable Rousseauian notion of the "Noble Savage." He goes on:

Know then, that the more barbarous a people are - that is, the more alive, the more freely acting (for that is what the word means) - the more barbarous, that is, the more alive, the more free, the closer to the senses, the more lyrically dynamic its songs will be, if songs it has. The more remote a people is from an artificial, scientific manner of thinking, speaking and writing, the less its verses are written for the dead letter.

The attraction of this national voice is its proximity to nature; and thus, proximity to a kind of raw reality. Herder makes clear that this "ancient" verse is a superior form for it is from "Nature" and not from "Art." The present age, he observes, has made the mistake of foregrounding Art over Nature:

And if that is the way our time thinks, then of course we will admire Art rather than Nature in these ancients' poems; we will find too much or too little Art in them, according to our predisposition, and we will rarely have ears to hear the voice that sings in them: the voice of Nature.

Indeed the general thrust of this essay is to cry out for a natural poetic voice, the kind of voice that he found so evident in the Ossian fragments. He complains at the recent German translation of Ossian, by Michael Denis, because he used the polished hexameters of the German neo-classical idiom; a hated, artful masking of the Natural Voice.

At the end of the essay, Herder calls to his countrymen for a collection of German folk-songs. They are badly needed; he feels, to remind the nation of their own collective voice, a voice that has been suppressed. Herder holds up England's Bishop Percy as the great example. He says that, "the sturdy Englishmen were not ashamed of [their ballads], nor did they need to be." Whilst invoking the Elizabethan "Hearts of Oak" quality in the phrase "sturdy Englishmen," Herder reminds his public that they have theirs—and we should have ours. It is a national necessity. Eventually Herder fulfilled his own wish, and he edited a two volume collection of folk-songs, entitled Volkslieder, which emerged in 1778-9. This collection was well-known among literary circles in Europe; when Coleridge visited Hamburg in 1798, he made a point of buying "a Luther's Bible, 3 marks & 4 pence — and Herder's Popular Songs, 7 Marks."

Herder was writing about Ossian around eight years after the first publication of Percy's Reliques of Ancient English Poetry, which came out in 1765. Although Percy was later to be hailed by many Romantics as a precursor to that movement, he underplays his contribution to any development in aesthetics, calling his collection "the barbarous productions of unpolished ages," and worrying that these poetic fragments are unworthy of patronage. However under this veneer of care and worry is a sly advancement of Herder's division between natural spontaneity and superfluous decoration. Percy immediately continues:

But this impropriety, it is presumed, will disappear, when it is declared that these poems are presented to your ladyship, not as labours of art, but as effusions of nature, showing the first efforts of ancient genius, and exhibiting the customs and opinions of remote ages.

Percy, in his famous phrase, "effusions of nature," anticipates the explosion of Romantic voices. But in a similar vein to Herder, he points to the collective importance of the ancient fragments. Voices are not singled out in these minstrels' lays; partly because they are anonymous, but partly also, I think, because Herder and Percy saw the fragments as in fact a kind of corpus, which in some way represented the collective ancient whole of a nation. Thus Percy refers to the works as the efforts of "genius," not "genii." For the generations who grew up with Percy's Reliques, this collection of songs would prove extremely influential.

By the end of the century, publication of songs had become even more popular and profitable. One of the most influential of these, as well as one of the most comprehensive, was Sir Walter Scott's Minstrelsy of the Scottish Border, of 1802. Here was the historical archive of ancient Scotland; the second chapter of Ossian, perhaps. Scott emphasized the link between poetry and national history, thus:

The historian of an individual nation is equally or more deeply interested in the researches into popular poetry, since he must not disdain to gather from the tradition conveyed in ancient ditties and ballads, the information necessary to confirm or correct intelligence collected from more certain sources.

Hugh Trevor-Roper states that, "Before he had ever written a novel, Scott had eclipsed the two founding fathers of the romantic revival. He was at once the new Percy of his country, the new Ossian of his time." Trevor-Roper's thesis in this 1969 Coffin Lecture is that Scott changed the writing of history, by peopling it. Enlightenment historians—Hume, Gibbon and Robertson, for example—"saw history as a process, and a process, moreover, of improvement, of "progress." "But", as he goes on to say,

If they thus penetrated to the inner meaning of history, they did so, too often, by overlooking the human content. The men of the past entered their story only indirectly, as the agents or victims of 'progress': they seldom appeared directly, in their own right, in their own social context, as the legitimate owners of their own autonomous centuries. The romantic writers changed all that.

Appearing "directly," in one's "own right," becomes of crucial importance when considering the emergence of an individual voice in Coleridge's early ballads.

Thus Britain at the end of the eighteenth century, according to Dianne Dugaw, "was being swept, bottom to top, by a spirit of antiquarianism, a sentimental and revivalist love for old ballads and histories." Wordsworth and Coleridge were caught up in this surge of sentimental interest and, whilst walking on the Quantock Hills in the late nineties, would conceive the idea of the Lyrical Ballads. In the later Supplementary to the Preface (1815), Wordsworth makes clear his, or their, debt to Percy:

I have already stated how much Germany is indebted to this... work; and for our own country, its poetry has been absolutely redeemed by it. I do not think that there is an able writer in verse of the present day who would not be proud to acknowledge his obligations to the Reliques; I know that it is so with my friends; and, for myself, I am happy in this occasion to make a public avowal of my own.

Wordsworth and Coleridge were undoubtedly influenced by Percy. But, as Mary Jacobs points out, the English romantics were equally stimulated by a descendent of Herder, the German balladeer, Gottfried Burger. In the nineties, ballad imitations—rather than the ancient originals so praised by Herder and Scott—were becoming increasingly sensational and poorly written. Burger was a welcome relief. Jacobs comments: "As no-one in England had done, Burger transformed the traditional ballad into something both novel and contemporaneous." Burger's ballad, "Leonora," had been in circulation in England from the early nineties, and it thrilled the English writers. Charles Lamb wrote to Coleridge in 1796, "Have you read the Ballad called 'Leonora', in the second Number of the 'Monthly Magazine'? If you have!!!!!!!!!!!!!!

Coleridge found himself at a time of intense interest and debate over the ballad form. His closest friends were writing to him about the Burger ballads; he talked about the ballad form with Wordsworth, in particular; and he was deeply interested in German aesthetics. He had taught himself German in the mid-nineties, because, as Richard Holmes puts it, "he considered [it] to be far more advanced, both scientifically and philosophically, than French and English." During the Lyrical Ballads months, he composed many experimental ballad poems: between September 1797 and April 1798 he began The Rime of the Ancient Mariner, Christabel, "The Three Graves," and "The Ballad of the Dark Ladies." Soon after, he traveled to Germany with the Wordsworths; he spent virtually a year there, reading German philosophy and aesthetics voraciously, particularly Kant, Schelling, and the Schlegels. It was during this visit that he bought Herder's Volkslieder.

He returned to England in July, 1799. And in the autumn of that year, amid his failing marriage, he traveled to Durham and met Sara Hutchinson whilst with the Wordsworths. He fell in love with her. Holmes comments: "This love affair underlay, and to some degree undermined, almost everything he did and wrote in the next ten years. It broke his marriage, it helped to break his health, and it very nearly broke his will to go on with his work." But at this time, Coleridge was ignited, regenerated in a passion for life and for writing. "His notebooks, previously used largely for memoranda of his reading, lists, addresses and accounts, suddenly explode into life with descriptions of the rivers and mountains, and the subtle effects of light and weather." From this regeneration, came immediately the poem "Love"—another experimental Gothic ballad. It was the only other ballad apart from the Mariner which he actually completed.

Coleridge's personal explosion here, although important, is somehow not unexpected. His life seemed to be a series of violent outbursts and then of silences, of tremendous energy, and then of procrastination. Dorothy Wordsworth, impressed by Coleridge in at least the early years of their friendship, describes the energy of his arrival at Racedown in June 1797: "he did not keep to the high road, but leapt over a gate and bounded down the pathless field by which he cut off an angle." One of the more famous, early, descriptions of Coleridge is from William Hazlitt. Hazlitt describes the scene, when Coleridge arrived at his local town to preach in 1798:

> He did not come till late on the Saturday afternoon before he was to preach; and Mr. Rowe, who himself went down to the coach in a state of anxiety and expectation, to look for the arrival of his successor, could find no one at all answering to the description but a round-faced man in a short black coat (like a shooting jacket) which hardly seemed to have been made for him, but who seemed to be talking at a great rate to his fellow-passengers. Mr. Rowe had scarce returned to give an account of his disappointment, when the round-faced man in black entered, and dissipated all doubts on the subject, by beginning to talk. He did not cease while he staid; nor has he since, that I know of. He held the good town of Shrewsbury in delightful suspense for three weeks that he remained there.

Coleridge himself, in describing his habit of procrastination, says, castigating, "It is a deep & wide disease in my moral Nature... Love of Liberty, Pleasure of Spontaneity, &c&c, these all express, not explain, the fact."

Such "Pleasure of Spontaneity" is, as Thomas McFarland notes, most fully felt in Coleridge's notebooks and marginalia. These fragmentary effusions of the poet's mind work well with McFarland's thesis, which to simplify, sees expressions of ruin and fragmentation as a core or bedrock of Romanticism. He says, "It is my judgment, and I believe of many and perhaps most scholars actively engaged in Coleridge studies, that Coleridge's most pregnant, vital and idiosyncratic work is to be found in his pure fragments: in the haphazard entries of his notebooks, and in the immediacies of marginal notations in books he was reading." Many of Coleridge's poems are fragmented, too; Christabel was written in a series of pieces, over a period of time; and Kubla Khan's form, actually described by the poet as "A Fragment," is a result of interruption and forgetfulness. Friedrich Schlegel, in one of his own "Fragments," responds to this modern habit, and relates it to the ancient tradition: "the works of the ancients have become fragments; the works of the moderns are fragments at their inception."

But the poem "Love" is a completed ballad. If there is fragmentation here, it seems to be of a more subtle kind. I suggest that the "ruin," to use McFarland's word, is that of the ancient national tradition. In this balladic experiment, Coleridge works within the by now predictable voices of the tradition, and from their ruins builds a personal emergent voice. The poem "Love" reminds us that you cannot have ruins without having a castle in the first place; Coleridge's own voice is new, but it is the product of a knowledge and love of the historical voice which Herder and Scott refer to in their own ways. Stephen Parrish, in his article, "The Wordsworth - Coleridge Controversy," simplifies nicely the difference in approach for Wordsworth and Coleridge in writing songs and ballads:

The crucial difference lay in Wordsworth's adoption of the dramatic method in his ballads. And Coleridge's rejection of it. To put it in the simplest way, the passion that Wordsworth expressed in poetry was likely to be that of his characters, the passion that Coleridge looked for was mainly that of the poet. For Wordsworth, the passion could appear only if the poet maintained strict dramatic propriety; for Coleridge, the passion was obscured unless the poet spoke in his own voice.

Coleridge approaches the balladic tradition and takes what he needs in order to experiment with his own voice. The voice speaks out of generations of voices.

At the time when he met Sara, Coleridge's notebooks teem with jagged shards of life, to use a McFarland turn of phrase. Not only are the entries for November 1799 about as long as all the entries for the preceding six months, but the mental leaps of imagination, excitement and wonder as revealed in the entries is disorienting:

576 — O God! When I now think how perishable Things, how imperishable ideas — what a proof of My Immortality — What is Forgetfulness? —

577 May not Time in Association be made serviceable & evidence Likeness/.

578 The Long Entrancement of a True-Love's Kiss.

579 In the North every Brook, every Crag, almost every Field has a name — a proof of greater Independence & a Society more approaching in their Laws & Habits to Nature —

Less than a month after these entries, "Love" was published in the Morning Post, on 21 December 1799, as "Introduction to the Tale of the Dark Ladies." It was considerably edited and newly titled "Love" for the 1800 edition of the Lyrical Ballads. It appears on the page as a controlled, completed, twenty-five stanza poems; evidence of romantic fragmentation here will certainly not come from the format of the verse. The ballad structure is rigid; every stanza is four lines long, the first three of eight syllables, and the last of six syllables. Coleridge dots the poem with the obligatory archaisms of the "ancient tradition": for instance, "ladies," "lay," and "minstrel." The story within the poem is recognizably of the antiquarian tradition, too: the wooing of a Lady by a Knight, "that wore / upon his shield a burning brand." This story is told by a minstrel, who himself is wooing a woman. When it first appeared, the poem was prefaced by a letter which Coleridge wrote to the editor of the newspaper, and the letter makes a case for his modern ballade ring. Coleridge's list of excuses makes interesting reading in the light of our discussion today:

> [A]s it is professedly a tale of ancient times, I trust that 'the affectionate lovers of venerable antiquity' (as Camden says) will grant me their pardon, and perhaps may be induced to admit a force and propriety in it. A heavier objection may be adduced against the Author, that in these times of fear and expectation, when novelties explode [Coleridge's emphasis] around us in all directions, he should presume to offer to the public a silly tale of old fashioned love; and, five years ago, I own, I should have allowed and felt the force of this objection. But, alas! explosion has succeeded explosion so rapidly, that novelty itself ceases to appear new; and it is possible that now, even a simple story, wholly inspired [sic] with politics and personality, may find some attention amid the hubbub of Revolutions, as to those who have resided a long time by the falls of Niagara, the lowest whispering becomes distinctly audible.

Coleridge is coy in this letter. We should not believe that he, of anyone, has not been affected by the explosion of "novelties" in "these times of fear and expectations." "Personality," or the individual person, is actually deeply involved in this poem; we do not need, in this case, the benefit of Holmes' and other modern biographical scholarship, for E.H. Coleridge glosses the history of this poem in the Poetical Works, and he points out a clear connection between this pseudo-medieval fable and Coleridge's personal life. He details the visit to Sock burn, and goes on to show direct links between the poem and this visit; for instance, he says that lines 13-16 describe scenes from Sock burn church and the "field near the farm-house."

More than plain biographical and topographical links, an individual personality or voice emerges from the story of the minstrel singing to his princess, the story which frames the Knight's tale. Because the minstrel/poet is the real subject of the poem, the ballad form is taken from historical fragment to personal, romantic song. The poem becomes less of an ancient imitation, less of a "simple song," than an expression of love, and at the same time, a statement of personal poetic ambition. The poet's love for Genevieve seems more concrete, more real, than the Knight's story, which is transparent by comparison. The Knight's story is constantly interrupted by the poet observing Genevieve react to him; her blushing, and finally, their embrace. "Love" does not end with the Knight, but with the minstrel: "And so I won my Genevieve, / My bright and beauteous bride." The poem foregrounds the minstrel's vocation as a poet, a singer and a teller, by repeating verbs which emphasize such a role: "I told her of the Knight"... "I told her how he pined"... "I sang an old and moving story." From this, the reader is encouraged, I think, to realise the triple relationship occurring; at the same time, three sets of voices compete for love's sake; Knight and Ladies, Minstrel and Genevieve; Coleridge and Sara. The ninth stanza in particular seems to indicate the importance of finding your way through a poem's voices:

I told her how he pined: and ah!
The deep, the low, the pleading tone
With which I sang another's love,
Interpreted my own.

At the same time as the minstrel is interpreting his love from the Knight's, so too do we interpret Coleridge's love for Sara from the minstrel; Sara seems very close to the text here. But there are other issues of interpretation going on, too. In this poem, Coleridge has moved the balladic voice from an impersonal story-teller to a doubly personal voice: the minstrel/narrator and Coleridge behind the scenes. Layers of interpretation unfold in this poem: from historical legend to ancient minstrel to romantic poet. Coleridge, in the letter to the editor, complains at "novelty," but in fact what he is doing here seems new and characteristically Romantic. He delves into the historical, cultural archive of songs and ballads - the univocal, raw, voice of a nation as described by Herder - and works within such a frame to produce his own voice. It is a voice both of love and of individual poetic vocation. Parrish reminds us that, for Coleridge, "passion was obscured unless the poet spoke in his own voice." In his ballads, as shown in this example, Coleridge's is not the only voice; but in competing with other, older voices his emerges as dominant and individual. Coleridge, the explosive romantic, becomes one of the writers, according to Hugh Trevor-Roper, who would influence the way people thought and wrote about history. He did this by creating his own voice from the old voice of the nation; by writing "directly," and in his "own right."

Coleridge, the Return to Nature, and the New Anti-Romanticism: An Essay in Polemic

Definitions of English 'romanticism' are doomed because there is always an appeal to exception; and no exception may be ruled self-evidently irrelevant without presuming a definition before you begin. The significance of this impasse shouldn't be exaggerated: for most critics most of the time, it is quite unimportant; you simply don't need a definition of romanticism to write about Wordsworth or Coleridge (or Austen or Byron). On the other hand, you clearly depend upon one if you wish to establish anti-romantic credentials: you are honor-bound to define what you define yourself (or your chosen author) against. Polemical modernists like Hulme or Eliot might come to mind here; but anti-romantic definitions of the 'romantic' form a genre which long outlives modernism: critics like Leavis, and contemporary figures like McGann and his New Historicist followers, contribute to it too. These various authors write in very different contexts, to be sure; but the demerits of the romanticism they identify to deplore are fundamentally similar, as are the attributes of the anti-romanticism they each claim as their own to praise. Common too is an adversarial quality to their prose, which stems from a conviction that the issue is one of the most vital currencies: not just a matter of historical interest, romanticism has continued to the present day, nurturing unscrutinised assumptions from which we must break free, finally post-romantic, into health.

In this essay, I aim to sketch what seem to me the salient characteristics of anti-romantic writing, tracing the genre back to Coleridge and forward to recent 'historicist' criticism. This new school makes one interesting variation on the terms it inherits from the Coleridgean tradition, which is to apply them to the concept of 'History'; and with some remarks on this dubious innovation, I shall conclude. I should say at once that turning in this way to the tradition of anti-romanticism is not going to take us any nearer what romanticism 'actually is'; but it may spur us to think about what kind of activity defining it usually is.

For the anti-romantics, the business of definition is not a question of disinterested historical enquiry so much as the staking of one's own imaginative position, a self-assertion furthered by a definitive 'romantic' to anathematize. In some classic examples of the genre, Shelley occupies this exemplary role; but his place has been assumed in more recent criticism by Coleridge and those 'idealist' aspects of Wordsworth's poetry which might be thought especially Coleridgean. (Shelley's politics seem to have rescued him.) Coleridge is at once theorist and summation of romantic failings; and, at the same time, he is well known as founding father of modern 'formalism', thus establishing the double-focus - upon both literary history and contemporary mores - which characterizes anti-romantic writing. There is a twist, however: for not only the 'romantic' but also the 'anti-romantic' position can, in fact, be traced back to Coleridge. Of course, the implication of earlier anti-romantics within the romanticism they hope to spurn has often been remarked: Hartman, for example, says that '[t]he reaction [...] of T. E. Hulme, Eliot and the New Humanists, appears to us more and more as one within Romanticism'; and this argument makes 'anti-romanticism' one of the threads of a continuing 'romantic' tradition, which seems set to become a terrible paradox. But the mystery is mostly verbal: instead of 'continuing romanticism' we might refer (as I have already) to a 'Coleridgean tradition', something less univocal than someone after a definition of 'romantic' might hope for, and rather more diversely inclusive - something one might be 'within'. Maurice was righter even than he knew in seeing Coleridge's followers as a various gathering if among their unwitting number we can count professed anti-romantics and anti-Coleridgean.

THE RHETORIC OF ANTI-ROMANTICISM: THE EXAMPLE OF LEAVIS

by F. R.· LEAVIS

Leavis exemplifies the way that anti-romantic criticism is based on a small number of tropes: the twin metaphors of 'placing' and 'displacing'; and, associated with them, a rhetoric of substance, the concrete and the natural versus one of immateriality, self-involutes dreaminess, and the idealist. The 'placing' part of the critic's job is an exercise in a kind of cultural history, the upshot of which is to undermine a writer's otherwise assumed authority or good faith. Within Leavis's scheme, we can confidently understand as deluded a voice we might otherwise have taken on its own terms: the effect is to introduce an historical dimension to our reading, but only in the form of something like irony, rather as Leavis saw wrong-headed or fallible characters in Conrad or James 'placed' by an implicit but emphatic irony within the masterful 'controlling conception' of the novelist's 'severe' art.

This 'placing' is the work of the critic in the novelist: for instance, the character of Maggie Tulliver is weak because it is offered 'with a remarkable absence of criticism', Eliot momentarily failing in that 'skeptical intelligence' which Leavis attributes to Martin Decoud from Nostromo , a man perfectly able to 'place Charles Gould' - just as Lawrence is able to apply a '"placing" sardonic touch' to the characters of St. Mawr.

'Placing' is a matter of reading with less deluded eyes than one's sentimentalist peers and predecessors; 'displacing' is about the education of one's successors. One 'displaces' in order to establish that Great Tradition in which the young may grow healthily; or as we might now put it, one establishes new canons: 'Milton's dislodgement... was effected with remarkably little fuss', as Leavis announced (prematurely). Naturally, critics with whom one disagrees are likely to be under the sway of unscrutinised traditionalism, which simply inculcates all the bad literary habits which a critical 'placing' had brought into unforgiving light. When used with any terminological emphasis (when not just a loose period label), 'romantic' tends to be the pejorative label for precisely those elements and authors which must be 'displaced', the tenacious influence of which had led to that deplorable state of affairs sharply described in the first chapters of Leavis's New Bearings in English Poetry.

Leavis's concern to 'place', and thence to 'displace', based itself on a distrust of the 'romanticism' exemplified with especial glamour by Shelley - an instructive choice, since Shelley was a poet known to all Arnoldian as lacking that grasp of the 'concrete' and the 'palpable' which distinguished the truly vital genius: in place of a 'vivid concreteness of realization', wrote Leavis, Shelley tends to produce 'nothing but wordy emotional generality' which 'does not grasp and present anything'. Shelley's romanticism represents a real-life equivalent to Othello's self-enchanting music: a 'hypnotic rote of favourite images, associations and words' occurring in 'the void' (a clear echo of Arnold there), which lurches down at its worst to 'a mere tumbled out spate... of poeticalities'. All this the scrutinizing critic can see through, and then turn instead to the truly 'Shakespearean' attributes of the best Keats: 'a native English strength... sensuous firmness... a general concrete vigor', in short, 'that strong grasp upon actualities - upon things outside himself, that firm sense of the solid world, which makes Keats so different from Shelley'. No wonder that Hopkins, whom Leavis saw as enjoying such Keatsian strengths, might be called a 'nature poet' (by T. S. Eliot) 'with some justice'.

The under-argument to this anti-romanticism is a distrust of the 'literary', of 'poeticalities' altogether, which are conceived as the fruit of an unhealthy introverted self-consciousness, and a faith instead in a literature that somehow embodies the discretely sensuous in an art of natural self-evidence - what Leavis celebrated as the 'there' ('Ursula is astonishingly there'; 'Great art, something created and there, is what Lawrence gives us'.

A desire for palpable truth over merely 'poetic' beauty might be thought of as having a precedent in Wordsworth's 'Preface' to Lyrical Ballads, or, more equivocally, in Keats: 'What the imagination seizes as Beauty must be truth'; Shelley, who had a 'weak grasp upon the actual' is 'the ideal of what a poet should be' - Trelawny's praise for him - only for the dreaming nineteenth century. Pleasingly, then, the prime candidate for 'displacement' from the Tradition is a literary intelligence which is itself, so to say, 'displaced' - that is, removed from the concrete, ungrounded, ideal, 'romantic'. Shelley's symbolic role in the severe structure of Revaluation is as a warning example of poetic idealism before the introduction of Keats's happily concrete materiality, subject of Leavis's culminating chapter.

COLERIDGE DISPLACED: THERE WAS IN COLERIDGE A SORT OF DREAMINESS WHICH WOULD NOT LET HIM SEE THINGS AS THEY WERE.

It is not a great step to replace Shelley with Coleridge in this critical mythology: that Coleridge had an inaptitude for the actual seems universally acknowledged. After all, it is Coleridge who is the first on record to complain about 'a something corporeal, a matter-of-factness, a clinging to the palpable' to be found in the (presumably un-Coleridgean) parts of Wordsworth's poetry, thereby listing as demerits precisely the highest virtues of successfully anti-romantic art. That his philosophical commitment was to idealism is apparently unquestionable too: he was, I. A. Richards influentially announced, 'an extreme Idealist'.

Coleridge's reputation as an instinctive idealist, devoted to the internal spaces of dreamy consciousness rather than engaged with the external world, is already well established within his own lifetime. Wordsworth's portrayal of his friend, for example, frequently stresses Coleridge's removal from the saving solidities of the concrete: anticipating an Arnoldian argument (and thence Leavis), Wordsworth diagnoses in this removal a kind of spiritual disaster - a surprisingly severe view since it appears in what everyone who knew it thought of as the 'Poem to Coleridge':

> The self-created sustenance of a mind
> De-barred from Nature's living images,
> Compelled to be a life unto itself.

The rhetoric of triumphantly self-sustaining consciousness, the living unto oneself, is an important value in The Prelude; but here, such self-sustaining sounds imposed, and even diseased, as if consumptive. Wordsworth's excuse for including so negative a portrait is that this is meant to be true only of his friend at Cambridge: one of the poem's necessary fictions is that Coleridge has reached the same position as the author, albeit by a less instinctive route; but the suspicion must be that even in The Prelude Wordsworth tended to think of Coleridge as somehow damagingly immersed in internalities. Coleridge was, as he told someone later in life, unable to feel 'the influence of external objects': clearly a failing.

Wordsworth came to represent for Coleridge all the solidity of character which he felt himself to lack. His own self-absorbed weakness is a running theme: writing Godwin a wriggling letter, for instance, he explains that his unreliability stems from a 'diminished Impressibility from Things', the consequence of which was that his 'ideas, wishes, & feelings are to a diseased degree disconnected from motion and action': as he later famously table-talked, 'I have a smack of Hamlet myself, if I may say so'.

This removal from the sensuous and concrete is a familiar part of Coleridge's rueful self-portraiture; but it can also be more self-aggrandizing: 'I never regarded my senses in any way as the criteria of my belief,' he writes proudly to Poole of his childhood, so casting himself, as John Cornwell puts it, 'as a kind of precocious Berkeleian idealist'. Freedom from influence of the external need not be simply culpable: it can be a path to visionary power.

Kubla Khan , as Coleridge's 'Preface' tells us, records the experience of 'about three hours in a profound sleep, at least of the external senses'; and Wordsworth's attraction to this kind of creativity must have been one of the main reasons for the sudden intimacy of their friendship in the first place. And not just in the first place: for the triumph of the 'ideal' - freed of the smell of opium, naturally - continues to be an important ingredient in Wordsworth's descriptions of imaginative power. One thinks of the Fenwick note to the Intimations Ode, dictated in his old age; or the passage in Book VI of The Prelude, only two hundred or so lines after the description of Coleridge's sickly solipsism, in which Wordsworth contrasts the anti-climax of crossing the objective Alps with the compensatory subjective rush produced by his own powerfully hallucinogenic 'vapor', Imagination.

One thinks too of the de Manian-Hartmanian school who single out such passages as especially crucial to the interpretation of Wordsworth, and draw theoretical strength from the hope expressed in them that 'consciousness [...] exist entirely by and for itself, independently of all relationship with the outside world, without being moved by an intent aimed at a part of this world'. This conception of the good imaginative life is the target of McGann and his followers; and Coleridge certainly attributes something very like this state of affairs to 'the self-sufficing power of absolute Genius ', an evidently impressive and admirable power, whose exponents (he tells us) rest content in 'an intermundium of which their own living spirit supplies the substance, and their imagination the ever-varying form'.

For Coleridge to compare his own self-involution to the tragic nobility of Hamlet's is winning; but at the same time, Hamlet's aversion to externals was, as Coleridge told his lecture audience in 1813, 'morbid'. The down-side of living your life as an 'instinctive' Berkeleian, as the Infant Prodigy from The Prelude shows, is that one may discover what Thomas Reid found in Berkeley, 'that forlorn state of egoism': 'Vanity, / That is his soul: there he lives, and there he moves - / It is the soul of every thing he seeks'. Wordsworth recalled late in life that Coleridge suffered from 'a sort of dreaminess which would not let him see things as they were': for Wordsworth, portraying 'things as they are' is the first requirement of a morally healthy artistic relationship with reality, one which had received its finest explication as a literary principle in the 'Preface' to Lyrical Ballads , and in the third of the Essays on Epitaphs. 'I vindicate the rights and dignity of Nature,' Wordsworth there declares, an adherence which, reasonably though paradoxically (for an artist), leads him positively to distrust 'the adversary of nature, (call that adversary Art or by what name you will)'.

This strongly realist prescription goes on to form an important strain in later nineteenth-century criticism; and not only Coleridge, but also the more 'Coleridgean' aspects of Wordsworth, were found wanting when judged by Wordsworth's own realist criterion: indeed, it was, possibly, an important reason for Victorian neglect of The Prelude. Clough, for example, wrote of it that, instead of looking directly at an object, and considering it as a thing in itself, and allowing it to operate upon him as a fact in itself, [Wordsworth] takes the sentiment produced by it in his own mind, as the thing, as the important and really real fact. The real thing ceases to be real; the world no longer exists; all that exists is the feeling, somehow, generated in the poet's sensibility.

(Hamlet's flaw, thought Coleridge, was to be 'for ever occupied with the world within him, and abstracted from external things'.) Clough's language is a compelling mixture of epistemology ('object', 'thing in itself') and sensibility ('sentiment', 'feeling'); and it is no wonder that his friend Arnold, for whom the task of the critical intelligence was precisely to see the object 'as in itself it really is', should have taken so poor a view of The Prelude when set alongside Wordsworth's more really 'really real' poems: at their best, famously, a Wordsworth poem was so extraordinarily real that nature herself took Wordsworth's pen and 'wrote his poem for him'. A distrust of the literary naturally reserves its highest praise for this counter-Coleridgean poetry: it is not literary or even poetry at all - it is poetry of 'no style'.

Paul Hamilton observes that, 'from Thomas Love Peacock to McGann', anti-romantics give as the 'stock reason' for their distrust 'the fact that [romanticism] internalizes', a charge which he goes on at once to accept and to reject. Following rather a different tack, we might suggest that this 'stock reason' is already there within much of the 'romanticism' under attack. Wordsworth's manifestly split feelings about his friend's 'idealist' tendencies parallel an equivocation within his own poetry between, say, the mind as 'lord and master' and endeavoring at all times to look steadily upon one's object.

The division is one between a devotion to consciousness in its own right and consciousness as intentionally directed toward, even absorbed by, something other than itself; and Wordsworth's growing moral disapproval of Coleridge's supposed involution in immaterial reality seems the result of his using the figure of Coleridge as a way of trying to work into order elements of his own creative dilemmas. As Robert Young has commented, both transcendent and 'simple' Wordsworths exist, and both in The Prelude; but we should add that accounts of both kinds of imagination are in Coleridge too: which is doubtless how they come to feature in so prominently reconciled a way in the great 'Poem to Coleridge'. We might expect an emotive equivocation over the sufficiency or authority of the 'internal' to go along with a reluctance whole-heartedly to embrace a philosophy of idealism: of course, one is a question of psychology and the other of proper epistemology, but a parallel seems at least probable. Sure enough - pace the categorical judgments of such influential commentators as Richards and Shawcross, not to mention many since - we find no straightforward alignment with philosophical idealism in Coleridge either.

Iris Murdoch once said that a good question to ask of any thinker is 'What is he afraid of?' and we could reply for Coleridge that one prominent object of fear is nothing other than the epistemologist's obligation to decide between the rival claims of idealism and realism at all. Not only was their reconciliation the declared project of the philosophical chapters of Biographia (Biographia, 1: 260-61), but also his culminating requirement of Wordsworth's Recluse. In this continuing desire to have things both ways (traced, in different ways, by Thomas McFarland, Raimonda Modiano, and some others), we can perhaps see Coleridge's theoretical orientation as rather more complicated than the traditional anti-romantic case generally has it. We might even look to this divided character for anticipations of the anti-romantic method itself.

COLERIDGE AND THE CONCRETE

In the first chapter of Biographia, Coleridge recalls a crisis in his apprehension of objective fact; he is redeemed from this perilous state by poetry, though not by poetry as poetry ('which is essentially ideal': Biographia, 2: 45) so much as by poetry as a representative of nature. In this passage, he recalls how,

At a very premature age, even before my fifteenth year, I had bewildered myself in metaphysics, and in theological controversy. Nothing else pleased me. History, and particular facts, lost all interest in my mind.

In this state, 'In my friendless wanderings on our leave-days, (for I was an orphan, and had scarce any connections in London)', the boy sought out clergymen with whom to discuss theology; but despite this elevated company, he looks back at this interest as 'beyond doubt, injurious, both to my natural powers, and to the progress of my education'. Fortunately, he was saved:

> It would perhaps have been destructive, had it been continued; but from this I was auspiciously withdrawn, partly indeed by an accidental introduction to an amiable family, chiefly however, by the genial influence of a style of poetry, so tender, and yet so manly, so natural and real, and yet so dignified, and harmonious, as the sonnets, &c. of Mr. Bowles! Well were it for me perhaps, had I never relapsed into the same mental disease; if I had continued to pluck the flower and reap the harvest from the cultivated surface, instead of delving in the unwholesome quicksilver mines of metaphysical depths. But if in after time I have sought a refuge from bodily pain and mismanaged sensibility in abstruse researches, which exercised the strength and subtlety of the understanding without awakening the feelings of the heart; still, there was a long and blessed interval, during which my natural faculties were allowed to expand, and my original tendencies to developed themselves: my fancy, and the love of nature, and the sense of beauty in forms and sounds.

John Beer has written finely of the way a Coleridgean 'argument which seems to be pointing firmly in one direction turns out to contain within itself a statement which acts as a counter-current, suggesting somewhere an alternative motion of the mind'; and we can see such equivocating drama played out here between the rival attractions of the metaphysically 'abstruse' and the physically immediate. Like Wordsworth's Ode , which it echoes ('there was a time'), it is entirely lucid in expressing something unrealised: a refusal simply to mourn the past as holding all natural good, but also a hesitancy in embracing the progressive disease of adult life as adequate compensation. The retreat into the senseless world of metaphysics is disastrous and even diabolic (Milton is quoted, describing the fallen angels in wandering mazes lost); but how much of this is merely because of the boy's prematurely? In the elaborate metaphor, the infernal mercury mines of abstruse research are clearly unhealthy when compared to the pleasant meadows of the surface; but at the same time they have in their favour the implications of 'depth' (as opposed to superficiality), and, since Coleridge persists in mining them, he is even allowed a kind of heroism.

Nevertheless, despite the lingering appeal of metaphysical enquiry, the Biographia passage predominantly celebrates restoration to the natural and substantial, a 'Wordsworthian' moral. Later in Biographia, philosophical introspection similarly sets him 'all afloat', drifting in the undirected steaminess of consciousness, until he reaches the firm ground of 'an Ararat' (Biographia, 1: 200), a lifelong craving for solidity: 'My poor crazy ark has been tossed to and fro on an ocean of business, and I long for the Mount Ararat on which it is to rest'. The experience of Bowles's poetry and the new acquaintance with a family - the Evanses, we happen to know - work in happy parallel because they both affect kinds of rehabilitation, drawing Coleridge, a displaced and self-absorbed orphan, back into a state in which the self may find its true identity in relationship and connection.

This need of external support is a recurrent theme in the personal writings: 'My nature requires another Nature for its support,' he confides to his notebook; and elsewhere stresses 'man's dependence on some thing out of him'; and again, terribly, cries to his only confidant: 'Have Mercy on me, O something out of me!' 'Take away from sounds &c the sense of out ness,' as he records elsewhere '- what a horrid disease every moment would become', worrying at that key-term of Berkeley's idealism to which he repeatedly returns. Clearly, there is no untroubled celebration of self-sufficing consciousness or the glories of a life led unto itself in Coleridge's writing: 'I own myself no self-subsisting mind,' he told Beaumont; and the dependency upon relationship which this lack of autonomy creates need not be merely a kind of weakness.

Restoration in the Biographia passage is explicitly associated with the re-awakening of an outward-directed sensibility, experiencing beauty in 'forms and sounds' - a case of entering into a responsive relationship with the 'actualities [...] of the solid world' so valued by Leavis. By a kind of anti-artistic naturalness Bowles restores young Coleridge to health; by withdrawing him from the enervating internalities of metaphysics, this 'style of poetry' makes him one again with the 'natural' and 'real', just as Bowles's poetry is itself 'natural' - Bowles is, as he writes in an early letter, an 'always-natural poet'. As it happens, one old, and now mostly abandoned, sense of the 'romantic' was precisely the 'return to nature'; and if we think of this less as a reaction against the artifice of neo-classicism and more as a repeated moment in the life of the spirit, then it has some justice.

The realist counter-currents in Coleridge, which would initiate such returns, are strong and, when given their fullest expression, give rise to narratives, usually nostalgic, in which, like Wordsworth in Book XI of The Prelude, the return to nature effects an imaginative restoration, as we have seen in Biographia. Such moments do not obviously tally with preconceptions of Coleridge the idealist; indeed, if any philosophical precursor need be found, the structure of the Biographia episode is less like the neo-Kantianism of the pages that come after it than it is like the emotive resort to nature (of a rather different variety, it is true) made by the empiricist Hume when his nerves are troubled by dark metaphysics, an anecdote memorably recounted in the Treatise of Human Nature.

Nature occupies an equivocal place in Coleridge's philosophical speculations: his celebrated commitment to the ideal and supernatural spaces of 'the Vast' is qualified, as Humphry House put it, by 'one of his greatest qualities... "delight in little things"'; and nature's role is similarly undecided in his conceptions of poetic genius. The Miltonic sublime is a sovereign self-sufficiency, negligent of the external and incapable of escaping the ego to conceive true drama: all the characters are in truth revelations of John Milton. This sublimity, 'the pre-eminent characteristic of the Paradise Lost', exemplifies with especial distinction that 'fleeting away of external things, the mind or subject greater than the object' which Coleridge thought typical of modern poetry; and which I suppose modern commentators to consider definitively 'romantic'. But there is an alternative Coleridgean sublime: the triumphant, self-oblivious impersonation of the Shakespearean imagination, 'that sublime faculty, by which a great mind becomes that which it meditates on'.

With such a genius, for example, Shakespeare 'became Othello and spoke as Othello would have spoken'. Such a poet is naturally 'universal', and, like Arnold's Wordsworth, has 'no manner'; so, 'instead of making artificial puppets he brings the real being before you'. Shakespeare, of course, has always been celebrated for being the poet of nature, for the startling kinship of his art to nature itself (Dryden's praise - 'when he describes any thing, you more than see it, you feel it too'); and, despite his idealist inclinations, Coleridge is no exception to this tradition of realist praise. Indeed his claims for Shakespeare's recreative mimetic powers are more extravagant even than most - despite this involving him in all kinds of theoretical gymnastics when he tries to reconcile it with the ideal bias of his 'Miltonic' enthusiasm: 'Shakespeare [is] in all things the divine Opposition or antithetic correspondent of the divine Milton'.

These paired, opposed versions of the poetic genius lead a various life in Coleridge's writings, and moral approval shifts about the terms accordingly, from idealist self-creation to realist sympathy, from Miltonic autonomy to Shakespearean sensibility, from male egotism to feminine selflessness, and back again, and again, from page to page of his works. But the pattern of possibilities on offer remains strikingly consistent - and, what is more, proves extremely tenacious in the work of later critics: it was, for example, precisely sensory blindness to the external universe, construed as a failing that moved T. S. Eliot to attack Milton. On this point Leavis concurred, criticizing Milton for the romantic failing of 'focusing rather upon words than upon perceptions, sensations or things', and celebrating instead the palpably self-evident realities of Shakespeare. 'True & easy Test of Poetry,' proposed Coleridge to his notebooks, 'If it relate to sight, might a well educated man born blind have written it: if he could , then presumably the poetry was written insufficiently from 'actual individual Experience ,' as he says elsewhere, and to much 'from Book-knowledge'. By the time we reach Eliot, Coleridge's fluid and shifting valuations of the different positions have hardened into a simple dislike of Milton's ideal, 'literary' or 'poetical' sovereignty; but the positions themselves remain thoroughly Coleridgean. And it is here, I think, in this provision of opposites, that we should locate the continuity of a Coleridgean tradition.

THE NEW ANTI-ROMANTICISM

– Lionel Trailling

If we can trace the rhetoric of Leavis's anti-romanticism back to the metaphors and associated preoccupations of Wordsworth and Coleridge, then we can also trace them forward into the work of the modern anti-romanticists, who similarly base their writings on the notion of a restorative return to the concrete. To take some swift examples: Marjorie Levinson hopes to 'bring "Tintern Abbey" back to earth'; while Alan Liu tells us that the imagination must be returned to 'the grounded or demystified Nile that is history' (a river is hardly the happiest instance of grounded ness, I suppose, but the rhetorical move is familiar). And a third case: an essay by other hands finds that Coleridge's lines on the Bastille 'preclude any attention to concrete historical processes', while his career as a whole emerges as 'the triumph of metaphysics and reverie over an attempt at direct engagement with politics and society' - which (leaving aside his manifest, though admittedly not left-wing, concern with politics and society) can be seen precisely to redeploy Coleridge's own terms of dreamy reverie and concrete solidity.

These assessments of failure imply that the historicist's perfectly anti-romantic poem would be the text which somehow embodied the very texture of its moment's history: hiding nothing, it would come before its reader with complete ingenuousness, 'the literature of the Whole Truth', as opposed to the 'Partial Truth'. The phrases are Huxley's, whose hero is Homer, reminding us that the artist of the Whole Truth would have less to produce poetry than reproduce nature ('Nature and Homer were, he found, the same'). Such art would be the work of a magically responsive realism, a triumph of always-natural art - precisely analogous, in fact, to the art Coleridge imagines for Bowles or Shakespeare: an art which becomes the thing contemplated and so brings before you the very thing - there - while its own literariness happily dissolves into immediacy.

Where, on earth, might we look for such a poem? McGann once singled out for praise Crabbe's 'human, non-transcendent approach', and made his poetry sound altogether what every anti-romantic materialist would want - 'time- and place-specific', full of 'illustrative' stories, illuminating 'social, psychological, and historical' 'problems' and so forth - but no surge of interest in Crabbe followed, not even, as far as one can see, in McGann himself.

The point is significant of more than the charms of Crabbe. It is not just that the whole method happens to be better in attack; it is rather that it has no positive voice, and can have none: for as soon as one thinks one has found a text which comes 'closer' to material history than (say) Coleridge's poems do, one sees, irritatingly, that it is still a text, still written. Nature, in the guise of 'History', has still not taken the poet's pen. This seems a simple-minded way of putting it, but, despite its often sophisticated general accounts of hermeneutic intricacy, 'History' is customarily introduced by historicist anti-romanticism in a much more bluntly positivist spirit. The desire to gain what Lentricchia calls 'direct access to history's gritty ground-level texture' (Veeser, 234) tips Leavis's poised distrust of the merely 'poetic' into creativity and its politics per se. (This seems an after-effect of one kind of Marxism; though not, one might add, a necessary effect). If one has a constitutional suspicion of the literary, then it is difficult to conceive the kind of literature which could possibly satisfy one's taste, 'really real' art being an obvious pipe dream.

My point here is that this dream, like its 'romantic' opponent, recognizably exists within a Coleridgean inheritance, formed about a division between idealist and realist aesthetic orientations: against the ideality of Coleridge's Miltonic aesthetic, the New Historicists are effectively invoking the super-realist, concrete representation of Coleridge's Shakespeare, who 'brings the real being before you'. If any praise is to be offered of the ideal counter-aesthetic, it inevitably sounds dutiful, as if making polite noises about the craftiness of an opponent: what, to the historicist, could be less 'brilliant' than 'the distancing of culture from politics that Romantic writers often brilliantly proposed' (Klancher; in Veeser, 77)? The brilliance can only be in the form of dazzling sophistication, like Satan's in Paradise Lost.

But if one cannot reasonably hope to encounter the perfectly realist text, then one might at least look forward to the historicist perfection of the texts we have. This perfection would explain what appears to be the text's self-sustaining, ideal Coleridgean existence as in fact the product of its determining historical occasion, revealing poetic inevitability to be actually the mystified form of contingency; the spuriously autonomous text would be forced, under historicist pressure, to come clean about its secret relationships with the external world.

The critic has now assumed the adversarial task of, as Levinson puts it, 'locating the body': the agenda is explicitly political - a way of 'finding a use 'for' Romantic transcendence and the 'use' depends on detecting the 'History' it is attempting to evade. For 'History' features in romantic poetry only by its pretended absence, by tell-tale bumps of the body in the would-be 'literary', 'idealist' text: thus, 'Levinson restores social history as a willfully repressed content', Jon Klancher writes, bringing to light 'what the poem should have shown' (Veeser, 81; my italics). Liu's Wordsworth:

The Sense of History repeats this turn over and over again: 'the georgic meditation of nature projected in Book 6 of The Prelude can only bury history out of sight provisionally before turning it up once more' - at which moment spurious, literary (= 'georgic') nature is supplanted by the real nature of things (Liu, 20). The rhetoric of a restoration to the concrete is recognizably a version of Coleridge's return to the authentically substantial and natural: what should have occupied the mind.

The very mode of existence of a literary work has by now become a species of false consciousness, for it comes into being in the first place only as a kind of misperception of its historical occasion, seeking to be, like Coleridge's Quixote, 'an unlimited monarch over the creations of [its] fancy'. But once the actual historical implication of the work is revealed, the work, as a work of art ('poetry as poetry'), disappears into the seamless continuity of the History which in fact provoked it: 'The inventor of the watch did not in reality invent it; he only looked on, while the blind causes, the only true artists, were unfolding themselves,' as Coleridge satirically put the position (Biographia, 1: 119-20). By retrospective critical intervention, 'History' reclaims the pen and writes (or implies) the poem that would have been written had the odd superfluity of consciousness not interfered.

Perfected, the work then leaves the mystified category of the 'literary' behind, just as the idealist consciousness finds itself returned to the material actuality of impersonal forces; and, like the poems of Coleridge's Bowles or Shakespeare, returns to the proper plenitude of the externally real. The poem is thus restored to its vital identity with what is really important, the non-literary; and, relieved, the critic may say to the redeemed poem, as Bob Dylan once put it, 'You're invisible now, you've got no secrets to conceal'. The study of literature at all then comes precariously close to being a specialism in the varieties of ideological obfuscation; and the very possibility of poetry's integrity - in both senses - is utterly forfeited.

And where does this leave us? To establish a parallel between the historicists' return from shadowy illusion to natural substance, and Coleridge's, may be surprising; but it is not valid to go on then to say that the historicists are therefore really 'romantic' all along, as if blowing their alibi: the entire structure of the argument between 'romantic' and 'anti-romantic' exists within a Coleridgean tradition in the first place. The important point lies elsewhere: for in one respect, of course, there is a remarkable difference between Leavis and the modern anti-romanticist: the 'material' reality from which Coleridge and his fellow romantic ideologues are said to turn away is not the felt materiality of stocks and stones, but the so-called concreteness of 'History', which replaces 'nature' in the unsteady, informal dialectic between object and poet-subject.

For the historicists, as Liu proclaims, '[t]here is no nature' (Liu, 38); but, although the historicists are keen to stress the de-naturalizing intent of their work, their 'History' actually keeps the important attributes of the 'nature' it replaces. Like Nature, 'History' brings relief: as Coleridge felt Nature save him from the self-absorption of metaphysics, so its latter-day replacement, 'History', has not infrequently been invoked as a solution to the spurious and harmful autonomy of the formalist 'Text', and the attendant, quasi-epistemological imponderables of 'Theory' ('the object as in itself it really is' or 'one's impression as it really is' or 'the object as in itself it really isn't'). Like Hume's resort to nature, this is actually a determination not to worry about the problems, rather than their solution, a frame of mind which Brook Thomas has satirically diagnosed as 'How I learned to stop worrying about theory by forgetting about it' (Veeser, 187). The felt need for such redemptive solidity tends to cast History in anti-romantic writing as, in Robert Young's words, 'an outside, a concrete, that somehow remains exterior to "theory", unaffected by it, capable of enclosing it and even swallowing it up' - like the patient appearances of Nature before the troubled metaphysician.

But this is not the only reason why a historicist version of anti-romanticism has become so popular: another is the (illusory) sense it offers of hardening up the notion of 'context' and thus solving an old problem. 'If a social-historical situation can be said to exist in a determinate way, then why not a text?' asks Kelvin Everest; but can it be so said? Without a Marxist confidence to know what is and is not self-evidently significant as 'history', the problem of relevance will properly remain insoluble because context is, logically, endless (really, universally, relations stop nowhere); and the 'readings' it allows may be quite as indeterminately various as those of the most un rooted of formalists. In one sense, as a pragmatist like Stanley Fish would doubtless respond, this means there is simply no problem: all contexts must be ad hoc, and an older generation of literary historians accepted as much without making that the basis of a style or an anti-metaphysical metaphysic.

On the other hand, to reconceive the relationship between poet and world in terms of an immaterial subject or text and a 'material' object (Wordsworth's Imagination or The Prelude and Napoleon, for example) appear to reduce the matter happily into the manageably schematic shape of an epistemological paradigm. It insists on 'a material reality in relation to which texts are secondary' (as Stanley Fish finds in Jon Klancher: Veeser, 304); but the 'materiality' of this 'history', its 'concreteness', the 'grounded ness' it offers, its ability to 'place' the text, are all wholly rhetorical. This latest anti-romantic exploitation of the Coleridgean idiom, one sometimes suspects, allows all the firm-mindedness of Marx's 'materialism' without any of the nuisance of having to believe in what Marx actually said.

Coleridge has a comprehensive intellectual virtue, and says many things about Shakespeare, by no means all of them develop or depend upon the enabling critical mythology of his super-realism: indeed, Coleridge's personal experience that attaining an artless nakedness in art was actually a matter of assumption anticipates his later discovery that elevating the principle of 'nature' into the sole criterion of excellence leaves you with nothing praiseworthy worth saying. One can only say 'It's like Nature' so many times, as Ruskin found too; and the praise is self-defeating anyway, since, if an art-work is good because it is rather like Nature, it can never be as exactly like it as Nature is.

The new anti-romantics are typically much more single-minded than Coleridge, and find things to say by describing the ways in which poems fall short of such natural excellence; but, if the merit of any critical method is to be assessed by the intricacy of the readings it encourages, this one runs a big risk: for, as part of its single-mindedness, it practices a kind of necessary violence on the diversity and complexity of the 'History' it ostensibly champions. ('History' = 'Napoleon', say; or 'History' = 'the rural poor'.) Ironically, then, the greatest victim of the historicists' committed use of the anti-romantic paradigm may be the very history they are so publicly enthusiastic to save.

The new anti-romanticism tends to delineate the margin between immaterial 'text' and concrete reality by an uncross able line, defining literariness by opposition; and yet also to deplore the bad ideology that pretends the line is there at all, making it inevitably complicit with the textual metaphysics it exists to deplore. Liu's work, for example, as David Perkins has argued, depends on assuming a positively 'oppositional relation of text to context' (Perkins, 146): accordingly, his extremely sophisticated book shows an almost bizarrely naive faith in the objective immediacy of his source material, a faith which naturally partners his practically programmatic distrust of Wordsworth's poetry. But to pretend, even if initially for one's own rhetorical self-confidence, that history is somehow as substantial as the stone Dr Johnson kicked can only be misleading: one does not need to believe that all history is just more text to disbelieve that history is, somehow, object to the text's subject. The 'History' which is referred to, appealed to, and returned to, is held to be simply 'self-evident, and needing no elaboration'.

Why Napoleon? Well, the only defense can be his self-evidence: it is natural to choose Napoleon, because he was the really real object of the poem in the first place. Every poem is a poem which takes the place of a mountain - and we want the mountain, for it is Ararat. I appreciate - and indeed share - the sense of spiritual need secretly motivating such 'materialism'; but surely this is not a very subtle way of thinking about history and historical sources: one cannot imagine historians getting very far with it, for example. It contains an argument without appeal which justifies itself only by its rhetoric's implicit appeal to naturalness.

But, finally, why should there be any general law governing the relationship between 'romantic' poetry and history anyway? Critics are only seduced into positing one, I think, because their language has reified 'History' into something as substantial as a stone and the 'text' into its idealist rival: with epistemology as your role-model, the lure of a general theory appears too tempting to resist; and one is drawn into describing relationships which, if translated back into the older and less glamorous language of psychological likelihood, would often seem ludicrous. It seems at least tolerably likely that literary works exist within historical time in rather more complex ways than the antagonistic stand-off suggested by the anti-romantic paradigm can allow, and very possibly in entirely various and quite distinct ways which are the results of authors having different kinds of mind.

There seems no reason why we should expect a general rule; and realizing this involves the critic once again in the more-or-less empirical, more-or-less guessing and uncertain evaluation of a writer's psychology or personality, far away from the (by definition) universal claims of an epistemology. This need not involve us treating art as simply 'self-expression', whatever that is, for it is not to deny art a kind of autonomy:

indeed, normal critical procedure takes that entirely for granted, in a un emphatic and practical sort of way. It merely suggests that art's relations with the world without art are mediated through the contingencies of imaginative individuality (which may be deplorable, I do not deny), rather than through the universal rules of a general case. This makes criticism a good deal more interesting to do, in my view, placing on the critic the duty of the balancing act described by T. S. Eliot (a good Coleridgean) who sought to maintain the autonomy and disinterestedness of literature, and at the same time to exhibit the relations of literature—not to 'life', as something contrasted to literature, but to all the other activities, which, together with literature, are the components of life.

Of course, that is easier said than done; but at least it says it: and success is not to be brought nearer by the new historicist form of the anti-romantic idiom.

Chapter 10

Further Study Questions

BIOGRAPHIA LITERARIA, PART 1, CHAPTER 1

- How does Coleridge compare the relative faults and merits of poets before his time and of his contemporaries?
- What does Coleridge write concerning any poem whose words can be rearranged? What is wrong with such a poem? What method of composition does his observation suggest?

BIOGRAPHIA LITERARIA, PART 1, CHAPTER 4

- How does Coleridge distinguish "fancy" and "imagination" in this chapter?
- What is "the only way to imitate without loss of originality"? Why? Against what doctrine of imitation is Coleridge writing here?

BIOGRAPHIA LITERARIA, PART 1, CHAPTER 13

- According to Coleridge, what is the "primary imagination"? What relationship does this term posit between the human and the divine?
- What Coleridge calls, in Chapter 13, the "secondary imagination" is the creative imagination of the artist. How does he describe the relationship of this power to the world of objects? What characterizes all objects as objects, and how does the secondary imagination differ? What does it do to the world of objects?

BIOGRAPHIA LITERARIA, PART 2, CHAPTER 14

- What two sorts of poems does Coleridge say became the stuff of the Lyrical Ballads? What seems to be the respective purpose of the two sorts?
- Before moving to his points of agreement and disagreement with Wordsworth, Coleridge, on 679 top, says that he must give us his notions about poems and poetry. What, then, distinguishes a poem from a work of science or ordinary prose? How does Coleridge further define poetry?
- What is the relationship of parts to parts in a "legitimate poem"? How does a genuinely satisfactory poem engage the reader's attention with respect to its parts? With respect to the whole? What does the poet do? What comment, in other words, does Coleridge offer about the value of poets to their fellow human beings?
- What is the "synthetic and magical power"? In what special activity does this power reveal itself?
- What are some of the "opposite or discordant qualities" balanced or reconciled by imagination?

BIOGRAPHIA LITERARIA, CHAPTER 17

- Coleridge has his disagreements with Wordsworth about poetic language. What reasons does he give for disagreeing, and what are his own views about the matter?

BIOGRAPHIA LITERARIA, CHAPTER 13 (XIII)

- What Coleridge calls, in Chapter XIII, the "secondary imagination" is the creative imagination of the artist. How does he describe the relationship of this power to the world of objects? What characterizes all objects as objects, and how does the secondary imagination differ? What does it do to the world of objects?

BIOGRAPHIA LITERARIA, CHAPTER 14 (XIV)

- What distinguishes a poem from a work of science or ordinary prose? How does Coleridge further define *poetry*?
- What is the relationship of parts to parts in a "legitimate poem"? How does a genuinely satisfactory poem engage the reader's attention with respect to its parts? With respect to the whole?
- What does the poet *do*? What comment, in other words, does Coleridge offer about the value of poets to their fellow human beings?
- What is the "synthetic and magical power"? In what special activity does this power reveal itself?
- What are some of the "opposite or discordant qualities" balanced or reconciled by imagination?

BIOGRAPHIA LITERARIA, CHAPTER 17 (XVII)

- Coleridge has his disagreements with Wordsworth about poetic language. What reasons does he give for disagreeing, and what are his own views about the matter?

Bibliography

Burgoyne, Daniel. "Coleridge's 'Poetic Faith' and Poe's Scientific Hoax." Romanticism On the Net 21 (February 2001).

Drummond, Gavin. "Coleridge and the Explosion of Voice." How Coleridge developed a unique Romantic voice. Prometheus Unplugged, Emory Univ.

Ford, Jennifer. A review of *Coleridge on Dreaming:* Reviewed by Nicholas Halmi in Romanticism on the Net, 18 (2000).

Gibson, Matthew. A review of *Yeats, Coleridge and the Romantic Sage.* (St. Martin's, 2000). Reviewed by Mark Sandy. In Romanticism on The Net, Issues 32-33 (November 2003-February 2004).

Haney, David. A review of *The Challenge of Coleridge.* Reviewed by Nicholas Reid in Romanticism on the Net, 29 (2003).

Hogsette, David S. "Eclipsed by the Pleasure Dome: Poetic Failure in Coleridge's 'Kubla Khan,'" in Romanticism on the Net 5 (February 1997).

Jones, Steven E. "'Supernatural, or at Least Romantic': the Ancient Mariner and Parody." Romanticism On the Net 15 (August 1999).

Koenig-Woodyard, Chris. "A Hypertext History of the Transmission of Coleridge's 'Christabel,' 1800-1816." Romanticism On the Net 10 (May 1998).

Magnuson, Paul. "Coleridge's Discursive 'Monody on the Death of Chatterton,'" as an example of the instability of textual origins. In Romanticism on the Net, 17 (February 2000).

Mahoney, Charles. "The Multeity of Coleridgean Apostasy." In Romantic Circles edition on Irony and Clerisy, August 1999.

Newlyn, Lucy. A review of *The Cambridge Companion to Coleridge*. Ed. Lucy Newlyn. (Cambridge UP, 2002). Reviewed by Nicholas Reid. Romanticism on the Net, Issues 36-37 (November 2004-February 2005).

Perry, Seamus. A substantial introduction to Samuel Taylor Coleridge from the Literary Encyclopedia.

Priestman, Martin. "Temples and Mysteries in Romantic Infidel Writing." Romanticism On the Net, 25 (February 2002).

Reid, Nicholas. "Coleridge, Language, and Imagination." Romanticism On the Net, 22 (May 2001).

Scott, Matthew. "The Circulation of Romantic Creativity: Coleridge, Drama, and the Question of Translation." Romanticism On the Net, 2 (May 1996).

Vallins, David. A review of David Vallins, *Coleridge and the Psychology of Romanticism*. Reviewed by Mary Perkins in Romanticism on the Net, 18 (2000).

Wallace, Catherine M. Coleridge's Theory of Language, in Philological Quarterly, 59 (1980).

Wallace, Catherine M. The Function of Autobiography in Biographia Literaria, from The Wordsworth Circle, 12 (1981)

Wallace, Catherine M. Unlikely Theologians and the Coleridgean Imagination in the Anglican Theological Review, vol. 86, no. 1 (Winter 2004).